CRITICAL PERSPECTIVES ON RESEARCH WITH CHILDREN

Sociology of Children and Families

Series editors: **Esther Dermott** and **Debbie Watson**,
University of Bristol, UK

The *Sociology of Children and Families* series brings together the latest international research on children, childhood and families and pushes forward theory in the sociology of childhood and family life. Books in the series cover major global issues affecting children and families.

Forthcoming in the series

Post-separation Relationships, Gendered Power and Single Mothers' Lives: Supplication, Mothering and Resistance
Kristin Natalier

Out now in the series

Race, Class, Parenting and Children's Leisure: Children's Leisurescapes and Parenting Cultures in Middle-class British Indian Families
By **Utsa Mukherjee**

Childcare Provision in Neoliberal Times: The Marketization of Care
By **Aisling Gallagher**

Black Mothers and Attachment Parenting A Black Feminist Analysis of Intensive Mothering in Britain and Canada
By **Patricia Hamilton**

Sharing Care Equal and Primary Carer Fathers and Early Years Parenting:
By **Rachel Brooks** and **Paul Hodkinson**

Find out more at
bristoluniversitypress.co.uk/sociology-of-children-and-families

Sociology of Children and Families series

Series editors: **Esther Dermott** and **Debbie Watson**, University of Bristol, UK

International advisory board:

Harry Brighouse, University of Wisconsin-Madison, US
Sara Eldén, University of Lund, Sweden
Mary Jane Kehily, The Open University, UK
Zsuzsa Millei, University of Tampere, Finland
Tina Miller, Oxford Brookes University, UK
Meredith Nash, University of Tasmania, Australia
Emiko Ochiai, Kyoto University, Japan
Gillian Ranson, University of Calgary, Canada
Anna Sparrman, Linköping University, Sweden
Ulrike Zartler, University of Vienna, Austria

Find out more at
bristoluniversitypress.co.uk/sociology-of-children-and-families

CRITICAL PERSPECTIVES ON RESEARCH WITH CHILDREN

Reflexivity, Methodology, and Researcher Identity

Edited by
Sarah Richards and Sarah Coombs

First published in Great Britain in 2024 by

Bristol University Press
University of Bristol
1-9 Old Park Hill
Bristol
BS2 8BB
UK
t: +44 (0)117 374 6645
e: bup-info@bristol.ac.uk

Details of international sales and distribution partners are available at bristoluniversitypress.co.uk

© Bristol University Press 2024

British Library Cataloguing in Publication Data
A catalogue record for this book is available from the British Library

ISBN 978-1-5292-1677-6 hardcover
ISBN 978-1-5292-1678-3 paperback
ISBN 978-1-5292-1679-0 ePub
ISBN 978-1-5292-1680-6 ePdf

The right of Sarah Richards and Sarah Coombs to be identified as editors of this work has been asserted by them in accordance with the Copyright, Designs and Patents Act 1988.

All rights reserved: no part of this publication may be reproduced, stored in a retrieval system, or transmitted in any form or by any means, electronic, mechanical, photocopying, recording, or otherwise without the prior permission of Bristol University Press.

Every reasonable effort has been made to obtain permission to reproduce copyrighted material. If, however, anyone knows of an oversight, please contact the publisher.

The statements and opinions contained within this publication are solely those of the editors and contributors and not of the University of Bristol or Bristol University Press. The University of Bristol and Bristol University Press disclaim responsibility for any injury to persons or property resulting from any material published in this publication.

Bristol University Press works to counter discrimination on grounds of gender, race, disability, age and sexuality.

Cover design: blu inc, Bristol
Front cover image: gettyimages/trilokso

To our families and reflexive researchers yet
to come

Contents

List of Figures		xi
Notes on Contributors		xii
Acknowledgements		xiv
Introduction		1
Sarah Richards and Sarah Coombs		
1	Do No Online Harm: Balancing Safeguarding with Researchers and Participants in Online Research with Sensitive Populations	10
	Michelle Lyttle Storrod	
2	The Ethical Challenges of Researching Sexting with Children and Adolescents	29
	Tsameret Ricon and Michal Dolev-Cohen	
3	Responding Reflexively, Relationally, and Reciprocally to Unequal Childhoods	42
	Pallawi Sinha	
4	Researching Children's Experiences in a Conflict Zone and a Red-light Area: Conducting Ethnographic Fieldwork in India and Kashmir	63
	Ayushi Rawat	
5	Capturing Narratives: Adopting a Reflexive Approach to Research with Disabled Young People	82
	Marianna Stella and Allison Boggis	
6	Youth Social Action: Shaping Communities, Driving Change	96
	Katie Tyrrell	
7	A New Panorama of Child Voice in the Child Protection Context	117
	Samia Michail	
8	A Bump on the Head in the Graveyard: Palimpsests of Death, Selves, Care, and Touch	138
	Sarah Coombs and Sarah Richards	

9   Owning Our Mistakes: Confessions of an Unethical Researcher   157
    Heather Montgomery

Index   172

List of Figures

1.1	Word cloud	19
1.2	Word cloud	19
3.1	Cube of Hope (CoH) activity – Sabar children in classroom; Sabar child using scissors for the first time; a Sabar boy's final net; and girl's constructed cube	51
4.1	Free hand drawing by Anwar	70
4.2	Mapping activity – Budhwar Peth	74
4.3	Mapping by Nazira	75
4.4	Mapping activity – Kashmir	76
4.5	Self-portrait – Budhwar Peth	77
4.6	Self-portrait II – Budhwar Peth	78
4.7	Self-portrait – Kashmir	79
7.1	Component structures and relationships in child protection	129

Notes on Contributors

Allison Boggis was an Associate Professor at the University of Suffolk until her retirement in 2020. Allison specialised in Disability and Childhood Studies.

Sarah Coombs was a Senior Lecturer in Childhood Studies at the University of Suffolk and is currently a Visiting Senior Fellow. Sarah's research interests include the sociologies of death and childhood, and qualitative research with children.

Michal Dolev-Cohen is a Senior Lecturer and researcher in cyberpsychology. She is the head of the Centre for Learning and Research Online Vulnerability, in the Educational Counselling Program, Faculty of Graduate Studies, at Oranim Academic College of Education. Michal specialises in researching online sexuality among adolescents.

Michelle Lyttle Storrod is an Assistant Professor of Criminal Justice at Widener University. Michelle's research focuses on how phones and social media are involved in the victimisation and criminalisation of young people in the criminal legal system.

Samia Michail is a Lecturer and researcher at Western Sydney University. Samia is interested in participatory research methodologies that employ children's rights to determine their own well-being and explore the impact of social structures and processes on child voice.

Heather Montgomery is Professor of Anthropology and Childhood at The Open University. She is currently writing a book on the history of violence against children in the home to be published by Polity in 2023.

Ayushi Rawat has a PhD from the Department of Sociology, University of Delhi. Her thesis, entitled 'Researching Children's Experiences in Kashmir: Perspectives on Conflict and Resistance', highlights children's perspectives on a controversial and challenging topic.

Sarah Richards is an Associate Professor and currently Head of the Doctoral College at the University of Suffolk. Sarah's research interests include inter-country adoption and research with children.

Tsameret Ricon is Head of the Educational Counselling Program and a Senior Lecturer in the Faculty of Graduate Studies, Oranim Academic College of Education. Her research interests include parenting and adolescent relationships, sexual education, childhood stress, professional development of educational counsellors, and parental involvement in education systems.

Pallawi Sinha is a Lecturer in Childhood Studies at the University of Suffolk. Her research interests include comparative and international childhood and education, indigenous, 'peripheral', and marginalised communities, socially responsive and arts-driven research, and the ethics and politics of education and research.

Marianna Stella is a Senior Lecturer in Education and Childhood at the University of Suffolk. Marianna specialises in dyslexia and primary education.

Katie Tyrrell is a Research Fellow at the University of Suffolk. Katie has expertise in qualitative research focused on social justice and well-being in childhood and youth.

Acknowledgements

We would like to express our gratitude to the contributors to this volume for their hard work and their dedication to its overall aims. We recognise the challenges that our requests for reflexivity represented and are grateful for their commitment in delivering such thought-provoking accounts of their individual research.

Introduction

Sarah Richards and Sarah Coombs

This Introduction outlines key themes of the volume. The centrality of reflexivity is emphasised by its introduction, application, and arguably neglected status in much research with children. As the chapters are outlined, the reader is taken on a journey representative of the research process. This begins with content that explores ethical governance, followed by an examination of methodology and methods. The focus moves onwards through critical reflexive discussions of how particular voices are privileged and/or marginalised. Finally, through reflexive considerations of the emotional labour embedded in doing research with children and the possible mistakes we make along the way, we demonstrate the usefulness and adaptability of reflexivity as a research tool hitherto mostly overlooked in childhood research. The reader has the opportunity to see how this reflexive approach is applied across sensitive topics such as sex, gang membership, conflict, death, and disability in the international, empirical discussions offered here. This volume emphasises the need to make such reflexivity far more prevalent in research with children.

Reflexivity is a nebulous, complex, and expansive concept that calls for our ongoing acknowledgement and engagement with participants, selves, positions, research fields, and wider contexts. Furthermore, reflexivity requires the researcher to continually survey themself as an integrated part of the research landscape and recognise the effect that they have on all aspects of research, through the topics chosen to the questions asked and the knowledge produced.

We argue that research with children is often ethically, emotionally, and morally charged, and yet little evidence of this is to be found in journal articles, research books, and conference presentations. Perhaps this absence is in part due to prevalent discourses, which surround and immerse children in constructions of vulnerability that in turn dictate how we present our research discussions. This vulnerability rightly makes ethical practice paramount in our research and yet leaves little room for self-doubt, reflection, or contemplation of the moment-by-moment decisions we make in the field. As researchers, we meet the academic rigour of the discipline and are confident in presenting the ways in which we have privileged children's voices but nonetheless, often remain silent in relation to our dilemmas, decision making, and any particular incidences that may occur. We do not seem to want to reveal ourselves or share the nuances and arguable 'imperfections' of our craft. Yet, we argue that this anxiety is unfounded: participatory research with children is well established with sound methodological underpinnings, is ethically robust, extensively used, and has tried and tested key concepts and methods. Despite this methodological maturity, such reflexivity remains predominantly neglected. In feminist methodology, the centrality of the researcher is commonly made explicit as a research instrument, and the multifaceted features of reflexivity evidenced as an invaluable methodological tool. If reflexivity, and its companion concept positionality, were to become more overt in research with children, then conversations about researcher identity, the emotional labour involved, the ethical and moral dilemmas we face, the ambiguity of the decisions we make, and the mistakes sometimes made, could occur.

Positionality as a concept refers to the attributes and characteristics that we each bring as researchers to the field. These shape our perspectives and understandings of what we see and inform our interpretation and analysis. Who we are as individuals characterises who we are as researchers, and informs not only what we see and how we respond, but also what our participants see and respond to when interacting with us. Our ethnicity, gender, age, for example, all become relevant to our data and its interpretation. Yet few of these characteristics are identified within texts that explore research with children, as we seek to understand the claims made by individual researchers. In contrast, this volume reveals some of the positionalities of the authors, which illuminates why they make the claims they do and enables the reader to more fully situate their analysis. It can be argued, therefore, that positionality enhances the validity of research with children by exposing the attributes of the researcher and providing more transparent and trustworthy accounts. Making our positionalities explicit begins the process of reflexivity.

Why have these ideas become so embedded throughout feminist research but not within research with children? With the proximity of childhood and feminist methodologies it seems perplexing that our research discussions lack these debates. We consider that one aspect continues to relate to the assumed vulnerability of children and therefore the implications this holds for research and the actions of researchers. This constructed vulnerability ensures that we are hesitant to disclose the complexities and extent of our experiences for fear of 'doing the wrong thing' and being identified as unethical. The consequences of this can be detrimental to careers and reputations. As identified by Heather Montgomery in this volume, 'owning our mistakes' is something we may feel more comfortable with from the security of a well-established career, rather than from the outset, but even here it is rare.

We argue that this absence of dialogue is detrimental to the field of study and to early-career researchers who interpret our published discussions as unburdened, unproblematic, and washed clean of all uncertainties the researcher may have faced. New researchers may therefore enter the field with idealised notions of the ease with which this methodology can be exercised. Consequently, they are often unprepared for the multiple ways in which their research identities will be challenged and changed, their ethical practice tested, key concepts confronted, and the inevitable emotional labour and involvement demanded of them. The longer we stay silent the further we become complicit in the perpetuation of the 'cherished conceits' of this methodology (Clark and Richards, 2017). Furthermore, a great disservice is done to those who follow. Our edited volume seeks to address this deficit and expose the messiness, challenges, and realities of this approach, and the choices that we make. Such discussions reverse the perceived vulnerability away from the child and onto the researcher by calling us to openly highlight our own uncertainties and dilemmas in the field.

To prevent wrongdoing in research with children we quite rightly have robust ethical principles, ethics committees, and guidelines to follow; we also have gatekeepers, layers of supervision, and peer review practices. These are in place to ensure that our practice is beyond reproach, but it could also be argued that they effectively mute discussion of predicaments that we all face both in the field and in pivotal moments during our research. Yet feminist methodologies manage to embrace these reflexive discussions in a more honest, open, and transparent way, while still adhering to these principles. Reflexivity, from this perspective, strengthens rather than undermines the methodology. Researchers learn from the discussions, struggles, and dilemmas articulated by others. We argue, therefore, that feminist researchers are more prepared for the unpredictability of research, the emotional intensity of fieldwork, and the recurring self-doubt involved in decision making. In contrast, childhood researchers have seldom read about, and therefore do not expect to encounter, such intricate predicaments. It is the decisions we make in such moments, both mundane and extraordinary, that reveal who we are as individuals and researchers. Furthermore, it is our continued consideration of the research decisions we make that reveal our ethical and moral positions. Reflexivity therefore becomes an ethical and moral endeavour, essential for the researcher and for childhood research methodology.

Contributors to this volume take steps towards embracing reflexivity within their research in all its complexity. Within this volume the reader encounters ethical discussions, where governance and approval are interrogated. This theme is followed by consideration of how reflexivity can be embedded in methodological debates, methods used, and the doing of research. This volume then provides critical discussion of how voice, as a key methodological concept, is situated and reproduced within research and practice. Finally, we explore how our research decisions can remain with us, as unresolved dilemmas, far beyond the life of our research. This structure provides the reader with insights into how reflexivity can be rooted in, and utilised across, each stage of the research process and beyond. The reader will witness, through the disparate chapters within this volume, the expansive nature and application of this concept from the individual and personal to the methodological and philosophical. Reflexivity therefore provides us with new ways of seeing, being, and thinking within our research, thus making childhood methodologies stronger and the researcher arguably more resilient.

Research with children is quite rightly organised through a robust set of ethical principles that inform the ways in which children should be involved, and what topics are considered appropriate for investigation. Despite the rigours of these guidelines, Michelle Lyttle Storrod explores their limitations in regard to consideration of the researcher. She highlights the neglect of ethics committees to support the well-being and mental health of researchers. Lyttle Storrod's choice of topic and population exposed her to viewing extreme online violence and explicit online content, as a result of decisions made by an ethics committee and gatekeepers, who exclusively focused on the implications for the children and young people involved. Tsameret Ricon and Michal Dolev-Cohen confronted a similar ethical emphasis when unsuccessfully applying to explore an aspect of sexuality with young people, ethical approval being refused on the grounds of it being an unsuitable topic for children to be exposed to. It is therefore the confrontation between the social constructs of childhood and sexuality that they interrogate.

Sensitive topics, populations, and geographies are also picked up in the following chapters. Pallawi Sinha reflexively interrogates childhoods on the peripheries. She equally explores the consequences and impacts of colonialism on perspectives of childhood and how these childhoods are researched. In observing reflexivity broadly, across ontological, epistemological, and methodological debate, she successfully delegitimises established knowledge positions. Ayushi Rawat challenges the notion of what a taboo topic is within the realms of childhood research by engaging children's perspectives of a red-light area and a conflict zone. Rawat highlights the necessity to perform various identities in order to be socially accepted, culturally competent, and successful in her research. Rawat then reflexively considers the usefulness and application of her methods, in examining such sensitive topics with vulnerable populations. Marianna Stella and Allison Boggis demonstrate how thinking about our decisions across the whole of the research process must be open to adaptation and change in order to fit participants, topic, and context. This consideration extends to what we do with the research in the final instance and how we might disseminate or share it with others.

The next chapters then confront our understandings of the voice of the child. Katie Tyrrell challenges the notion of voice as a singular entity and instead considers the co-production and collaboration that constitutes voice. She identifies the significance of safe spaces and contexts, where young people are more comfortable and empowered to share their views, and calls for greater recognition of the co-production of research more generally. Samia Michail then examines the limitations of child voice, identifying its use as more rhetorical than realised within safeguarding policy. She speculates how voice might be implemented in practice, in order to increase the relevance and application of children's perspectives in policy development and social work practice.

The final two chapters consider the emotional labour involved in research with children and how we reflexively interrogate and continue to question and reconcile ourselves with the incidences that occur. Sarah Coombs and Sarah Richards consider how the methodologies that literally and metaphorically underpin their research, the palimpsests that lie underneath it, inevitably influence their responses in the moment and the subsequent tensions and anxieties they experience afterwards. In this chapter we see how a 'sensitive topic', a 'vulnerable population', the central tenets of feminist methodology, our present and past identities, collide to form a mass of entanglements. Fully conversant in acknowledging the expected emotional labour of caring for their young participants, they found themselves faced with unexpected and more searching questions to answer. Reflexivity challenged them to share their experiences, rather than hide them away.

Heather Montgomery, retrospectively wrestles with trying to make sense of what we do as researchers; the decisions we make, the promises we break, and the impact this has on us personally. Montgomery, like Lyttle Storrod, questions if examining the emotions, feelings, relationships, and ethical dilemmas within our research might appear rather self-indulgent. However, Montgomery goes on to contend that in acknowledging the moral and ethical dilemmas we face, by exploring our often 'turbulent' feelings within and about our work, we become more honest about our experiences and uncover an often 'uncomfortable and ambivalent relationship between researcher and informant' (Chapter 9). Such insights call for greater reflexivity, even though this scrutiny might make us uncomfortable and perhaps reveal details we would rather forget.

The chapters illustrate key ideas that we wish to promote further in research methodologies with children. The first being the multiple selves we each bring to research. Twenty-five years ago Reinharz (1997) was arguing that we not only bring ourselves, but also create ourselves in the research field, and this self emerges as a result of both context and the relationships we develop with our participants. Furthermore, she contends that these identities that we bring and create in the research process, shape and/or obstruct the relationships we develop as researchers, and thereby inform the knowledge constructed. It is ourselves, therefore, who shape our research endeavours and its outcomes. Reinhartz categorises the variety of selves we bring to the field: primarily the research-based self, who is a good listener, a researcher, and someone who can ultimately leave the field; the brought self, where attributes supposedly outside of the research encounter actually play a significant role, such as gender, ethnicity, parenthood, age, and our personal interests; and finally, our situationally created self, which can only emerge in each specific context and through particular interactions with our participants. We argue that these claims remain salient today and highly pertinent to childhood research, yet they seem to have gained limited traction in normative research debates within the field. This volume will provide examples of the multiple selves we each bring to our research, as well as the selves we create with our participants.

Stella and Boggis explore research-based selves and the need for those selves to be flexible and continually adaptive to the situations that arise throughout and across the research process. Rawat discusses her situationally created self as 'guest-daughter', in her interactions with gatekeepers and the hosts that made it possible for her to reside and be accepted within the community in which her research took place. Tyrrell focuses on the co-production of research, emerging through her relationship with the young people, which calls for a recognition of the researcher-based self as plural and inclusive of participants. Ricon and Dolev-Cohen explore their brought selves as mothers in a topic relating to young people and sexting. Lyttle Storrod identifies a brought self as a social worker, yet acknowledges a vulnerable self when exposed to online gang-related activity. Ultimately, she accounts for the emergence of a more resilient self that was situationally required in order to complete her studies. As a consequence of her experiences, her research-based self demands change in ethical governance, to protect other researchers intending to research this field. Nevertheless, she continues to carry the resulting traumatised self. Coombs and Richards identify several brought selves, which were shaped by the sensitivity of the topic, the particular context, and the characteristics of the participants. The emotional labour required by this research ensured the centrality of other selves as pivotal to the nurturing interactions with young participants and the resultant responses in the moment. Montgomery subsequently identifies the ways in which her brought self is confronted by the actual context in which she finds herself and the experiences her participants shared. Furthermore, she highlights the ways in which research identities and brought selves are changed as a result of research encounters and the implications this has for current selves after the fieldwork is completed. Therefore, our brought and situational selves are inextricably linked to our research-based selves and the knowledge we produce. We argue that the presence of these selves and our positionalities should be more explicit in our published texts, and reflexivity provides us with the means to do this.

If we are willing to bring ourselves into our research landscapes, then our emotional selves inevitably accompany us. Excitement, anxiety, hope, ambition, determination, and stress all form part of the emotional tapestry we weave into our research encounters. Like positionality, our emotions, hidden or overt, are productive in determining what we do, how we respond in situations, and the emotions felt by our participants. Therefore, emotions become embedded in research encounters and, we argue, should be explicit in our reflexive practice. As researchers, we are emotionally invested in our work, and conducting research can represent emotional labour, perhaps particularly so when working with children in difficult and challenging circumstances, where injustice, abuse, and marginalisation are evident. However, emotional labour is also present when exploring sensitive topics with children such as death, sex, gangs, and war, as many authors have done in this volume. Being ethically sensitive, while nevertheless probing children's lives for information and knowledge about contentious topics, calls for sensitivity, nurturance, and a willingness on the part of the researcher to emotionally invest in the children. Emotional detachment, therefore, has no place in such endeavours and we argue that this emotional investment should be made explicit in our reflexive writing.

A further unifying theme across the chapters is a call for change and for research with children to move beyond the simple celebration of agency, voice, and participation. This methodological and political clarion call asks us, as childhood scholars, to follow where disability studies has led, by demanding greater benefits and more action for our participants. Sinha critiques the universal construction of childhood and highlights the ways in which such dominant concepts are not useful in exploring the experiences of all children. In a similar way to Rawat she emphasises the need for an Indian sociology of childhood, to better situate and understand the lived experiences of these children through the application of more appropriate discursive concepts. In a further challenge, Michail argues that the implementation of child voice from research into practice is sporadic, inconsistent, and ultimately a betrayal of children's participation. She calls for the resituating of children's voices into the wider political landscape to better apply their perspectives into social work practice. Stella and Boggis also illustrate this call for change in how, as researchers, we use the voices of arguably marginalised participants, and question who these voices belong to. Furthermore, they then explore how to continue the privileging of such voices within the dissemination of findings, where the researcher's voice is muted in order to retain the integrity and authenticity of the participant's voice. Tyrrell extends this discussion of voice by emphasising its relational and co-produced nature, whereby as researchers, if we acknowledge such co-productivity, then the authoritative singular voice, found in research texts, would be undermined. Refusing children a voice, in research, is confronted by Ricon and Dolev-Cohen as they challenge the regulations and boundaries around the topics in which children are allowed to participate, calling for a relaxation of the rigid ethical boundaries that tie up and impede research into so-called sensitive topics. Rawat further justifies this claim by demonstrating the ways in which children can successfully be included in such topics, whereby ethical governance too often acts to refuse rather than permit access. While still focusing on ethical governance surrounding children, Lyttle Storrod moves the focus onto the lack of welfare and consideration for the researcher. She calls for ethical consideration of the impact that witnessing such unadulterated data can have on their well-being. The researcher as an emotional self is further highlighted by Coombs and Richards, as they call for the recognition of emotional labour in research to be more transparent. Research with children can be fun yet intensive and can hold a degree of uncertainty. Revealing such emotions in our research texts would enable the emotional burden of doing research with children to become more explicit. Such emotional revelations are found in Montgomery's discussions, where she provocatively and persuasively demands that we recognise our privilege as researchers, acknowledge our limitations, and reveal our uncertainties, as well as account for and own the mistakes we make.

The aim of this volume was to gather together research that utilised reflexivity, and engaged reflexively in research with children. Clearly, reflexivity is an expansive notion that can be applied widely across all aspects of research, from ontological positions to epistemological and methodological questions, and further to global and political context and issues. Through the chapters that follow, we see multiple ways in which this concept has been incorporated as a central tenet of research methodologies with children, and the intricacies and insights it reveals. Furthermore, we see how it is used to shine a light on the quiet decisions we make, grant us permission to share and discuss these, and bring our emotions and uncertainties to the forefront of debates rather than hiding them away for fear of the repercussions.

What emerges through these chapters is a call to move beyond simply capturing the voices of children, and, rather, to involve ourselves in a more reflexive, meaningful, and far-reaching encounter with our co-producers of research, the children. This call for change is challenging, it demands an extensive paradigm shift in how we research, the topics we choose, and the populations we involve. It seeks a deeper acknowledgement and exposition of self, position, power, and thinking. It involves further consideration of how we present our research, including revealing our omissions, errors, and indeed our multiple selves. Finally, it anticipates a moral imperative to do something that improves the lives of our participants, if we can. Clearly, this is a broad ask but, as the following chapters show, it seems the time is right to move forward in methodologies that research children and their childhoods reflexively.

References

Clark, J. and Richards, S. (2017). The cherished conceits of research with children: Does seeking the agentic voice of the child through participatory methods deliver what it promises? In Castro, I.E, Swauger, M., and Harger, B. (eds) *Researching Children and Youth: Methodological Issues, Strategies, and Innovations* (pp 127–47). Bingley: Emerald Publishing Limited.

Reinharz, S. (1997). Who am I? The need for a variety of selves in the field. In R. Hertz (Ed.), *Reflexivity and Voice* (pp 3–20). London and Thousand Oaks, CA: Sage.

1

Do No Online Harm: Balancing Safeguarding with Researchers and Participants in Online Research with Sensitive Populations

Michelle Lyttle Storrod

Introduction

How do we safely research the role of social media and mobile phones in young people's offending and/or delinquent behaviour? How do we ensure that in exploration of digital lived experiences both the young participants and the researcher are equally protected?

In assessing the implications of my digital 'gang' ethnography, this chapter will demonstrate the complexity of researching young people who are considered deviant both off- and online. As children are identified as a vulnerable population by nature of age, within research there are vast amounts of literature on how to conduct ethical research with them offline (Morrow and Richards, 1996; Farrell, 2005; Alderson and Morrow, 2020) and some about online studies (Zelezny-Green, 2016; Livingstone and Bloom-Ross, 2017; Standlee, 2017). Less attention is paid to research with populations of children deemed as sensitive due to child protection concerns and/or involvement in offending behaviour. Digital research regarding children within sensitive populations is largely absent. Ethical digital research with gangs has recently received some attention (Urbanik, et al, 2020), although there is little focus on how the age of participants affects research.

This chapter will demonstrate how principles of 'do no harm' (which guide research to ensure that no harm is done to the participants, researcher, and the research community) presented specific obstacles within my research. Concerns over the protection of participants as vulnerable minors and the perceived physical threat to me from children who carried knives dominated methodological choices, according to university ethical board approval. As a practitioner I had worked with young people involved in serious youth violence for over ten years. Despite this depth of front-line experience, strict limits were placed on the way in which young people could be involved in my research. As a result, I was placed in the difficult and powerless position of a covert researcher 'lurking' (Hine, 2000) online, without the young people's knowledge or consent. The impact of emotional trauma on me as a researcher was not considered, which left me unprepared for witnessing traumatic images and videos of physical and sexual violence towards children that auto-played on social media feeds. My experience raises questions about how we safeguard ourselves as researchers not just from physical harm, but from vicarious traumatisation.

The emotional impact of fieldwork on qualitative researchers is a growing field of concern (Dickinson-Swift et al, 2009; Newell and MacNeil, 2010; Coles et al, 2014; Drozdzewski and Dominey-Howes, 2015; Markowitz, 2019), however the inclusion of digital research and its impact is rare (Hanna, 2019). This chapter will show what trauma, stemming from the digital world looked like for me as a researcher and how reflexivity helped me to acknowledge signs of stress and deal with trauma during and after the research. Like others who have shared their difficult and very personal research accounts, the sharing process feels somewhat self-indulgent, raising concerns about researcher privilege and 'de-centring the lives of our participants, in favour of our own' (Markowitz, 2019, p 13). I am sharing my experience here as part of a reflective journey in the hope that it supports other researchers who may have been emotionally impacted through their research. I hope also to encourage debate and questioning about how harm is defined and thought about within digital research with vulnerable young people. This chapter has been developed from several conference presentations; I would like to thank the many audience members who participated in these presentations, including the editors of this collection, who saw value in my experiences and encouraged me to write this chapter.

'Digital Artefact vs Digital Fingerprint'

'Digital Artefact vs Digital Fingerprint: An Ethnography of Gangs Online' was conducted for my master's thesis in 2015. The inspiration for this research came from issues that presented in my working life. Working for a charity that aimed to prevent young people becoming involved in serious violence, I was increasingly aware of the impact that social media was having on young people's well-being, particularly those who were gang involved. Young people who were involved in YouTube rap videos seemed to be getting physically hurt on a regular basis, yet increasingly others still wanted to appear in these self-produced digital artefacts. Coming from an Interpretivist perspective, I was interested in gaining an insight into young people's relationships with social media and the social meanings that they draw from online interactions. Were young people using social media to commit crime or to go viral? Were the online activities of gang-involved youth expressive of or instrumental in gang activity? These research questions became the foundation of the study (see Storrod and Densley, 2017 for findings).

Over a six-month period, a total of 270 young people between the ages of 13 and 15 were involved in 12 focus groups across six schools in one London borough. The field site was designated as an Ending Gang and Youth Violence Borough by the government due to high levels of youth violence (HM Government, 2011). Eight semi-structured interviews with practitioners working in the same area were also conducted. In addition, I conducted countless hours of social media content analysis, which will be the focus of this chapter.

Plan A

My initial method choice was to conduct a digital ethnography based in a pupil referral unit (a school for those excluded from mainstream education). The majority of the young people at this particular school were known to the local youth offending team and welfare services. Many of them were thought to be gang involved, with several of the young people self-nominating as gang associated to the school staff and support services.

Data collection would take place across a school term, from January to July. To immerse myself in the field I planned to conduct participant observation in classes and during break times at the school, also following students on social media. Much like boyd's landmark study (2014), I would simultaneously compare students' interactions online and offline. Orgad suggests that to 'break down the dualism between online and offline, you need to meet participants', but this needs to be assessed based on the context of the research (2005). It is advised that you interact and create a network of key informants to add to the understanding of the interrelationship of online/offline activities and announce your presence and purpose of research (Orgad, 2005; boyd, 2014). Therefore, the young people would need to consent to my following them on social media and be aware of my presence. Students would also have the opportunity to interpret their own data, which is often considered good practice when researching with children. This process helps to diminish stark power differentials between the adult and child, ensuring adultist interpretations of children's worlds are reduced (Best, 2007). Data would be triangulated with expert interviews conducted with practitioners working alongside the students, such as social workers, teachers, and youth offending team workers. Practitioners would provide contextual information about how services around the young people dealt with social media concerns.

As a practitioner working in the borough for several years, I had formed positive and trusting relationships with gatekeepers who supported my request to conduct the study. However, a month before data collection was due to begin the deputy headmaster of the school informed me that due to safeguarding concerns the research could not take place. The school were concerned that knowing the participants on- and offline could compromise the school's child protection policy and legal requirement to report any concern of significant harm (Children Act 1989). Concerns included the following: sharing information from online data would have directly intervened in the participants' lives (intrusive); and the school would have to deal with making referrals to police and social care, which would not only be resource intensive, but could also cause conflict between parents and students, and parents, students, and the school. On reflection the intrusion and reporting mechanism built into this design would have been difficult to navigate and emphasised a position of authority that I held as an adult over the children.

The school's decision is an example of how children's welfare, and in particular how services are organised around child protection, outweighs children's rights to take part in research (Ost, 2013). The young people in Plan A went from being centred in the research to having their research decision made for them by the adults around them who had a 'duty of care' to them. This was my first indication that wanting young people to be active research participants, speaking as competent social actors, who are experts in their own lives (James and Prout, 2015) could be difficult to put into practice. The elevated status of risk around this group of young people meant that they were deemed as vulnerable by age but also due to their involvement in deviant behaviour and/or risk of victimisation.

Working within child protection policies would continue to limit children's voices in my final study, making it difficult for them to take an active part in the research. Historically, children involved in the juvenile justice system have been constructed according to their innocence as angels in need of saving in contrast to devils who need containing, with labels of angel or devil ascribed according to race and gender (Valentine, 1996). This conception of childhood operated to construct my participants as both angels and devils and potentially disrupted their right to participation in research 'on matters affecting them', according to Article 12 of the UN Convention on the Rights of the Child (UNCRC, 1989).

Becoming a lurker

To avoid concerns over child protection issues stemming from including the same young people in digital and non-digital methodologies, I made the difficult decision with my supervisor not to triangulate data with the same young people on- and offline. I was still committed to including a digital methodology which could represent young people's experiences. Lurking online, which involves a researcher watching live social media interactions, was at the time justified to investigate sensitive research topics (Beckmann, 2005). In particular, observing social media was considered as a way to access the silence of marginalised communities, in particular 'excluded and disenfranchised youth' (Edwards et al, 2013, p 49). Observation without interaction was thought to reduce intrusion and disruption in young people's lives while providing a rich and naturalistic digital environment (Richman, 2007; Standlee, 2017). As social media is considered a public space there was also no ethical board approval needed (Standlee, 2017). I attempted to imagine myself as a researcher like Amy Best who would sit in fast food restaurants and watch young people interact (Best, 2017). I simply transferred this observation technique to an online environment.

Lurking was a difficult and an ethically uncomfortable position for me as I wanted young people to voice their own experiences. I felt extremely uncomfortable watching young people's feeds without their knowledge, as I recognised that although they were posting in public, they were not expecting their social interactions to be used within research. Using Lee's (1993) covert approach, I felt at the time I was taking a 'pragmatic' approach, whereby I openly acknowledged negative difficulties and did not employ manipulative techniques to get data. To protect young people's privacy, I exclusively observed publicly available material, nothing that was password protected. To protect young people's confidentiality, I use pseudonyms when talking or writing about a young person I have encountered online. To ensure that posts cannot be searched online and traced back to the young people, I refrain from sharing exact copies of any posts or screen grabs (Shklovski and Vertesi, 2012). My main focus was on analysing written comments and looking at how digital artefacts were shared across platforms. I did not analyse or store any of the abusive videos or images I observed. I actively tried to avoid them by scrolling quickly, however videos would play automatically on social media feeds.

Focus groups

I was (and still am) unconvinced by the idea of a pure 'virtual ethnography' (Hine, 2000) which involves digital methods only. Like others, I want to ensure that online data can be contextualised according to the offline environment of young people and the positions that they occupy in society (Beckman, 2005; Orgad, 2005; Richman, 2007). This approach 'creates the opportunity to better understand the online interactions and the meaning-making process, there is a greater possibility for more complete valuable data'

(Richman, 2007, p 199). Although I was not able to follow the same young people online, I decided that focus groups with young people would help me contextualise what I would see online. Talking to young people would also allow me to ask clarifying questions.

To gain a breadth of experiences focus groups were used in several schools. To overcome child protection concerns, I entered schools with a representative of a charity who was already going to speak with students about gangs and social media. A teacher and charity youth worker were present in all focus groups so they could respond to any safeguarding concerns (Ost, 2013). While the presence of an adult from the school meant that the young people's voices were potentially constrained and produced within the context of authoritative power dynamics (Clark and Richards, 2017), this was the only way I could get authorisation to speak directly to young people. I acknowledge that adult presence and the school setting may have impacted how young people chose to use their voice and share their experiences. Schools were deemed as a safe environment for me to talk to young people in and around gangs and had established child protection protocols which met ethical approval. Even with the restrictions placed on young people's ability to speak to me directly as a researcher, focus groups provided invaluable support for my digital methodology.

Inspired lurking

During the focus groups young people spoke about how they utilised YouTube when they wanted to see what was happening with 'gang beefs'. Watching a 'trap rap' video was only the beginning. From YouTube they could click on the people that made comments on the video and find links to personal bios, Instagram, Twitter, and other social media accounts. They could also hashtag the names of people and their gang from the video on similar social media feeds to find out more about them. After several focus groups I began to attempt to replicate this process based on the two YouTube videos that the focus group participants mentioned most frequently. What I wanted to do was reproduce the method of young people while paying attention to the feelings and responses I had as a researcher. I am convinced that online research conducted in a reflexive way can be a valuable qualitative experience, which is far from passive for the researcher.

So, although it took more time than, for example, using a system like Python to scrape numerous social media accounts at once, I manually skipped from one profile to the next following threads, pictures, and videos. I was following incidents online which I had heard about in focus groups. On Twitter I used 'hashtag sociality' (Postil and Pink, 2012, p 9) searching for 'gang names' or words used by young people to describe their local area and other terms found in the YouTube videos. Research across multiple platforms is very 'messy' (Postil and Pink, 2012, p 3). I often got lost when skipping from one place to another, so I used my internet history to record my movements. On average I viewed 50 profiles per session, including videos, pictures, and conversations. This inevitably resulted in 'information overload' (Postil and Pink, 2012, p 9).

I also followed 'social media events', defined as events that are occurring offline but have a large presence and impact online (Hines, 2000; Postil and Pink, 2012). The events I would follow would be discussions surrounding, and sometimes even video footage of, stabbings in the local area, dawn raids conducted by police, or the reaction to a young person being killed. I watched real-time reactions through comments, likes, and shares.

Unprepared 'lurker'

I heard in focus groups about videos of people 'getting shanked', 'nudes' of naked teenage girls, and videos of people having sex or 'giving head' (oral sex). I was not a stranger to discussion of these events by young people so was unsurprised to hear about them. However, what did surprise me was how many of these images and videos were present and publicly available on profiles. Hearing about these events and seeing them (especially as a 'lurker') are two vastly different experiences. Even with a clear defensible position, this situation left me in an extremely difficult position as a 'pracademic' (Posner, 2009) and also as a human. Repeatedly ingesting such visceral imagery online and not being able to do anything about it left me very traumatised.

What should I do?

On finding so many abusive images and videos, I sought advice from my supervisor and other academics researching similar topics. I searched for examples of other studies with young people to try and assess whether I should report images and videos to Child Exploitation and Online Protection Command (CEOP) or local police. I could not find any supporting studies at the time that considered child protection concerns when conducting digital research.

I formed a 'defensible position' to help guide my digital research. Outlining a defensible position is common practice when studying criminal behaviour, helping researchers to decide at which point they should inform on criminal acts by participants (Lee, 1993; Yates, 2004). For my study, my defensible position covered not only criminal acts, but also child protection concerns and evidence of victimisation, all of which were complicated by my position as a lurker.

My defensible position:

- All online information was publicly available to authorities charged with protecting young people online, so could have been reported already.
- Other professionals were already aware of some of the images/videos as they had mentioned them in interviews.
- Information was not directly disclosed to me by anyone involved and thus did not fall into the category of child protection or safeguarding.
- I could not authenticate the images/videos.
- I did not have any of the young people's names, addresses, or contact information.
- I could not identify the young people personally.

When I came across what seemed to be a substantive death threat against a 14-year-old boy, with details of the location and potential perpetrators of the crime, I did pass this on to the appropriate professionals. I recognise here that what I was prioritising was preventing something from happening and not the effects of assaults that had already occurred. I felt guilty. I did not report every image/video. I did repeatedly and markedly prompt and remind practitioners whom I worked with, interviewed, or spoke with of the routes that they should be using to report online concerns.

Upon reflection I find my defensible position to be clinical and almost minimising of the harm I saw young people experiencing. Like other researchers, my lack of action left me feeling empty, overwhelmed, and in a constant state of concern, not knowing what happened to the young people, especially when they disappeared from the online space (Hanna, 2019). This is some of the unexpected 'emotional baggage' incurred from my research and some of the factors that contributed towards my experiences of vicarious trauma, of which guilt is one of the most common features for researchers (Drozdzewski and Dominey-Howes, 2015).

Vicarious trauma?

Vicarious trauma is defined as 'the effect of chronic day to day exposure to clients and the distress they experience which becomes emotionally taxing' (Newell and MacNeil, 2010, p 8). Research suggests that the interaction and relationships built between participants combined with research on sensitive subjects often pertaining to deeply personal experiences can have a lasting emotional impact on researchers (Dickson-Swift et al, 2009; Newell and MacNeil, 2010; Coles et al, 2014; Drozdzewski and Dominey-Howes, 2015; Markowitz, 2019). Researchers, unlike therapeutic professionals are not trained to deal with the emotions of others. Furthermore, there is a lack of formalised support for emotional experiences within academia

(Dickson-Swift, et al, 2009; Drozdzewski and Dominey-Howes 2015; Hanna, 2019; Markowitz, 2019). Academia as an institution often favours objectivity and therefore can be sceptical of incorporating emotion within research (Dickson-Swift et al, 2009). 'Trauma and exposure to it is frequently buried, unrecognized and repressed' (Drozdzewski and Dominey-Howes, 2015, p 15). Academic culture potentially leads to researchers suppressing their emotions within research to prevent raising concerns about their credibility, neutrality, and rigour as researchers (Dickson-Swift et al, 2009). By centring reflexivity and privileging interpersonal communication and relationships, feminist researchers have supported the integration of emotions within academic work (Russo, 2017), arguing that emotions can enhance understanding of others' experiences. However, it is still rare that emotional harm to the researcher is considered within ethics or research design, never mind actually reported in findings in on- or offline research.

As vicarious trauma is defined according to its relational nature it is even less likely to be considered in digital research. The presence of a computer or smart phone screen could be considered as obscuring the emotions felt between the researcher and participants. Hanna (2019) argues that we can be 'emotionally engaged researchers online' and therefore feel traumatised or stressed by what we are encountering. In particular as a lurker online, seeing multiple people share emotional narratives without being able to demonstrate empathy and offer support can make the researcher feel powerless and overwhelmed, causing feelings of depression and anxiety (Hanna, 2019). This bystander role was particularly difficult for me and fed into much of the vicarious distress that I felt from watching the impact of trauma on the young people, coupled with witnessing actual footage captured on video.

Signs of stress

Figure 1.1 depicts word clouds created from entries to my field notes. The first was made early in my research and the second four months after data collection began.

Figure 1.1 reveals some of the early signs of the trauma I was experiencing without realising: rising adrenaline, normalisation of violence, and paranoia. At this point I had not even started my deep-dive chain referral across platforms that would ultimately uncover deeply abusive material. I was not expecting my online trips to be so addictive. I was nightly checking in, to watch drama unfold. I decided to see what my response was telling me; I would keep a check on it by writing a stream of consciousness in my field journal after each session. The further I got into my research the excitement and entertainment of the research were silenced by the horror of the abuse between young people that I was witnessing.

Figure 1.1: Word cloud

Figure 1.2: Word cloud

Feelings of fear, guilt, and panic are much more present in the second extract (Figure 1.2). I was not only overwhelmed, but I also felt powerless. This was a strange and difficult set of emotions to deal with, further exacerbated by my role as a practitioner. For years I had been using my empathy to advocate and support young people through trauma; I could do something to help. As a lurking researcher I just watched, even though I knew which professional bodies in the local area could and should be offering support to the young people. This was devasting to me and went against who I was as a person and served as a stark reminder that 'researchers are not robots' (Hanna, 2019, p 531).

Where these events were geographically occurring in the physical world was also difficult: parks, 'trap houses', alleyways, schools, transport stops, and prisons. I frequently felt that the institutions where these events were occurring were not effectively doing their job. I needed someone to blame. Everything seemed so public both on- and offline, yet it did not seem as if anyone was seeing what was happening. As experienced by other researchers (Coles et al, 2014; Markowitz, 2019) my world view was shifting; I was rapidly losing faith in the services meant to protect people, which was a very isolating and terrifying place to be.

I was so consumed by the trauma of my research and its seriousness that everything else became trivial; all I wanted to talk about was injustice and abuse. Similar to researchers also affected by their research experience, stories about abuse I was seeing would almost fall out of me when asked a simple question about my research (Markowitz, 2019) I was not fun to be around; I was aware of this but could not prevent it. I became emotionally unavailable to everyone around me, becoming withdrawn from friends and family. I surrounded myself with other people doing similar work, which was supportive but would often result in competitive trading of war stories. I retrospectively have no doubt that this was emotionally triggering for all involved. What I needed was the comfort and support of my already trusted friends who could provide an alternative and more balanced view of life.

At no point was I emotionally prepared to do prison research, but the online world transported me there as it has and knows no bounds. Watching videos of young people being brutally assaulted in their cells was vastly different from my experience of working with young people under the supervision of a guard in a meeting- or classroom. Those who do prison research in the 'real world' stress the importance and the need to prepare emotionally for this exposure, especially for new and inexperienced academics (Sloan and Wright, 2015). I could not smell, nor did I have to touch the environment (Sloan and Wright, 2015) in the same way as offline researchers in prisons do, but my emotions were still being overloaded; I heard the virtual prison screams and saw what some of them were caused by.

Although I was doing this research on my own, in my own home (often in my bedroom or living room) I felt unsafe. Online researchers have gone to great lengths to justify the online space as place (Hine, 2000; Postil and Pink, 2012), yet this is abstracted from where the researcher is physically located. At home I could close my computer, but the embodied trauma filled the atmosphere and remained in my body, which would often be frozen or stiff from tension. It felt like there were no boundaries to my research. When I was out in public, I would encounter young people I had seen being victimised online or at least people I thought might be them. I would worry that they might think I knew and chose to do nothing. The guilt was suffocating. I also had nightmares that involved young people I had known as a practitioner experiencing the abuse I was seeing online. These nightmares still occur, although less frequently.

Stress management

Putting things in place to manage your own stress (Lee, 1993) is important for any researcher but when researching vulnerable populations, planning ahead for this may be more effective, it is a lot harder to do *in situ*. I decided to limit myself to two hours of 'deep hanging out online' (boyd, 2014) at a time. I also tried to gather online data in the day rather than at night, so the adrenaline did not affect my sleep. I stopped doing this research in my bedroom to try and create a safe space. I would swim or go to a dance lesson to release tension in my body. Swimming has been used by other academics as a way to cleanse themselves from negative experiences with participants (Sloan and Wright, 2015). I continued to keep a check on myself through reflective journalling, a further technique used by others (Connolly and Reilly, 2007; Dominey-Howes, 2015). I also limited my exposure to any and all media that might remind me of the young people's experiences, avoiding certain genres of music, films, television programmes and, most specifically, the local news. Again this is a tactic that others have used to create distance (Coles et al, 2014). I actually returned to watching TV programmes from my youth to find reassurance, predictability, and comfort. Watching sci-fi or other worldly things really helped.

Positionality and trauma

It would be impossible to separate myself from my own history of trauma or working with those who had experienced traumatic events (Coles et al, 2014). I may have already been suffering vicarious traumatisation as a result of years of this frontline intervention work. The insight that I had developed over the years put me in the optimal position with the necessary expertise and resilience to do this research, or so I thought. The years of exposure may, in fact, have made me more vulnerable. My feelings of guilt were also associated with feelings of betrayal that I felt from the space I was occupying in between an outsider and insider (Muhammad et al, 2015). I had shared multiple traumatic experiences with young people. We had lost friends and community members to gang violence through death, disability, and/or prison. I had cleaned gunshot and stab wounds. I had taken girls and boys to sexual health clinics following rapes and/or sexual assaults. What was different about the research was that I saw traumatic events happen and had a bird's eye view of the repercussions online but remained inactive. In my practitioner life I was reactive after a disclosure of abuse but rarely saw what actually happened. As a researcher and as a practitioner I felt like I was letting the young people down in one way or another.

In my work as a practitioner and a researcher I was aware of my privileged position as a white adult, occupying a higher socio-economic position than the young people who were often of colour and from lower-income areas. Based on race, class, and my adultness, my view could be seen as alarmist due to an 'inability to transcend cultural and linguistic barriers that could lead to incomplete or inaccurate interpretations of the communities' (Richman, 2007, p 103). I would argue against this. I was not extra-traumatised or misunderstanding the interactions I saw online because I occupied contrasting social locations. I was extra-traumatised because I had bonded with young people over experiences similar to what I was seeing online and felt I was betraying them and myself by not acting. I had intimate knowledge of the very community that I was researching, which can increase the responsibility researchers feel towards and for participants (Muhammad et al, 2015).

Recovery after research?

Hanna (2019) suggests that those conducting 'emotionally engaged research' on sensitive populations online should, like offline researchers, have a managed and careful 'coming offline' process at the end of the research (Hanna, 2019, p 535). On completion of my research, I shared my findings with others to raise awareness of the harm that was occurring as depicted in the online space. I also shared my methodological challenges and ethical dilemmas at conferences. And I took a complete break. Unknown to me, what I was actually doing was taking the crucial steps that others frequently identify as positive techniques to overcome researcher trauma.

The extant literature suggests that feeling compelled to act on behalf of participants to seek justice or change responses to their harm is perhaps the most common response to researcher trauma (Connolly and Reilly, 2007; Dominey-Howes, 2015). Making a difference may be in the best interests of the researcher and participants (Coles et al, 2014). I wanted to do something to better protect the young people from the victimisation that was displayed online but also protect researchers and passive young participants online.

I created a training session based on the findings of my research, which highlighted the safeguarding issues and harms that young people were facing online. One of the primary points of the training was for practitioners to take social media seriously and not minimise young people's experiences. Providing frontline practitioners with information and practical advice on how to deal with social media issues did help to heal some of my anxiety and guilt, while hopefully indirectly supporting young people. However, due to the nature of my research, often professionals were more interested in gangs and the sale of drugs across county lines than the harm the young people were experiencing. Presenting to a room full of powerful professionals and showing them how to find videos of sexual violence towards children, being met with blank faces, and then fielding questions about drug lines is not only frustrating, but also disheartening, triggering feelings of powerlessness all over again. I recount this as a cautionary tale to those who will want to get out there and help as soon as possible. A little time for reflection and being choosey about whom you feel is privileged and safe enough to look after the young people you speak about may be helpful.

While academics have been incredibly supportive, just talking about the research's methodological and ethical issues can be stressful and triggering. It is important to stay attuned to human and embodied responses to vicarious trauma (Connolly and Reilly, 2007; Dickson-Swift et al, 2009), which does not just go away once research stops. I have an emotive response every time I talk or write about 'Digital Artefact vs Digital Fingerprint'. The first time I presented my research on gangs and social media at a conference I opened my mouth and nothing came out. When I was able to speak, my voice was shaking and gruff as if it were being restricted or forced. I was unprepared for this; I am a confident public speaker. I had also talked publicly about sexual violence at conferences, meetings, and trainings as a consistent part of my job. I did not feel nervous. More generally at conference presentations, no matter how much I try to contain my adrenaline, my heart races, my muscles tense, my temperature rises, my eyes widen, my forehead tenses, and my frown becomes fixed. I also tend to have memory lapses where I subsequently struggle to remember what I said. When this happens my brain typically chooses to recount the very worst of what I saw during the research. This concerns me as I want to provide a representative and contextualised account of my research and not just the worst case scenario. As I end my presentations and my adrenaline starts to drop it can be hard to focus on questions. I often record my presentations to ensure that I answered questions appropriately. Often my presentation state is interpreted by audiences as passion. I do not doubt that I am passionate about my research, or more specifically about getting justice for young people, but there is definitely something more nuanced occurring.

At every conference some people, 'the empaths' in the audience, feel my trauma too. People have approached me with a concerned look to say they have worked with people experiencing trauma and how difficult it is, which is reassuring. Some people want to hug me after presentations. I think sometimes they are in shock and need comfort. The hug is the hardest: containing myself only works if I build an imaginary wall around me, I am always concerned that a crack in the wall will break me and reflect badly on my professionalism. It is exhausting. Ensuring you take time out during conferences is a must when presenting on emotive research. Taking a walk outside or skipping a drinks meeting can be helpful breaks. This advice may be at odds with the networking style of academic conferences but staying in control of your own networking will make sure that you are representing yourself and not the personal impact of your research.

Future research

Covert lurking online is sanctioned by ethics boards due to social media's public nature. The way that young people choose to obscure their identities online is seen as a benefit for confidentiality (Standlee, 2017). However, I will never lurk again. From my experience, I believe lurking not only to be an invasion of privacy, but also representative of a deeper level of harm. I witnessed significant harm done to young people online, without their knowledge and without being able to personally intervene or support them. In addition, while the videos, pictures, and comments were in the public domain, they had not been put there by the young, victimised person. Instead, these artefacts of both physical and sexual abuse had been shared by perpetrators or voyeurs of technology-facilitated abuse. By displaying trauma to an audience this action was intended to further humiliate, harass, and victimise young people. In effect, I was causing harm by witnessing harm.

Balancing safeguards to young people and myself as a researcher was at the centre of my recently completed doctoral dissertation, which looked at the role of phones and social media in the victimisation and criminalisation of girls in the juvenile justice system in the United States. To avoid lurking and ensure more control and agency over digital data, this time I used a more 'participant-driven' digital method. As trialled with young people from disadvantaged communities, I utilised social media tours with participants (Campos-Holland et al, 2016). This 'enhanced qualitative method' involves the researcher moving through social media accounts or phones alongside participants who are explaining what is happening as they respond to posts or messages (Campos-Holland et al, 2016). Young people provide meanings to artefacts and actions online, putting them in firm control of interpretation and their own privacy. This method also allowed space for young people's dissent and research refusal (Clark and Richards, 2017), providing opportunities for girls to decide how and when they would like to proceed with the research (Lyttle Storrod, 2021). The control the girls had in this research is in stark contrast to that which I observed online back in 2015/16.

To address issues of vicarious traumatisation, Dominey-Howes (2015), who experienced both 'direct personal' trauma in the field and 'indirect professional' vicarious trauma through supervising young academics, suggests having a least one more experienced academic supervising sensitive research. This can help combat feelings of isolation and complete responsibility for devasting issues you cannot control (Dominey- Howes, 2015). I chose a chair for my committee who had experience working with vulnerable girls involved with welfare systems. My chair had shared a pracademic experience and was familiar with the frustrations of this position. I was also upfront with my committee members regarding my previous experience of vicarious traumatisation. Such disclosure could be seen as a risky strategy for a new academic who is also being graded by the same people from whom she is hoping to gain emotional support. I believe that offering openness about my concerns and difficult past experiences was a key part of preparing my network (Connelly and Reilly, 2007).

Throughout my PhD fieldwork and writing-up stage I had clinical supervision, the funding for which came from successful applications for research grants. Reflective of a trauma-informed approach that recognises 'that trauma can be contagious' (Newell and MacNeil, 2010), affecting those experiencing it directly and those who work beside them, I identified supervision as an opportunity to strengthen resilience. Formalising funds and time to dedicate to emotional support is an important shift for academia. Ignoring the emotional impact of research and dealing with its effects privately reinforces negative inferences about emotions within academia, allowing funders and institutions to be let off the hook for money needed to support the entire research process (Dickson-Swift et al, 2009). Support for researchers dealing with sensitive topics needs to be institutionalised within academia. For many of us it is part of the job.

Conclusion

I still battle with my methodological choices for studying young people, gangs, and social media. Researching young people's experiences within digitalised society is complex but should not be saved for the youth we consider to be angels (Valentine, 1996). When researching the experiences of young people who are involved in crime or who are deemed at risk, their status as children and 'offenders' complicates research but does not make it impossible. Protection of children from harm within research is of course paramount, however this should not prevent them from playing an active role within research, as it did here.

As I have explored in this chapter, the digital method of lurking adopted due to perceived lack of risk to young people (Standlee, 2017) did nothing to prevent ongoing harm to young people and prevented them from having an opportunity to talk about these experiences. The lack of consideration of the emotional impact of lurking also put me at risk of emotional harm. Ethics boards, researchers, and supervisors should ensure online research methods are factored in to assessments' harm, taking the context of the participants and the researcher into strong consideration. The boundless nature of online research and the inability to act left me vulnerable as a researcher, causing vicarious trauma. Committing to a reflexive process was key to the recognition of the difficulties I was experiencing. Keeping track of periods of stress and how the research was affecting me, my view of the participants, and the overall research ultimately enabled me to complete the study. Reflexive accounts, such as this chapter, provide an insight into the emotional labour of research, which can help guide and support future researchers in the planning and conducting of research. I hope this chapter is also helpful for ethics boards and academic institutions in helping to demonstrate how reflexivity is integrated within qualitative research on sensitive topics which may be on- or offline, providing insight into the time, space, and resources that are needed to conduct safe research for all. Utilising digital methods with children is in its infancy. Finding a balanced way to conduct research which centres the welfare and emotions of all involved off- and online is needed.

References

Alderson, P. and Morrow, V. (2020). *The Ethics of Research with Children and Young People: A Practical Handbook*. London: Sage.

Beckmann, S.C. (2005). Sensitive research topics: Netography revisited, *Qualitative Research Topics*, June, Research Gate.net/publication/233742156.

Best, A.L. ed. (2007). *Representing Youth: Methodological Issues in Critical Youth Studies*. New York: NYU Press.

Best, A.L. (2017). *Fast-food Kids: French Fries, Lunch Lines, and Social Ties* (Vol. 4). New York: NYU Press.

boyd, D. (2014). *It's Complicated: The Social Lives of Networked Teens*. Newhaven, CT: Yale University Press.

Campos-Holland, A., Dinsmore, B., and Kelekay, J. (2016). Virtual tours: Enhancing qualitative methodology to holistically capture youth peer cultures. In Robinson, L. Cotton, S.R. and Schulz, J. (eds) *Communication and Information Technologies Annual: [New] Media Cultures*. Bingley: Emerald Group Publishing Limited.

Clark, J. and Richards, S. (2017). The cherished conceits of research with children: Does seeking the agentic voice of the child through participatory methods deliver what it promises? In Castro, I.E, Swauger, M., and Harger, B. (eds) *Researching Children and Youth: Methodological Issues, Strategies, and Innovations* (pp 127–48). Bingley: Emerald Publishing Limited.

Coles, J., Astbury, J., Dartnall, E., and Limjerwala, S. (2014). A qualitative exploration of researcher trauma and researchers' responses to investigating sexual violence. *Violence Against Women* 20(1): 95–117.

Connolly, K. and Reilly, R.C. (2007). Emergent issues when researching trauma: A confessional tale. *Qualitative Inquiry* 13(4): 522–40.

Dickson-Swift, V., James, E.L., Kippen, S., and Liamputtong, P. (2009). Researching sensitive topics: Qualitative research as emotion work. *Qualitative Research* 9(1): 61–79.

Dominey-Howes, D. (2015). Seeing 'the dark passenger' – Reflections on the emotional trauma of conducting post-disaster research. *Emotion, Space and Society* 17: 55–62.

Drozdzewski, D. and Dominey-Howes, D. (2015). Research and trauma: Understanding the impact of traumatic content and places on the researcher. *Emotion, Space and Society* 17: 17–21.

Edwards, A., Housley, W., Williams, M., Sloan, L., and Williams, M. (2013). Digital research, social media and the sociological imagination. *International Journal of Social Research Methodology* 16(3): 245–60. https://doi.org/10.1080/13645579.2013.77418

Farrell, A. (2005). *Ethical Research With Children*. Berkshire: McGraw-Hill Education.

Hanna, E. (2019). The emotional labour of researching sensitive topics online: Considerations and implications. *Qualitative Research* 19(5): 524–39.

Hine, C. (2000). *Virtual Ethnography*. London: Sage.

HM Government (2011). *Ending Gang and Youth Violence: A Cross-Government Report Presented to Parliament by The Secretary of State for the Home Department by Command of Her Majesty*. London: HM Government.

James, A. and Prout, A. eds (2015). *Constructing and Reconstructing Childhood: Contemporary Issues in the Sociological Study of Childhood*. London: Routledge.

Lee, R.M. (1993). *Doing Research on Sensitive Topics*. London: Sage.

Livingstone, S. and Blum-Ross, A. (2017). Researching children and childhood in the digital age. In Christensen, P. and James, A. (eds) *Research with Children* (pp 45–62). Oxon: Routledge.

Lyttle Storrod, M. (2021). *Digital Justice: Girls, Phones, & Juvenile Justice*, Doctoral Dissertation, Rutgers University, Camden.

Markowitz, A. (2019). The better to break and bleed with; Research, violence and trauma. *Geopolitics* 26(1): 94–117.

Morrow, V. and Richards, M. (1996). The ethics of social research with children: An overview 1. *Children & Society* 10(2): 90–105.

Muhammad, M., Wallerstein, N., Sussman, A.L., Avila, M., Belone, L., and Duran, B. (2015). Reflections on researcher identity and power: The impact of positionality on community based participatory research (CBPR) processes and outcomes. *Critical Sociology* 41(7–8): 1045–63.

Newell, J.M. and MacNeil, G.A. (2010). Professional burnout, vicarious trauma, secondary traumatic stress, and compassion fatigue. *Best Practices in Mental Health* 6(2): 57–68.

Orgad, S. (2005). From online to offline and back: Moving from online to offline relationships with research informants. In Hine, C. (ed.) *Virtual Methods: Issues in Social Research on the Internet* (pp 51–66). Oxford: Berg.

Ost, S. (2013). Balancing autonomy rights and protection: Children's involvement in a child safety online project. *Children & Society* 27(3): 208–19.

Posner, P.L. (2009). The pracademic: An agenda for re-engaging practitioners and academics. *Public Budgeting & Finance* 29(1): 12–26.

Postil, J. and Pink, S. (2012). Social media ethnography: The digital researcher in a messy web. *Media International Australia* 145(1): 123–34.

Richman, A. (2007). The outsider lurking online: Adults researching youth cybercultures. In Best, A. (ed.) *Representing Youth: Methodological Issues in Critical Youth Studies* (pp 182–202). New York: NYU Press.

Russo, A. (2017). Brokenheartedness and accountability. *Journal of Lesbian Studies* 21(3): 289–305.

Shklovski, I. and Vertesi, J. (2012). 'Un-Googling': Research Technologies, Communities at Risk and the Ethics of User Studies in HCI. In *The 26th BCS Conference on Human Computer Interaction* 26 (September): 1–4.

Sloan, J. and Wright, S. (2015). Going in green: Reflections on the challenges of 'getting in, getting on, and getting out' for doctoral prisons researchers. In Drake, D.H., Earle, R., and Sloan, J. (eds) *The Palgrave Handbook of Prison Ethnography* (pp 143–63). London: Palgrave Macmillan.

Standlee, A. (2017). Digital ethnography and youth culture: Methodological techniques and ethical dilemmas. In Castro, I.E, Swauger, M., and Harger, B. (eds) *Researching Children and Youth: Methodological Issues, Strategies, and Innovations*, Vol. 22 (pp 325–48). Bingley: Emerald Publishing Limited.

Storrod, M.L. and Densley, J.A. (2017). 'Going viral' and 'Going country': The expressive and instrumental activities of street gangs on social media. *Journal of Youth Studies* 20(6): 677–96.

United Nations Committee on the Rights of the Child (1989). E/CN.4/RES/1990/74. https://www.refworld.org/docid/3b00f03d30.html

Urbanik, M.M., Roks, R., Storrod, M.L., and Densley, J. (2020). Ethical and methodological issues in gang ethnography in the digital age: Lessons from four studies in an emerging field. In Melde, C. and Weerman, F. (eds) *Gangs in the Era of Internet and Social Media* (pp 1–21). Switzerland: Springer.

Valentine, G. (1996). Angels and devils: Moral landscapes of childhood. *Environment and Planning D: Society and Space* 14(5): 581–99.

Yates, J. (2004). Criminology ethnography; Risks, dilemmas and their negotiation. In Mesko, G., Pagon, M., and Doboresk, B. (eds) *Policing in Central and Eastern Europe: Dilemmas of Contemporary Criminal Justice* (pp. 1–21). Maribor: University of Maribor.

Zelezny-Green, R. (2016). Can you really see what we write online? *Girlhood Studies* 9(3): 71–87.

2

The Ethical Challenges of Researching Sexting with Children and Adolescents

Tsameret Ricon and Michal Dolev-Cohen

Introduction

Childhood is viewed as a period of innocence and vulnerability that demands special attention (Daly et al, 2019). These concepts have held such dominance over time that they can now be construed as hegemonic in nature. Within this discourse, sexual maturity, with its accompanying knowledge and loss of sexual innocence, is one of the dividing boundaries between childhood and adolescence, leading to an impediment in discussions around sexuality during the period of childhood (Robinson, 2008). Furthermore, the public consensus is that the sexualisation of culture, as a construct of childhood, is damaging and negative (Moore and Reynolds, 2018). Consequently, there is little discussion with children about sexuality, at home or in school; rather, any discussions mainly focus on parental concerns and specific negative outcomes for children (Flores and Barroso, 2017).

However, the online arena allows exposure to a wide range of sexual content, and children surf the internet (Ybarra and Mitchell, 2005). Since the message for children, from adults, is that sexuality is not relevant to them, they learn about it from a variety of media sources, including the internet (Longo et al, 2002). The significant adults in their lives are not always sufficiently active in the learning process and may not play a mediating role in young people's emerging sexual activities. Sometimes, they are even oblivious to all the aspects of sexuality on the internet and are unaware of what their children are being exposed to. Sexual socialisation is a process through which children acquire their essential beliefs, attitudes, values, cultural symbols, concepts, and meanings on sexuality (Kunkel et al, 2007) and this process is affected by the attitudes and beliefs of the family, school, and society with respect to sexual topics. Children's sexual behaviours are influenced by their age and by their socialisation (Ganji et al, 2017).

Aspects of sexuality accompany a person from infancy. When children are still at pre-school age, it is the parents' responsibility to discuss this subject (Ganji et al, 2017). However, conversations on sexuality can be uncomfortable for parents (and for their children), so they may avoid raising the topic. Alternatively, parents may only talk about the positive sides of healthy sexuality, such as love and partnership, and less on potential harms (Ashcraft and Murray, 2017). This is also true in the case of parents who conduct conversations on sexuality with their children in a more open way (De Looze et al, 2015). Thus, a wider verbal discourse is needed, one that encourages dialogue covering the full range of vulnerability to security. If the mandate for this subject lies with the education system, parents can sometimes refrain from discussing it in the family, though the way school systems address this subject can vary widely. Most parents acknowledge their role as educators of sex and sexuality, and yet can feel that they lack the skills and confidence in effectively communicating with their children about sexuality (Teo and Morawska, 2021).

In this chapter, we wish to reflect on the ethical issues that emerge through the social constructs of childhood and sexuality when trying to research what is often constructed as a taboo subject (Richards et al, 2015). Here we focus on a particular issue prevalent in young people, that of sexting (sending and receiving sexual messages) among children and adolescents throughout the world. After reviewing the relevant research literature, we discuss our dilemmas and positionalities as researchers and mothers when conducting such research.

Sexting among children and adolescents

Technology is an inseparable part of the life of adolescents (Lenhart et al, 2010), who can enter cyberspace via their smartphones for both social and academic needs at any time and from any place (Anderson and Rainie, 2010). Therefore, it is only natural that their developmental processes are also expressed in the online environment, through the use of a variety of apps that cater to their needs (Campbell and Park, 2014). The smartphone can create a sense of privacy, which eliminates inhibitions and enables authentic self-expression (Suler, 2004); at the same time, the role of peers in their lives becomes increasingly important. These circumstances, which constitute the backdrop to the adolescents' significant changes (Steinberg, 2008), also lead them to examine various aspects of their sexuality in cyberspace (Gordon-Messer et al, 2013).

The term 'sexting' refers to the sending and receiving of sexual messages intended to arouse a person sexually. A sext message can include photographs, video clips, texts, or even emojis only; it can be part of romantic or sexual relationships (Burén and Lunde, 2018). Sexting is presented in the research literature as part of a developmental stage in which young people experiment with their sexuality (Henderson and Morgan, 2011; Dir et al, 2013), yet it also raises issues of consent and privacy (Albury and Crawford, 2012; Gillespie, 2013; Hasinoff and Shepherd, 2014), as well as abuse, pressured sexting (Wachs et al, 2021), sextortion (Wolak et al, 2018) and online grooming (Kloess et al, 2019). Studies examining the frequency of the phenomenon have found that it is widespread among adolescents worldwide and is not typical of any specific culture, nationality, or gender. For example, a study by the EU Kids Online project revealed that 12 per cent of adolescents (ages 11 to 16) in the United Kingdom had seen or received sexual messages online (Livingstone et al, 2010). Research conducted in the Czech Republic (Kopecký and Szotkowski, 2018) found that more than 15 per cent of Czech children (ages 8–17) had sent sexting messages. A meta-analysis of 39 studies conducted among minors in the United States, Europe, Australia, South Africa, Canada, and South Korea found that 14.8 per cent had sent sexts and 27.4 per cent had received such messages (Madigan et al, 2018). A Canadian study found that 14.4 per cent of the adolescents (ages 14 to 17) in the sample group had sent sexts and 27 per cent had received such messages in the 12 months prior to the study. A study encompassing 3,223 Spanish adolescents (ages 12 to 17) found that 3.4 per cent of the 12-year-olds and 36.1 per cent of the 17-year-olds had engaged in sexting (Gámez-Guadix et al, 2017).

Thus, it appears that the phenomenon is widespread and its frequency among adolescents increases with age, particularly due to their access to smartphones and the dominant perspective that sexting has today become a normative, legitimate way to express one's sexuality (Casas et al, 2019; Mori et al, 2019; Van Ouytsel et al, 2020). This behaviour is often considered a type of flirtation or a source of harmless fun, which allows those involved to feel good about themselves and their sexuality (Lenhart, 2009; Dir et al, 2013). Sexting also provides body image reinforcement (Bianchi et al, 2019) and contributes to identity construction (Chalfen, 2009). Moreover, it appears that the use of sexting is motivated by adolescents' desire to experience sexual intercourse (Yépez-Tito et al, 2019). Nevertheless, adolescents tend to comport themselves in the way they think corresponds to the peer group's behaviour (Brechwald and Prinstein, 2011) and, indeed, the predominant view is that peers who are part of the in-group engage in sexting. This perception increases the likelihood that other adolescents will follow suit (Maheux et al, 2020). Posts written by young people on a variety of online forums tend to reveal personal stories and various motivations for sending sexts, for example a need for attention as part of developing relationships, and to encourage feelings of being sexy and attractive to others (AskPeople).

It seems clear that children and young adolescents, a population not often examined in regard to sexual practices, due, in part, to the dominant ideals held in the social construct, are exposed to this phenomenon of sending and receiving sexts. As researchers, we are aware of the risks of sexting – whether as a sender or as someone who has been exposed to the sexual content – and we are troubled by the emotional and even legal consequences, and by the dilemma this poses: should we refrain from asking young people about sexting in order to protect those who have not yet been exposed to it, or will we (as a society) pay a higher price (risks, ignorance, prevention) if we fail to study the sexting practices of young adolescents in order to create educational materials and prevent at-risk behaviours? Failure to explore aspects of children's everyday lives reduces the opportunity for children to give voice to a potentially important feature of their lives and reinforces the idealised notion of childhood and sexuality being disparate. Yet, to attempt to engage in such research presents distinct challenges in overcoming ethical barriers imposed to protect a potentially vulnerable group in society.

Notwithstanding the perception among young people and researchers that adolescent sexting is a frequent and acceptable phenomenon, it is known to have potential risks: it can lead to bullying, privacy abuse, sextortion, and revenge porn (Van Ouytsel et al, 2017; Madigan et al, 2018). Furthermore, adolescents may engage in sexting as a response to social pressure or emotional difficulty (Klettke et al, 2014; Gámez-Guadix and de Santisteban, 2018). These implications mainly (but not only) affect young women, who are judged severely by society for their involvement in sexting, alongside almost all other sexual practices (Lippman and Campbell, 2014). A study conducted in Belgium found that gender minority adolescents (such as transgender, gender fluid, gender non-conforming, gender diverse and non-binary youth) are under enormous pressure to send sexts (Van Ouytsel et al, 2020). The research literature reveals that the pressure exerted on young girls is greater than that exerted on boys (Burén and Lunde, 2018), and male adolescents report the desire to demonstrate their ability to obtain texts with sexual content as a way of increasing their popularity and proving to their peers that they are sexually experienced (Ringrose et al, 2013; Lippman and Campbell, 2014).

Despite the risks associated with sexting, adolescents tend to avoid sharing this experience with significant adults, and refrain from consulting with them about sexting and its implications. Although research about sexual activity is construed as being sensitive, research with young people on this particular topic is considered doubly so, and yet we feel it is tremendously important to examine this phenomenon among children and young adolescents. Studies show that sexting can begin before the age of 12, which can be a problematic age for data collection as some children may already be dealing with their sexuality, while others are not. For the latter, exposure to sexting through research encounters may leave them confused, embarrassed, or harassed, and undermines the idealised notion of innocence in the social construct.

A request to study sexuality in childhood is likely to be rejected by an ethics committee, in part to prevent premature exposure to sexual content. Requesting parental consent for such research may also stir up opposition and meet with rejection, perhaps in some measure because many parents are unfamiliar with, or are unaware of, their children's engagement in sexual activity. However, such research, which makes central the voices and experiences of children, allows for a more informative discourse to emerge, which potentially creates a deeper social understanding of this under-researched issue.

Widman and his colleagues (2021) conducted research with 226 US high school students (median age = 16.25) who reported their digital sexual behaviour and sexual communication during the past year. Rates of sexting, viewing pornography, and starting relationships online were high: 89 per cent said they had engaged in at least one of these behaviours and 35 per cent reported engaging in all three behaviours. Yet communication about these topics was generally low: only 7 per cent of the youth said they had discussed all three digital topics with their parents, while 19 per cent reported discussing all three with their best friends (Widman et al, 2021).

Based on these findings, it appears that the sexting phenomenon is widespread among youths but is not necessarily revealed to parents. Parents can feel uneasy about discussing sexuality with their children, perhaps because they fear they lack sufficient information to do so effectively or that they might be putting ideas into their children's heads prematurely. Alternatively, parents might consider that such conversations can be construed as granting approval for this type of behaviour (Hosseinkhanzadeh et al, 2012; Ashcraft and Murray, 2017). Such feelings can intensify when it comes to discussing sexual behaviour in cyberspace. Nevertheless, the research literature underscores the need for parents to be involved in their children's sexual education, while also finding that only a low percentage of parents are, in fact, involved in this area of education (Nair et al, 2012). Hence, seeking information from parents alone about sexting is problematic and does not necessarily reflect the prevalence of the phenomenon in children's lives.

Given that sexting is seldom discussed in the family framework, adolescents do not often have the opportunity to have a significant conversation about this topic with their parents or rely on their support, when necessary, that is, when they are asked to send a sext to someone, or if they are the subject of sextortion, privacy abuse, or revenge porn. The research shows that in such cases, the percentage of adolescents who seek help is very low (Wittes et al, 2016; Wolak et al, 2018), which, in turn, leaves the adolescent not only to cope alone with the resulting distress, but also vulnerable to ongoing abuse. The impact of this is that reticence to discuss a so-called a taboo subject with childhood, can have a negative impact on children's lives.

The research literature offers several explanations for the low reporting rates of online sexual abuse, including: the victim's young age, a sense of shame and guilt, attitudes about asking for help, a fear of repercussions if the information is revealed, and a belief that they are beyond help or that they will be perceived as responsible for the situation (Tomczyk and Kopecký, 2016; Wolak et al, 2018; Dolev-Cohen et al, 2020).

The phenomenon of sexting by children and adolescents has been widely discussed by educators, therapists, researchers, lawmakers, and parents. Despite the accepted definition of sexting (sending and receiving sexual messages), the research literature addresses different aspects of sexting. Consequently, the research method of gathering data also varies. Sometimes the data pertains to the sender, sometimes to the receiver, and other times to the distributor of the content. Nevertheless, despite the variability of assessment measures, the findings indicate a high frequency of all types of sexting. We argue here that research in this field should focus predominantly on the young people themselves, focusing on and including their perceptions, frequency of involvement, whether they seek help from adult figures, and the reasons behind their choices. This would more fully embrace young people's inclusion on wider topics about their everyday life experiences, moving beyond well-trodden and safe themes such as education, and into the lived realities of their nuanced and often complex lives. Attention to the methods with which we gather such data should be given careful consideration. We contend that gathering data online allows the participants to remain within a context where they feel comfortable about expressing themselves.

Gaining ethical approval: childhood and sexuality

Ethical research is the process of being truthful in the negotiation of relations between the researcher and the participants. Ethical dilemmas are often complex. The ability to resolve ethical dilemmas is often found in the context of a wide variety of research activities and researcher experience (Head, 2020). In this section, we address ethical issues in the specific context of collecting online data from children. The research literature addresses many ethical aspects of data collection, including important legal contexts, which may touch on privacy laws, pornography, sexting (without consent), and distribution of photographs and/or sextortion (Lee et al, 2015; Holoyda et al, 2018).

Ethical frameworks, which seek to protect the participants, in particular children and young people, from harm in taboo subjects such as sex and sexuality, among others, tend to reproduce the marginalisation of the child's voice. The basic assumption that children do not understand, or do not know, or that the subject is inappropriate for children because the exposure is harmful is quite patronising (Oates, 2020) and is not sustainable in the era of the internet. The proliferation of ethical guidelines limiting the opportunities to conduct research with children in different social, cultural, and geographical contexts has raised the need for a more robust debate regarding the promotion of ethical research in these areas (Abebe and Bessell, 2014).

As experienced researchers, we have faced, and continue to face, significant challenges posed by ethical frameworks in our institutions. The ethics committee at our academic institution has been unwilling to approve proposed research on sexting among children. Every series of studies we have put forward on and around issues of sexuality and sexual abuse has been rejected, and yet we strongly argue that research into this area is important and neglected and requires further investigation. Such a stance from ethics committees only serves to emphasise the vulnerable child, and positions them, the ethics committee, as responsible for protecting the dominant construct of childhood at the expense of the agentic child as expert in their own lives. As a result of these challenges in getting approval, there is a paucity of research that examines this phenomenon among at-risk populations, which is very much worthy of study.

Furthermore, if research such as this is perceived as forbidden, this implies sanctioning and penalties, and makes ethical approval even more problematic. Sexting, for example, could in consequence be considered a less legitimate subject for research, which, in turn, will be used to convey messages that promote deterrence. This forbidden perspective also potentially undermines the agentic construct of childhood, which is so prevalent in the research accounts across childhood studies. However, this issue could be approached differently, for example as a matter of protecting the public from potential defamation or other implied risks, especially those relevant to children and adolescents. Such risks might include drug abuse (Ševčíková, 2016), unprotected sexual intercourse (Rice et al, 2012), and online bullying. This protective stance, which focuses on the welfare and support of children, could potentially ease the passage of an ethics application, due, in part, to its positioning of children as vulnerable and in need of protection, rather than agentic participants of sexting. It should also be noted that some studies have differentiated between sexting that takes place in the context of romantic relationships versus sexting that occurs outside of such relationships and have identified lower risks when romance is involved. However, as previously discussed, the evidence suggests that children as young as 11 and 13 years are engaged in sexting, and therefore could be considered too young to be fully engaged in a romantic, consensual relationship.

Another ethical issue is related to the manner of data collection. On the one hand, it is very important to collect the information directly from the young people in a way that is accessible and a normative part of their everyday lives. Therefore, it is important that the method provides opportunities for in-depth insights into the lives of children and young people and their emerging sexuality. On the other hand, using social networks to collect information about sexting raises complications, such as maintaining structures of information and support that the young people might need. While the online data collection method might be popular among young people, due to their readiness to engage in online activities and the clear ability to maintain their anonymity (Barak and Dolev-Cohen, 2006), this can potentially impede the provision of what might be considered to be appropriate welfare information. However, when researching so-called sensitive topics such as sexting with young people, we argue that the use of cyberspace for anonymous data collection presents a considerable advantage over methods of face-to-face qualitative research, and that this method is particularly valuable when studying the phenomenon in a culture that shuns sexual behaviour among adolescents.

As mothers of young children and adolescents, attempting to conduct research in this field stirred discussions in our own families. We found ourselves discussing the phenomenon with our children and their friends. It was clear that once we raised the topic, the children were extremely interested, they asked questions, checked what is and is not acceptable, and showed interest in the ethical aspects of sending and receiving sexts. Some of our teenagers managed to name the phenomenon, perhaps for the first time, understanding that they had unwittingly been exposed to sexting. In the discussion, they shared their feelings regarding the encounter with this content and the confusion they had felt. As mothers we were able to gain insights into this phenomenon, yet as researchers we were denied the opportunity. This discourse allowed us to provide meaningful educational messages, while also teaching us to become more open. It enabled us to lend our own children and their friends a friendly, accepting, and attentive ear, one that does not judge, but wants to hear more. We learned that the dilemma should not be whether to study sexting among children and adolescents, but rather how to accompany them during the research process and how to uncover deeper layers within their perceptions. Such opportunities are lost when the social constructs of sexuality and childhood are positioned in opposition, and therefore incompatible in the research process.

Conclusion

The social structures of childhood, which create vulnerability and the need for protection from inappropriate content, especially vis-à-vis subjects like sex/sexting, inhibit the discourse between adults and children and underscore its complexity. Child-centred research advances our understanding of the characteristics and needs of children, and shifts it from focusing exclusively on the anticipated dangers to children. As researchers, our attentiveness to the voices of children and their abilities, as opposed to their vulnerability, innocence, and need for protection, affirms their rights, including the right to be involved in discussions about their own life experiences.

The existing literature clearly shows that sexting among minors, despite its potent risks, is common in the era of internet technology, when everything is quickly and easily accessible. Young people use cyberspace and all of the related apps extensively, including to express their sexuality and conduct intimate relationships. Research in this field has confirmed that it is indeed a widespread phenomenon throughout the world and has raised awareness of the risks involved, highlighting the paucity of reported abuse and the need for educational, therapeutic, or law enforcement intervention. Research based on data collected directly from children and adolescents also provides the most authentic findings. This chapter has highlighted the complexity related to researching such sensitive topics and reveals the ongoing limitations of how research with children and young people continues to be constructed through ethical frameworks that perpetuate and privilege innocence in childhood and thus deny the agency and voices of children.

References

Abebe, T. and Bessell, S. (2014). Advancing ethical research with children: Critical reflections on ethical guidelines. *Children's Geographies* 12(1): 126–33.

Albury, K. and Crawford, K. (2012). Sexting, consent and young people's ethics: Beyond Megan's story. *Continuum* 26(3): 463–73.

Anderson, J. and Rainie, L. (2010). Millennials will make online sharing in networks a lifelong habit. *Pew Research*. http://pewresearch.org/millennials

Ashcraft, A.M. and Murray, P.J. (2017). Talking to parents about adolescent sexuality. *Pediatric Clinics* 64(2): 305–20.

Barak, A. and Dolev-Cohen, M. (2006). Does activity level in online support groups for distressed adolescents determine emotional relief? *Counselling and Psychotherapy Research* 6(3): 186–90.

Bianchi, D., Morelli, M., Baiocco, R., and Chirumbolo, A. (2019). Individual differences and developmental trends in sexting motivations. *Current Psychology* 40: 4531–4540.

Brechwald, W.A. and Prinstein, M.J. (2011). Beyond homophily: A decade of advances in understanding peer influence processes. *Journal of Research on Adolescence* 21(1): 166–79.

Burén, J. and Lunde, C. (2018). Sexting among adolescents: A nuanced and gendered online challenge for young people. *Computers in Human Behavior* 85: 210–17.

Campbell, S.W. and Park, Y.J. (2014). Predictors of mobile sexting among teens: Toward a new explanatory framework. *Mobile Media and Communication* 2(1): 20–39.

Casas, J.A., Ojeda, M., Elipe, P., and Del Rey, R. (2019). Exploring which factors contribute to teens' participation in sexting. *Computers in Human Behavior* 100: 60–9.

Chalfen, R. (2009). 'It's only a picture': Sexting, 'smutty' snapshots and felony charges. *Visual Studies* 24(3): 258–68.

Daly, A., Heah, R., and Liddiard, K. (2019). Vulnerable subjects and autonomous actors: The right to sexuality education for disabled under-18s. *Global Studies of Childhood* 9(3): 235–48.

De Looze, M., Constantine, N.A., Jerman, P., Vermeulen-Smit, E., and ter Bogt, T. (2015). Parent–adolescent sexual communication and its association with adolescent sexual behaviors: A nationally representative analysis in the Netherlands. *The Journal of Sex Research* 52(3): 257–68.

Dir, A.L., Coskunpinar, A., Steiner, J.L., and Cyders, M.A. (2013). Understanding differences in sexting behaviors across gender, relationship status, and sexual identity, and the role of expectancies in sexting. *Cyberpsychology, Behavior, and Social Networking* 16(8): 568–74.

Dolev-Cohen, M., Ricon, T., and Levkovich, I. (2020). #WhyIDidntReport: Reasons why young Israelis do not submit complaints regarding sexual abuse. *Children and Youth Services Review* 115: 1–9.

Flores, D. and Barroso, J. (2017). 21st century parent-child sex communication in the United States: A process review. *Journal of Sex Research* 54(4–5): 532–48. https://doi.org/10.1080/00224499.2016.1267693

Gámez-Guadix, M. and De Santisteban, P. (2018). 'Sex Pics?' Longitudinal predictors of sexting among adolescents. *Journal of Adolescent Health* 63(5): 608–14.

Gámez-Guadix, M., de Santisteban, P., and Resett, S. (2017). Sexting among Spanish adolescents: Prevalence and personality profiles. *Psicothema* 29(1): 29–34.

Ganji, J., Emamian, M.H., Maasoumi, R., Keramat, A., and Merghati Khoei, E. (2017). The existing approaches to sexuality education targeting children: A review article. *Iranian Journal of Public Health* 46(7): 890–98.

Gillespie, A.A. (2013). Adolescents, sexting and human rights. *Human Rights Law Review* 13(4): 623–43.

Gordon-Messer, D., Bauermeister, J.A., Grodzinski, A., and Zimmerman, M. (2013). Sexting among young adults. *Journal of Adolescent Health* 52(3): 301–6.

Hasinoff, A.A. and Shepherd, T. (2014). Sexting in context: Privacy norms and expectations. *International Journal of Communication* 8: 24.

Head, G. (2020). Ethics in educational research: Review boards, ethical issues and researcher development. *European Educational Research Journal* 19(1): 72–83. https://journals.sagepub.com/doi/pdf/10.1177/1474904118796315

Henderson, L. and Morgan, E. (2011). Sexting and sexual relationships among teens and young adults. *McNair Scholars Research Journal* 7(1): 31–39.

Holoyda, B., Landess, J., Sorrentino, R., and Friedman, S.H. (2018). Trouble at teens' fingertips: Youth sexting and the law. *Behavioral Sciences & the Law* 36(2): 170–81.

Hosseinkhanzadeh, A.A., Taher, M., and Esapoor, M. (2012). Attitudes to sexuality in individuals with mental retardation from perspectives of their parents and teachers. *International Journal of Sociology and Anthropology* 4(4): 134–46.

Klettke, B., Hallford, D.J., and Mellor, D.J. (2014). Sexting prevalence and correlates: A systematic literature review. *Clinical Psychology Review* 34(1): 44–53.

Kloess, J.A., Hamilton-Giachritsis, C.E., and Beech, A.R. (2019). Offense processes of online sexual grooming and abuse of children via internet communication platforms. *Sexual Abuse* 31(1): 73–96.

Kopecký, K. and Szotkowski, R. (2018). Sexting in the population of children and its risks: A quantitative study. *International Journal of Cyber Criminology* 12(2): 376–9.

Kunkel, D., Farrar, K.M., Eyal, K., Biely, E., Donnerstein, E., and Rideout, V. (2007). Sexual socialization messages on entertainment television: Comparing content trends 1997–2002. *Media Psychology* 9: 595–622.

Lee, M., Crofts, T., McGovern, A., and Milivojevic, S. (2015). Sexting among young people: Perceptions and practices. *Trends and Issues in Crime and Criminal Justice* 508: 1–9.

Lenhart, A. (2009). Teens and sexting: How and why minor teens are sending sexually suggestive nude or nearly nude images via text messaging. *Pew Research Center: Internet & Technology*. https://www.pewresearch.org/internet/2009/12/15/teens-and-sexting/

Lenhart, A., Ling, R., Campbell, S., and Purcell, K. (2010). Teens and mobile phones: Text messaging explodes as teens embrace it as the centerpiece of their communication strategies with friends. *Pew Internet & American Life Project*.

Lippman, J.R. and Campbell, S.W. (2014). Damned if you do, damned if you don't … if you're a girl: Relational and normative contexts of adolescent sexting in the United States. *Journal of Children and Media* 8(4): 371–86.

Livingstone, S., Haddon, L., Görzig, A., and Ólafsson, K. (2010). Risks and safety for children on the internet: The UK report. LSE, London: EU Kids Online. http://eprints.lse.ac.uk/33730/

Longo, R.E., Brown, S.M., and Orcutt, D.P. (2002). Effects of Internet sexuality on children and adolescents. In A. Cooper (ed.) *Sex and the Internet: A Guidebook for Clinicians* (pp 87–105). London: Routledge.

Madigan, S., Ly, A., Rash, C.L., Van Ouytsel, J., and Temple, J.R. (2018). Prevalence of multiple forms of sexting behavior among youth: A systematic review and meta-analysis. *JAMA Pediatrics* 172(4): 327–35. https://doi.org/10.1001/jamapediatrics.2017.5314

Maheux, A.J., Evans, R., Widman, L., Nesi, J., Prinstein, M.J., and Choukas-Bradley, S. (2020). Popular peer norms and adolescent sexting behavior. *Journal of Adolescence* 78: 62–6.

Moore, A. and Reynolds, P. (2018) *Childhood Sexuality: Contemporary Issues and Debates*. London: Palgrave Macmillan.

Mori, C., Temple, J.R., Browne, D., and Madigan, S. (2019). Association of sexting with sexual behaviors and mental health among adolescents: A systematic review and meta-analysis. *JAMA Pediatrics* 173(8): 770–9.

Nair, M.K.C., Leena, M.L., Paul, M.K., Pillai, H.V., Babu, G., Russell, P.S., and Thankachi, Y. (2012). Attitude of parents and teachers towards adolescent reproductive and sexual health education. *The Indian Journal of Pediatrics* 79(1): 60–3.

Oates, J. (2020). Research ethics, children, and young people. In Iphofen, R. (ed.) *Handbook of Research Ethics and Scientific Integrity* (pp 102–34). Cham: Springer.

Rice, E., Rhoades, H., Winetrobe, H., Sanchez, M., Montoya, J., Plant, A., and Kordic, T. (2012). Sexually explicit cell phone messaging associated with sexual risk among adolescents. *Pediatrics* 130(4): 667–73.

Richards, S., Clark, J., and Boggis, A. (2015). *Ethical Research with Children. Untold Narratives and Taboos*. Basingstoke: Palgrave Macmillan.

Ringrose, J., Harvey, L., Gill, R., and Livingstone, S. (2013). Teen girls, sexual double standards and 'sexting': Gendered value in digital image exchange. *Feminist Theory* 14(3): 305–23. https://doi.org/10.1177/1464700113499853

Robinson, K.H. (2008). In the name of 'childhood innocence': A discursive exploration of the moral panic associated with childhood and sexuality. *Cultural Studies Review* 14(2): 113–129.

Ševčíková, A. (2016). Girls' and boys' experience with teen sexting in early and late adolescence. *Journal of Adolescence* 51: 156–62.

Steinberg, L. (2008). A social neuroscience perspective on adolescent risk-taking. *Developmental Review* 28(1): 78–106.

Suler, J. (2004). The online disinhibition effect. *Cyberpsychology & Behavior* 7(3): 321–6.

Teo, S. and Morawska, A. (2021). Communicating with children about sexuality: A randomised controlled trial of a brief parenting discussion group. *Journal of Child and Family Studies* 30: 1487–500. https://doi.org/10.1007/s10826-021-01948-w

Tomczyk, Ł. and Kopecký, K. (2016). Children and youth safety on the Internet: Experiences from the Czech Republic and Poland. *Telematics and Informatics* 33(3): 822–33.

Van Ouytsel, J., Van Gool, E., Walrave, M., Ponnet, K., and Peeters, E. (2017). Sexting: Adolescents' perceptions of the applications used for, motives for, and consequences of sexting. *Journal of Youth Studies* 20(4): 446–70.

Van Ouytsel, J., Walrave, M., De Marez, L., Vanhaelewyn, B., and Ponnet, K. (2020). A first investigation into gender minority adolescents' sexting experiences. *Journal of Adolescence* 84: 213–18.

Wachs, S., Wright, M.F., Gámez-Guadix, M., and Döring, N. (2021). How are consensual, non-consensual, and pressured sexting linked to depression and self-harm? The moderating effects of demographic variables. *International Journal of Environmental Research and Public Health* 18(5): 2597.

Widman, L., Javidi, H., Maheux, A.J., Evans, R., Nesi, J., and Choukas-Bradley, S. (2021). Sexual communication in the digital age: Adolescent sexual communication with parents and friends about sexting, pornography, and starting relationships online. *Sexuality & Culture*. https://doi.org/10.1007/s12119-021-09866-1

Wittes, B., Poplin, C., Jurecic, Q., and Spera, C. (2016). *Sextortion: Cybersecurity, Teenagers, and Remote Sexual Assault*. Washington, DC: Center for Technology at Brookings.

Wolak, J., Finkelhor, D., Wals, W., and Treitman, L. (2018). Sextortion of minors: Characteristics and dynamics. *Journal of Adolescent Health* 62(1): 72–9. doi.org/10.1016/j.jadohealth.2017.08.014

Ybarra, M.L. and Mitchell, K.J. (2005). Exposure to Internet pornography among children and adolescents: A national survey. *Cyberpsychology & Behavior* 8(5): 473–86.

Yépez-Tito, P., Ferragut, M., and Blanca, M.J. (2019). Prevalence and profile of sexting among adolescents in Ecuador. *Journal of Youth Studies* 22(4): 505–19.

3

Responding Reflexively, Relationally, and Reciprocally to Unequal Childhoods

Pallawi Sinha

Introduction

Childhood remains a contested subject. With capitalist forces and neoliberal agendas driving forth the 'global child', universal development, and massification of education, tensions around the notions of childhood across the local–global and North–South divide have become emphasised. Social constructions of an 'ideal' childhood, countered by scholarship primarily from the South, have since matured and diversified in the 21st century, which may otherwise have been 'impervious to enlightened insights' (Nieuwenhuys, 2008, p 4) emerging from the rich peripheries of the majority worlds (Connell, 2007). Only by problematising 'childhood essentialisms' (Nieuwenhuys, 2010), 'global coloniality' (Escobar, 2008) in knowledge production and legitimisation, and reifying structural disjuncture, can a move beyond the monocultural logics (Santos, 2008) of childhood, and research with children and young people, begin to take shape and cater to difference (see Barad, 2007; Chen, 2010; Burman, 2019; de Castro 2020).

In recent years, post-developmental, postcolonial, and posthuman scholars and researchers have foregrounded the distinct material, geographical, social, discursive, and political conditions within which a myriad of childhoods occur and are constructed at the peripheries. The childhoods observed within this chapter remain entangled with such shifting and unequal topographies, which contour their lived worlds. It draws on my postdoctoral experiences and postgraduate research studies with children in disadvantaged and marginalised contexts of India between the years 2011 and 2019. A particular focus is cast on the indigenous Hill Sabar children of Jharkhand to contrast their embodied difference in contextual particularities with the hegemonic, globalised notion of childhood. The first section accordingly highlights how normativity reproduces essentialisms in thinking about childhoods at the peripheries. This is discussed in relation to postcolonial perspectives, briefly interrogating modernity and its habitual constructions of 'other' children, towards reframing the 'singularity of stories' (Balagopalan, 2019, p 231).

Reflections on these issues lead chapter discussions to meaningful ways of researching with children. At the core of such precedence is children's voice about the social phenomenon of interest. Here, research is thus understood as a social process, contoured by power and privilege, which urges strategies for reflexivity framed by the relational and ontological contexts of childhoods examined. Within my own studies, reflexivity underscored the implicit and explicit tensions between academia, the site and 'self'. It is important to note, however, that the performativity of reflexivity cannot be contained within the privileged realms of the researcher or issued as an abstract existentialist condition to validate 'truth' claims. Rather, with this text my intention is to draw out the reflexive 'turn' on contexts, conditions, concepts, and practices of children's lives, one's sites of inquiry, and the gaps in researcher knowledge that may be bridged by reflexivity or what Garfinkel (1967) proposes as 'uninteresting' conversations on ways of knowing and doing that make the familiar strange and the strange familiar.

The following sections then explore how reflexivity shaped the researcher and research only to be reshaped by the research sites and what particular reflexive approaches emphasised the invisibilised voice of the Sabar children. Such reflexive practice that engenders researcher positionality, situatedness of the study, authentic listening, reflections on the dominant socio-discursive agendas, and 'difference' has significant implications for ethical research – particularly those research practices framed by marginalisation, poverty, and emancipation – in terms of an ethic of care, multiple subjectivities, social justice, the rigour of the study, and realisation of professional practice, (see Finlay, 2002; Smith, 2012; Liamputtong and Kurban, 2018; Alejandro, 2021). In conclusion, deliberations urge consideration of ways in which knowledge generation may begin to become emancipatory, shaped by reflexivity, and foreground the ethical priorities for acknowledging difference in research.

Childhood essentialism and children at the peripheries

There is a growing recognition among scholars today that renderings of childhood emphasise modern Western ideologues and imaginaries (Burman, 2001; Cannella and Kincheloe, 2002; Nsamenang, 2005; Nieuwenhuys, 2009b; Balagopalan, 2011; de Castro, 2018). Concomitantly, the UN Convention on the Rights of the Child (1989) in its attempt to cater to the 'world's children', and later in universalising agendas for an equitable future for all, has endorsed and idealised the Western childhood (see Stephens, 1995; Burman, 2011; Nieuwenhuys, 2013; Balagopalan, 2019). Chen (2010) further highlights how Western social theories operationalised in non-Western nation-states have historically produced erroneous, and often delegitimised, knowledges of the 'Rest'. The 20th century, accordingly, prompted the visible continuum of hierarchical knowledge production and dissemination, first privileging then reproducing a singular childhood. This, in turn, has widened inequalities in education and research distancing 'peripheral' childhoods from the 'developed' North. The globalising tendencies of the neoliberal world have thus beset hegemonic contingencies transnationally that urge examination of the politics of childhood, particularly in relation to universal logics, knowledge erasures, and the ethics and practice of research itself.

Over the last three decades, scholars, particularly from, or working in, the Southern contexts, have attempted to foreground the varying constructions of childhood across the post-colonies. While Balagopalan (2011) is optimistic in asserting an 'exciting epistemic shift' towards 'multiple childhoods' releasing the notion of childhood from its 'normative moorings' (p 291), the realities of the children at the peripheries – including the rural, street, and indigenous children of my studies – have remained entangled with, and often suffocated by, the essentialising tendencies and universalisms propagated by the dominant 'gaze' on childhood, development studies, education, and research. This has been the failure of modernity's 'civilising' mission, also made evident by the crises of well-intentioned international programmes such as Education for All and the Millennium Development Goals. In the following section, I introduce one such childhood that challenges the Western 'gold standards for the contemporary world order' (Nsamenang, 2005, p 18), and which is raised with the intention to underscore 'difference' beyond cultural relativism and confront the insidious colonial legacies that continue to frame the lives of children in peripheral countries.

(Re-)imagining an 'Indian' childhood or orientalising a *boka* child?

Within the framework of multiplicities, children, particularly those that deviate from the norm, are often posited as 'objects of concern' (McLaughlin, 2015, p 7) by Western and dominant societies. With this reading of postcolonial childhoods performed at the *rich peripheries*, I hope to rearticulate childhoods beyond normativity. Thus, I draw upon, and contextualise, the lives of the 'particularly-vulnerable' indigenous Hill Sabar[1] children and young people (CYP) of Jharkhand, India, who remain invisibilised from the public arena and India's policy priorities. This is undertaken with the purpose of rethinking concepts, values, and practices of childhood towards envisaging meaningful ways of researching with 'other' children.

The indigenous communities or Adivasis (literally, First Inhabitants) of India are a heterogeneous group of more than 705 communities speaking more than 100 dialects. They vary greatly in terms of their histories, ethnicities, geographies, sociocultural practices, and politics but are officially notified in a monolithic group, the Scheduled Tribes. Indigenous peoples form 8.6 per cent of India's population (approximately 104 million people) yet account for 45.3 per cent of the poorest in the country (International Institute for Population Science survey, 2021). The Hill Sabar communities comprise a minute proportion of the indigenous population with their own distinct realities. While India's ratification of the United Nations Declaration on the Rights of Indigenous Peoples has been selective, it has foregrounded indigenous politics. Nevertheless, indigenous groups continue to struggle to preserve their identity and uphold their rights, and are barely consulted in matters that concern them.[2]

This was clearly illustrated by the Hill Sabar, who were never consulted and were denied access to their lands from their lands and forced to migrate while private corporations plundered the forest produce for pharmaceutical raw materials and industrial minerals. Similarly, the Sabar were rarely engaged in conversations related to their economic, educational, or ontological needs, priorities, and practices, given dominant presumptions that Sabar peoples and children are *boka* (useless, naive, buffoons). Contrary to the dominant world's portrayal of the Hill Sabar as *boka*, 'idle', 'lethargic' 'merry-makers', my study found them to be a hard-working group who rose by 3–4 am to commence daily chores and leave for work in the forest by 7 am, only to return home by sunset. Children often accompanied their families to 'learn by doing'. Their work is labour intensive, including foraging for medicinal herbs and edible foods, collecting wood for fires and the construction of buildings and tools, making *mahua* (fermented milk), and tending livestock for both personal use and trade.

In terms of education, the hegemonic essentialisms and universalisms advocated by the dominant societies have exacerbated inequalities. For Adivasi populations, this has affected their engagement with formal education systems. According to the Census in 2011 (Registrar General and Census Commissioner, 2011), a mere 59 per cent of indigenous children of all ages (68.5 per cent male and 49.4 per cent female children) are deemed literate in comparison to the 73 per cent literacy rate of children nationally, with boys at 80.9 per cent and girls 64.6 per cent. The Sabar adults and CYP were neither included in the Census reports nor were they a priority for teachers or third-sector bodies operating in the region. During my 11 months of fieldwork, the appointed teacher did not visit the school once. In fact, he, like other dominant members of society, warned me that the children "are boka, they will not understand", they had neither the "inclination nor capacity to engage", and if they did "they will not pay attention for longer than 15–20 minutes, you can try". Ironically, Sabar children undertook the research with me five days a week, working three to four hours daily.

India's project of modernity has subsequently produced the *boka* child, orientalising its own 'other' (see Said, 1978; Chakrabarty, 2000). As will be made evident further on, from the work generated by the Sabar children, the assumed limitations are hardly their onus to bear. Instead, there is an emphasis on the dissonance between indigenous peoples' ethico-onto-epistemologies (Barad, 2007) or ethical ways of knowing, doing, and being, and 'distant' dominant ideologies posited as education for (rather than by) indigenous peoples is yet concerned narrowly with measurements – of school enrolment numbers, literacy attainment, and vocational skills (Ministry of Tribal Affairs, 2021). This cultivates a 'flattening out of the particular albeit multiple local-national hierarchies and inequalities that mark children's lives' (Balagopalan, 2019, p 231). While the National Education Policy (2020) acknowledges that indigenous children 'find their school education irrelevant and foreign ... culturally and academically', its strategy to confront such disparities is limited to special hostels, bridge courses, and financial assistance, and appears merely tokenistic in its inclusion of 'tribal knowledge' (pp. 25, 16).

These concerns around universalist and essentialist thinking are pertinent also in addressing the undertones of the Western projects of 'saving' the 'undersocialised', underdeveloped 'Indian' childhoods from their wanting families, now made the subjects of global governance (Nandy, 1987; Balagopalan 2008; Nieuwenhuys, 2009a, respectively). As Kumar (2007) retorts 'the child's life at home was seen as an impediment to the attainment of goals for which the school was working under the direction of the colonial state' (p 201). The Hill Sabar CYP thus face a 'double apartheid' (Appadurai, 2000, p 2) of hegemonic powers not only delegitimising their languages, knowledges, and practices, but also rendering their families and 'self' invisible. Such contemplations and conditions foregrounded reflexivity as an ethical imperative for my research, offering crucial lessons in relation to the peoples, the site, and the wider contexts, and practical consideration for those interested in childhood, indigenous, and cross-cultural studies and research, as discussed next.

Research as a site for reflexivity

Given the conditions, in (re)imagining an indigenous childhood an analysis of the uneven topographies (whether historical, social, material, geographical, or discursive contexts) that shape indigenous children's lives becomes significant. Since the 'dualisms which continue to dominate western thought are inadequate for understanding a world of multiple causes and effects, ... historical and cultural specificities' a core tool to (re-)turn the researcher's gaze is reflexivity (Lather, 1991, p 21). Only by acknowledging and addressing the unequal and continually shifting topographies of postcolonial and indigenous research can the (re-)searching self locate possible means of navigating them and transform research. Here, research itself is envisaged as a site for reflexivity, albeit temporal, liminal, and philosophical. This situated the researcher and research across: the *paradigmatic* sites (South–North; ideological, political, or historical framings); the *academic* sites (say university/faculty, library, conference, or discipline), the *field* sites (for example, nation-state, specifically, where the Sabar were located and neighbouring villages); and *excavation* sites (research sites for 'knowing'; Sabar places for 'being' and 'doing'; spaces-places of researcher-'researched' un-learning); each folding and unfolding into the other to inform the study, reflexively.

Research with the Hill Sabar CYP living in contexts of multiple disadvantages (see previous section) necessitated a configuring and reconfiguring of these sites, first, by acknowledging the 'centre' (sites of privilege and power, sites I occupied, of knowledge production and dissemination) then a de-centring or moving away from the dominant gaze, of 'academic delivery and consumption' and the 'legitimation discourse of colonising states' (de Castro, 2020), followed by a re-centring to emphasise the epistemic formations, practices, and values, informed by the social actors of the research. It is from these situated locations in which the researcher becomes embedded that our perceptions, imagination and lived experiences emerge. Reflexivity, at the centre of research thinking, enhanced the capacity to configure and reconfigure the self and the said sites, broadened the study's fields of perception, and was not simply concerned with 'stepping back' to reflect on one's biases, elaborated further on.

Reflexivity in practice also led to my proposal of a personal theory of action which contoured the ontological, epistemological, and methodological aims of the study, always asking: why is the study of any importance; what are its aims, what matters and who will it affect; what else is there – between and beyond each site of inquiry? The underlying philosophy for such a theory is *dharma*[3] and emancipation intended to diminish the widening chasms of epistemologies, ethics, personal action, 'outsider' intentions, and researcher limitations. I found recognising, and eventually classifying, a theory of personal action to be particularly significant in appreciating the non-human and human entities, unforeseeable disruptions, reflexive conversations, moments of self-questioning, or dissonance with local work ethics as it continually reinforced my priorities for the study despite planned-for or unpredictable difficulties. In doing so, the study was able to overcome 'ethical singularity' in acknowledging that while responses emerged from all sides it is always the case that some things may not be heard (Spivak, 1999, p 384). While the personal theory of action foregrounds conceptualisations of research design as ethical praxis, ethics of listening authentically, and ethics as researcher reflexivity (see Sinha, 2017), for the purposes of the chapter, I will focus on elaborating reflexivity as an ethical tool for reconfiguring the entangled assemblage of research-researcher-researched. Yet, the path to qualitative research is one that cannot always be predetermined, thus the strategies offered may or may not find universal understanding. Instead, these reveal how, while remaining entangled with the mentioned sites, specific actions and priorities were enacted and have facilitated my own (un-)learning in the process.

The following sections then examine a reflexive turn on the researcher, thus research that situated research contexts, sites, peoples, and their own positionality. It extends this discussion on reflexivity by elaborating on the relationality of difference – that is, the multiplicity of voices engaged, what significance the study may have for the researcher personally, for the community engaged, and for the wider community, whether academic, social, or political – and the ethics of reciprocity to consider what the ultimate purpose of research may be, ways to 'give back', and how far the 'knowers' of research (the researcher-'researched' or the field) may be ready to go and embrace it.

A reflexive 'turn' on research

In studies such as mine that embark on unfamiliar terrains, an 'absence of formulas to guarantee social knowledge' demands 'vigorous self-reflexivity' (Lather, 1991, p 66). Researching with indigenous children is concomitantly underscored by the immeasurable valence of differentials (say, power, privilege, and socio-economic status), which, nevertheless embodies distinct hopes, beliefs, actions, morals, and possible contradictions. This prompted rigorous de- and re-construction of the 'self'- 'other', research paradigms and paradoxes, and the ethics and politics of research. My study thus looked to reflexivity as a process underscoring 'uncomfortable realities' (Pillow, 2003, p 193) of research and a tool to question the 'practical politics of cultural explanations' (Spivak, 1998, p 141).

It was imperative then that first I acknowledged and navigated my own positions of power and privilege, and as the 'outsider'. Initially, I drafted reflection notes on writing and rewriting the self (Freeman, 1993). At the core of such self-reflexivity lay locating the researcher-self within the 'self' manifested over the years. This beckoned introspection into the colossal question: 'who am I?' but suddenly across blurring boundaries of several 'self's – female-human, academic-practitioner, partially colonised-insider, scientific-artistic, spiritual-political Indian researcher living in the United Kingdom. The moment of transit, however, perpetuated complexities of difference, the 'other' and self-identity. This led to examining the nature of scholarship referenced (which until then had largely been drawn from Northern scholars), and the discourse employed within these and my own texts (say, how indigeneity and childhood were defined or adopting the term Adivasi for indigenous communities of India since scholars argued that due to its ancient history all its inhabitants are in fact indigenous).

Indeed, a self was being rewritten but while such self-examination started as an exercise in positioning oneself, it culminated as a self-seeking process that defined all future research action. For instance, reflexive considerations about my positions of power and privilege concomitantly urged building an understanding of the historical, social, economic, and political disadvantages confronted by the indigenous worlds before entering the field and *in situ*. This initiated a critical and thematic analysis of policies, government legislation and provisioning, and wide-ranging research and reports (on education, health, social welfare, and finance) across international, national, and regional contexts of indigeneity. Further, it directed examination of the hierarchical nature of language (which demanded I learn Kharia[4] instead of simply relying on a translator) and knowledges (say scientific over traditional, epistemologies over ontologies, or ways of 'knowing' over 'being', North over South), and how these may be overcome.

Such explicit 'self-aware meta-analysis' (Finlay, 2002, p 209) was significant also in positioning the research, its priorities, and eventual alignment with postcolonial and indigenous underpinnings. Reflexivity in methodological thinking offered a powerful resource for negotiations of power – whether in acknowledging 'other' ways, appreciating the entangled binaries (of the adult–child, dominant–subordinate, and insider–outsider), or examining the ongoing impact of colonialism (Smith, 2012; Vanner, 2015). This defined the ethical stance of the study beyond academic prescriptions, established strategies for enquiry and authentic listening, and diminished distortions of power and privilege. For instance, upon my initial visit, I found that the Hill Sabar were conventionally illiterate, which made my consent and information sheets redundant. In consideration of their oral traditions, consent was then obtained audiovisually before each research activity, while research intentions were elaborated verbally in Kharia, with drawings, and reiterated over different phases of inquiry.

Positioning research within indigenous ontologies that adhere to the 'circle of life' also enabled envisaging research not as a linear but as a cyclical process. Reflexivity about the wider contexts of research, researcher limitations (of language, uncharted terrains, and 'first contact'), and power disparities led to devising three advancing phases of enquiry.[5] This offered spaces for reflection between stages, allowing for all social actors engaged (including children, practitioners, field assistants, the third sector, and state officials) to explore and revisit relevant constructs, policies, provisioning and practices, tools of inquiry, difference, and research intentions. For instance, reflexive ethnomethodological[6] conversations undertaken with children during ordinary, ceremonial, and epistemic Sabar practices (say, foraging, death ritual, or making tools) enabled an understanding of the differentiations in language and notions, say the different values attached to education – *sheeksha* (teaching), *seekh* (life-lesson), *padhusu* (reading/studying), and *gyan* (education of the mind or wisdom). It departed from the limited definitions (related to formal education or social mobility) offered by the teachers and state officials, who were startled by children's broader understanding. This delegated some power to Sabar children as the experts on their lives, and infused confidence.

Following such insights, the study also made use of bespoke audiovisual and spatial participatory tools that reflected children's everyday realities and observed practices, which enabled listening authentically and elicited rich insights despite textual limitations. Take, for example, the sensory exploration tool 'Life, a Tree' (Box 3.1), which entailed participatory tours led by children locating and describing their favourite tree. Non-/participant observations of Hill Sabar children's lived world had made me aware of their proclivity for climbing, swinging from trees, collecting fruits and red ants, and engaging in creative play under the trees' shade. The activity not only reiterated their unique relationship with trees and informed research queries, but just as importantly propelled conversations to distinctive stories, garnered children's trust, and eventually allowed authentic access into their worlds. Reflexive spaces embedded in methodological thinking also offered opportunities for amending and designing tools in consultation with the CYP. An example of this was the Cube of Hope activity (Figure 3.1), which involved children drawing their ideas about formal education. However, children stated that they had barely had any lessons in the last three years, and so this altered the activity to investigate aspects of their lived world that involved learning (such as my life, a Sabar culture, a new learning, my future school, my rights, and my place) and deconstructing notions of indigeneity, education, and rights with children.

Box 3.1: Excerpt from 'Life, a Tree'

R: Ah so you all come here?
B3: We come with him to play. He showed it to us.
R: So, what do you all play? [Some of us climb up, some sit under, in the shade]
B1: Who climbs the highest? Sometimes, we just sit, sometimes hide and seek. Also, we split its big seeds, and play with that. [B3 climbs right to the top]
G1: [shyly] We make *bor-kanya* (bridegroom-bride) and the wedding party out of the leaves.

B3: I like to swing. We all do, isn't it?

R: Wow, you all must have fun. [B4 swings on the branches] Please be safe. [To G1: Will you show me? She nods. Returning to B1] How did you find this tree?

B1: When I was young [he is no more than 12 years old] I used to come to these jungles with my mother to collect the leaves.

R: Why did she collect the leaves?

B1: To sell for *biddi*-making [tobacco leaf roll-ups]. We would sit under it for shade when it was too hot. Ate food, collected again. Then carried piles back.

R: Do you still come with her?

B1: [quiet]

B2: She is no more.

R: Oh, I am so sorry to hear that.

B1: But I still come here. It is good, breezy, calm.

R: I can feel it. [gesture the same] So what else do you do here?

B1: Nothing. Rest. Sit. See things happening.

B5: [mumbles] He plays the flute!

R: Do you really? That's great, will you show me one day?

B1: [nods awkwardly] I am still learning.

R: Thank you. It is a good tree to sit under [I climb down, as do others] and play the flute. I had a tree when I was young, it got cut down, I was very sad. But it is good you have your tree.

B1: Yes but people are cutting our trees. Grandfather says that in his time trees were very big and green. He says now, they are so thin that even monkeys don't come, forget lions, bear or elephants.

Figure 3.1: Cube of Hope (CoH) activity – Sabar children in classroom; Sabar child using scissors for the first time; a Sabar boy's final net; and girl's constructed cube

 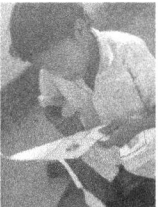  

As the section evidences, researcher positionality and reflexivity have proven effective in building relationships of trust, diminishing barriers of power and privilege, and emphasising 'other' knowledges. Instead of pre-manufactured tools designed within the confines of academic walls that

may have overlooked the Sabar history, ontology, or sociocultural realities, reflexivity situated the research within its global and immediate contexts, facilitated strategies for partnership, negotiated children's ownership of the study, and elicited rich insights where traditional methods may not have done so. The reflexive 'turn' of the researcher and research thus disrupted, not only the privileging of self over the other but also knowledge over being and scientific over traditional knowledges.

The relationality of difference

Indigenous ontologies observe life as interwoven with human and non-human entities, communality, and reciprocity. Reflexivity in researching with the Sabar children urged acknowledgement of the relational 'ways of being'. For the Sabar, the crucial elements of their entangled existence are *jal* (water), *jungle* (forests), *janvar* (animals), *jan* (people), and *jameen* (earth), and this relationality is not merely practical or material but is in fact at the core of 'being' Sabar. This foregrounded the everyday contexts that shaped Sabar lives despite the disparate agendas and 'distant' ideologies that frame it. Such deliberations, in turn, highlighted the fundamentally relational nature of the 'self' between the historically constituted and emergent self, the self-determining versus essentialised self. This prompted rigorous deconstruction of the relational 'self' and 'other', research paradigms and paradoxes, and the ethics and politics of research.

What these elucidations made evident was the inevitability of a relational framework of inquiry and knowledge making that engaged differing voices, concepts, practices, and priorities in engendering a comprehensive picture of Sabar children's realities and dismantling of dominant strategies. Before entering the field, a critical analysis of scholarship was imperative to grounding knowledge in the historical, social, material, political, and discursive conditions of Sabar lives in relation to the global and national contexts of indigeneity. This revealed the marked lack of academic research with indigenous peoples in India (none with the Sabar), particularly on childhood and education, and the over-reliance on the ethnographic 'gaze' or statistical measurements in the research that still exist. In reconfiguring the centre and generating an authentic study on Sabar lives, it was clear that the research would be enriched by listening widely and relationally. Ways of listening and emphasising Sabar participation in, and negotiation of, their everyday lives then could not be exclusionary in either merely reiterating the dominant hegemonies or isolating children's voice. The study thus relied on continued conversations across differing levels of Sabar children's engagement and marginalisation – namely, the home (parents, grandparents, extended family members, and siblings); the community (Hill Sabar Elders, chiefs, shamens, youth, and children); the school (headteachers, teachers, support staff); and the state (members of the bureaucratic and administrative apparatus and other elite bodies from the health, land, social welfare, and education sectors) – to learn directly from and challenge presuppositions. Moreover, 'methodological consciousness' (Finlay, 2002) underscored the significance of generating knowledge that did not put humans at the centre of the research, but instead extended 'knowing' to places-spaces of 'doing' and 'being', animals, and nature. This further devised a relational analysis of data offered by the study.

While a gargantuan task, such a relational analysis of, and conversations across, Sabar children's home–community–school–state nexus, across time and space, concomitantly emphasised commonalities and difference that facilitated a rigorous rendering of their lives and diminished cultural essentialisms. This has particular relevance for decolonising indigenous research where 'the problem of identity returns as a persistent questioning of the frame, the space of representation … confronted by its difference, its Other' (Bhabha, 1994, p 66). And this problematic of representation is magnified if the researcher is not reflexive about the relationality of representation (whether self, the 'other', or those participating in the study, directly or indirectly) since it invisibilises difference and the gaps in knowledge within each context. Achieving any worthiness in indigenous research then entails limiting representational errors that emerge from the dualities and disparities of contexts, conditions, and ontologies. Reflexivity about the relational nature of difference and representation enabled reading of data and drawing conclusions in ways that accentuated assumptions, value judgements, and blatant errors in perception, across contexts.

Nonetheless, representation and 'representability' are limited neither to the realm of the 'knowing investigator' nor to the '(un)knowing subject' (Gandhi, 1998, p 2). In this research encounter, interpretive accounts emerged from multiple perspectives and the work of social research could only begin when the assumed knowledges and representations had been dismantled. For instance, researcher assumption that Hill Sabar women suffered the same secondary status (based on literacy rates, health indicators, and participation in democratic and economic activity) as others in India was confronted by Sabar women's suspicion of my research intentions and confusion about 'why a woman would travel so far just to listen to them'. Only by creating spaces for mutual dialogue and relaying research information that reflected common values, hope, and concerns relationally was it possible to overturn such suppositions. Assumptions about the researcher across the different nexuses altered from a Maoist insurgent or a *badaa sahib* or civil servant, to "strong lady" and "just like us". In representing the Hill Sabar children, it was equally important to move away from cultural relativism and disrupt hegemonising essentialisms reproduced by the dominant world (say lazy, carefree truants or *boka*). Moreover, indigenous studies have been inextricably linked with colonialism, and in India, its ongoing legacy presupposes the indigenous individuals or groups to be at the centre of the 'indigenous problem' ("Sabar are not interested in education"; "these people are just lazy") rather than a structural, political, or social hinderance. Thus, the researcher, when presented with such a maxim, whether by the children or those in dominant positions, immediately produced children's works to counter it.

Epistemological reflexivity further reflected this relational and contextualised understanding during dissemination such that representations were not 'embedded ... in the culture, institutions, and political ambience of the representer' (Said, 1978, p 272), and resisted (re)description according to dominant interests. In practice this meant that while at the core of my dissertation was the Sabar voice, it wove in the relational voices that shaped children's lives. As importantly, it included texts in Kharia alongside an extensive glossary to emphasise the Sabar language and its textual and cultural registers. Relationality also espoused knowledge exchange, journalling, and analysis of notions between the researcher, academe, and the wider stakeholders. This was initiated before stepping into the primary site, conducted during fieldwork, and 'unpacked' during the process of writing up the thesis due to the observed dissonance between the mentioned contexts/nexuses. Such praxis not only extended my understanding of multiple subjectivities, but also delineated representational renderings to historical, sociocultural, material, and political difference and agendas, which was disseminated to the wider networks and rights- and stakeholders. It shifted the discourse within such exchanges from saviourship and dominance to children as experts and rightsholders of their lives, indigenous self-determination, legitimisation of 'other' knowledges, and wanting public provisioning.

Ethics of reciprocity

Reciprocity is a central tenet of indigenous ontology. Indigenous peoples have reverent and reciprocal relationships with nature, places they inhabit, and their community. As Hart (2010) indicates, it 'reflects the relational worldview and the understanding that we must honour our relationships with other life' (p 7). Indigenous research, particularly that which is situated in contexts of marginalisation, disadvantages and poverty, demonstrates how reciprocity addresses the unequal and often dichotomous relationship between the knowledge 'producer' and 'consumer' by offering spaces for mutual 'giving' between the researcher and 'researched' (see Kirkness and Barnhardt, 1991; Smith, 2012; Swartz, 2011; McGregor and Marker 2018). Liamputtong (2010) reiterates this, 'by giving something back ... researchers can reduce power inequality between themselves and the researched (pp 80–1). Due to the ontological priorities of the Sabar and the epistemological bearing of my study, considering ways of giving back was thus an imperative, however limited the extent of my influence may have been. Nevertheless, these were fraught with confrontations of personal-academic-professional ethics and responsibilities.

Researcher-research reflexivity directed recognising and enacting reciprocity with the intention to value participants sharing their knowledge, lives, and time with a relative stranger despite no material benefits. Often participating in my research meant that the Sabar could not go to work a full day in the jungle and if the support practitioners absconded there would be no way to communicate our absence and their day could be wasted. Also, at the onset of the study, I observed that field assistants and translators who were primarily from 'higher' castes or tribal communities frequently exhibited privileged behaviour – whether in referring to the Sabar in derogatory terms, deciding places of research for their convenience rather than the hills where the Sabar inhabited, demanding forest resources to be foraged on their behalf or water on a sunny day when the Sabar children and families have to walk 5–10 kms sometimes to fetch water, or expecting a cot to be brought out for them to sit on while the Sabar sat in circles on the ground. In acting reciprocally, I not only ensureed that I sat with the Sabar peoples as they did, but we also scheduled meetings to suit them, and reiterated that they were the experts while the research team were the learners. I also ensured that I undertook rigorous training of the field assistants to include punctuality, respect for the Sabar and their ways, on language employed, barriers of power-privilege in research, and the code of practice, as non-negotiables.

There are multiple epistemological and practical reciprocal actions that a researcher may undertake over the research cycle to act in the participants' best interests and demonstrate genuine concerns about their lives or for their community. The epistemological stance of the study itself may be a start; for instance, reciprocity in my research commenced with the prioritisation of 'deep' listening, and an empathy for adults' and children's anxieties about the research or 'real-world' issues, which led to crafting multitextual tools and deconstruction of core constructs. Practical aspects of reciprocity in my study related to responding to Sabar adults' and children's requests or addressing gaps in knowledge. In 'going beyond' the research priorities, this entailed helping participants develop a skill (say, writing their names, teaching maths to diminish anxieties about being cheated in markets, or familiarising Sabar with, and directing them to, relevant government/non-government bodies). It also led to addressing a gap in knowledge identified by Sabar children, women, and men and creating an activity where they were introduced to, and deconstructed ideas about, rights, necessities, needs and wants. For all groups, these ended with discussions on available policies and provisions, possible democratic action, and future participation. Moreover, upon completion of each activity and post fieldwork, I ensured that I returned to relate relevant information and findings to the participants. This small act upheld trust in my intentions and for future researchers.

Where possible, reciprocity engages in some form of social action, if not social change, for the immediate community. In my case, I organised two established NGOs to visit their hamlets, enabling children and adults to share their concerns and priorities for future development and schemes. Since I had been informed of Sabar concerns, post discussions with the community, I also took Sabar representatives to meet with the Deputy Commissioner such that they could relate their ordeals directly, register themselves for government rations and structural provisioning for water irrigation, and identify their lands for ownership. Post fieldwork, I returned to the site with books, stationery, and collected toys, shoes, and clothes for the indigenous children. These 'tangible rewards' were offered in consultation with the people and aimed to address the 'local ethics of immediate needs' (Nama and Swartz, 2002, p 295). During writing up, and post research, I revisited the sites twice, once to discuss findings with the community and offer children CDs and images of their works and research, and the next time to meet with stakeholders and the Sabar (to present findings, share the report drafted for state and non-government bodies, and deliver workshops) and see if any changes had been made. By 'going deep' and 'giving back', this study was able to diminish some of the power disparities.

With limited funds and time, such steps may seem unfeasible to novice researchers but there are diverse ways of being reciprocal. As with my research, researchers may find ways of disseminating knowledge generated in the field to create awareness (through conference and seminar presentations, workshops, or writing articles) to ensure the findings reach the people concerned with research. Personally, reciprocity has meant an ethical commitment to my social actors, even when academic and personal commitments have not always allowed physical contact. While I completed my fieldwork in July 2014, I still think about my research, reflect on what could have been done better, whether I have done justice to my participants' voice and been authentic in my representation of their lives, or how my positions of power and privilege may have (re-)manifested as I exited the site to move on to an academic life. I have since questioned if I have maintained the ethics of reciprocity deemed imperative to my research. Thus, reflexivity has been continual and is an ongoing process, despite disruptions and unintended distances.

Acknowledging 'other-ness'

This chapter has sought to emphasise reflexivity not merely as a tool to 'turn' the researcher's gaze, but also to problematise and extend the very nature, discourse, and dialectics of research and negotiate the available academic positions that may otherwise bind us structurally. In observing reflexivity broadly – across the ontological, methodological, and epistemic framings of research – the text evidences how an indigenous study was able to diminish power disparities, delineate relational engagements, and ascertain reciprocal encounters that foregrounded difference, agency, and legitimisation of 'other' knowledges rather than reproduction of dominant dispositions.

Scholars of childhood studies have argued that the notion of childhood reflects dominant adult imaginaries, morals, and political agendas rather than children themselves (see Valentine, 1996; James et al, 1998; Cannella and Kincheloe, 2002; Sircar and Dutta, 2011; Nieuwenhuys, 2013; Balagopalan, 2019). Ontological reflexivity, then, is particularly important in visibilising the 'contradictory, plural and heterogenous struggles' of the children that participated in my studies, 'whose outcomes are never predictable, even retrospectively' but has been postscripted by the acquisitional and modernising agendas of this 'imaginary Europe' (Chakrabarty, 2000, p 42) proficient at invisibilising their particular realities emerging from the peripheries. As Bourdieu (1993) reaffirms, such reflexivity about the paradigm and contexts of research 'opens possibilities for rational action, aiming at undoing or redoing what history has done' (p 1399). It is this criticality of 'gaze' on the 'mimetic' 'other' childhoods (Bhabha, 1990) which ahistoricises the histories, philosophies, and futures of children driven to the margins that ontological reflexivity foregrounds and confronts. Children in rich peripheral countries do not live in flattened, monochromatic, or easily scalable topographies that may appear so from the distant, high ground of dominant ideologies. This is not to valorize the labouring lives of children or dispense with the well-intentioned programmes of development of the last 70 years that have 'so miserably failed' (Nieuwenhuys, 2009b, p 245).

Rather, reflexivity about the unequal topographies that children inhabit, whether historical, material, socio-political, or discursive, has prompted the methodological 'turn', ethical priorities, and the social performativity of my research with Hill Sabar children. Methodological reflexivity then directed attention to how 'other' voices, perspectives, knowledges, and practices may be engendered. Since 'ways of being', 'knowing' and 'doing' are situated, relational, and continually evolving, reflexivity cannot be neutral. Such reflexivity, driven by meta-self-analysis, relationality, and reciprocity in my research, has espoused mutual spaces for dialogue, listening authentically, and building trust, in my intentions and for future researchers. In postcolonial and indigenous research such as mine, reflexivity about methodology addresses the varying social, ethical, educational, and political landscapes (via paradigmatic, situated, and reciprocal knowledges systems and practices) and the differing stages of its engagement (whether in hypothesising, fieldwork, or writing up). While this facilitates a critical lens on power differentials, it also recognises the need for partnership strategies, contextually relevant tools, and spaces for co-creating research, some of which may be informative for novice researchers. For reflexivity to even begin to devise a 'theoretical confession' (Willis, 2000, p 113), 'desire for "truth" as primary' (Pillow, 2003, p 186) or to move beyond a 'self-conscious existential condition' (Lynch, 2000), research must confront the inequalities and presumptions that may otherwise remain invisible to the 'ongoing-being-becoming' (Barad, 2014) subjects of research (including the researcher-'researched', the shifting sites and areas of inquiry).

This ontological and methodological dyad, in turn, drives epistemological reflexivity in transforming the cognitive empire (Santos, 2018) with difference, challenging coloniality's insidious linkages to projects of modernity (Bhambra, 2007) that have resulted in the erasure of 'peripheral' knowledges, and emphasising childhoods with differing subjectivities, epistemic priorities (say, embodiment of knowledge), and ways of 'knowing' and 'doing'. While the infantilisation of the monolithic 'East' and neocolonial discourses have been problematised to some extent, the 'West' still remains the 'silent referent' (Chakrabarty, 2000, p 28) for thinking about children and (re)producing socio-political constructions of childhood in the contemporary world. Reflexivity about the epistemic disparities between the self, sites, and social actors may thus begin to diminish some concerns about whether the knowledge we, as researchers and academics, generate can truly be emancipatory when our discourses continue to originate from the very centre we seek to disrupt. This is particularly significant for resisting any morally driven debates set on behalf of children and extending notions of childhood beyond saturated capitalist, racist, or universalist agendas. Reflexive praxis, in mapping and negotiating the ontological, epistemological, and methodological contours of one's study, can thus enable researchers and academics to de-centre the production of knowledge, discourses, and narratives by moving beyond normative, dominant, and elitist propositions and agendas.

Notes

[1] The Indian Constitution until recently categorised indigenous communities such as the Hill Sabar peoples as Primitive Tribal Groups, distinguishing them from other tribal communities since by comparison they are deemed 'primitive, geographically isolated, and shy' (Planning Commission Report, 2005, p 1). This, however, was justifiably questioned by the Twelfth Planning Commission of India, which recommended change, leading to the amended classification as Particularly Vulnerable Tribal Group (PVTG). The Sabar prefer not to be categorised within such generic terms applied to the indigenous peoples of India, including Adivasis.

[2] Take, for instance, the draft Indian Forest (Amendment) Bill 2019, which has been referred to as 'more colonial and frightening than before' and 'discriminatory and draconian' in a joint statement issued by indigenous human rights watch movements and women's forums (The International Work Group for Indigenous Affairs, 2020, p 245). In the name of conservation, the draft Bill sought to reinstate state power over forest lands at the expense of forest-dwelling communities' rights, ontological priorities or nature-driven

epistemologies. Furthermore, the committee was formed primarily of forest officials, marginalising relevant rights- and stakeholders, from the ongoing dialogue.

3   *Dharma* is a Hindu philosophy of being or living. To interpret this fundamental Law of Living, I employ Bipin Chandra Pal's (2010) elucidation of *dharma*, established on the characteristics of detachment and idealism. He elaborates that *dharma* 'holds together the different elements ... into one organic whole. ... It is –the Law of Being. And as every object, whether animate or inanimate, whether vegetable, animal or human has its own law of being ... dharma of one man cannot truly be the dharma of another' (pp 47–8). *Karma* (the doctrine of evolution systematised in the concept of *dharma*) is defined as '[a]ccording as a man acts and walks in the path of life, so he becomes. ... By pure actions he becomes pure. ... As his works are, so he becomes' (Mascaro, 1965, p 140).

4   Kharia is the deteriorating Sabar language, which, upon entering the field, I learned was no longer spoken at the sites; instead a dialect that synthesised Kharia, Bengali, and Oriya (languages of neighbouring states) was used. Yet, my knowledge of Kharia, and mistakes, amused the Sabra, which eased my access into their worlds.

5   Phase one, *construction* (to explore members' lives, research intentions and activities, prior knowledge); phase two, *deconstruction* (activities to make the familiar strange, creative strategies, critical analysis of mundane activities); and phase three, *reconstruction* (reflexive and arts-based activities, reconstruction of constructs).

6   As the term suggests, 'ethno' refers to the point of view of social actors (which includes the voice and practice of both the researcher and the researched) and 'methodology' refers to the processes employed by these actors towards accomplishing their mundane activities or specific phenomenon. Garfinkel (1967/1984), the founder of Ethnomethodology (EM), refers to it as 'practical sociological reasoning' (p 1), employed to analyse the 'formal properties of common sense activities as a practical organizational accomplishment' (p viii). Ethnomethodological directives – indexicality, accountability, reflexivity, and making the familiar strange – facilitate understanding of members' (all participants') situated practices.

References

Alejandro, A. (2021). Reflexive discourse analysis: A methodology for the practice of reflexivity. *European Journal of International Relations* 27(1): 150–74.

Appadurai, A. (2000). Globalization and the research imagination. *Public Culture* 12(1): 1–19.

Balagopalan, S. (2008). Memories of tomorrow: Children, labor and the panacea of formal schooling. *Journal for the History of Childhood and Youth* 1(2): 267–85.

Balagopalan, S. (2011). Introduction: Children's lives and the Indian context. *Childhood* 18(3): 291–7.

Balagopalan, S. (2019). 'Afterschool and during vacations': on labor and schooling in the postcolony. *Children's Geographies* 17(2): 231–45.

Barad, K. (2007). *Meeting the Universe Halfway: Quantum Physics and the Entanglement of Matter and Meaning*. Durham, NC: Duke University Press.

Barad, K. (2014). Diffracting diffraction: Cutting together-apart. *Parallax* 20(3): 168–87.

Bhabha, H. (1990). *Nation and Narration*. London, New York: Routledge.

Bhabha, H. (1994). *The Location of Culture*. London, New York: Routledge.

Bhambra, G.K. (2007). *Rethinking Modernity: Postcolonialism and the Sociological Imagination*. New York: Palgrave.
Bourdieu, P. (1993). Comprendre. In Bourdieu, P (ed.) *La Misère du Monde* (pp 1–7). Paris: Le Seuil.
Burman, E. (2001). Beyond the baby and the bathwater: Postdualistic developmental psychologies for diverse childhoods. *European Early Childhood Education Research Journal* 9(1): 5–22.
Burman, E. (2011). Deconstructing neoliberal childhood: Towards a feminist antipsychological approach. *Childhood* 19(4): 423–38.
Burman, E. (2019). Child as method: Implications for decolonising educational research. *International Studies in Sociology of Education* 28(1): 4–26.
Cannella, G. and Kincheloe, J.K. (eds) (2002). *Kidworld: Childhood Studies, Global Perspectives and Education*. New York: Peter Lang.
Chakrabarty, D. (2000). *Provincializing Europe: Postcolonial Thought and Historical Difference*. Princeton, NJ: Princeton University Press.
Chen, K. (2010). *Asia as Method: Toward De-imperialization*. Durham, NC: Duke University Press.
Connell, R. (2007). *Southern Theory*. Crows Nest: Allen & Unwin.
De Castro, L.R. (2018). The self under domination: A dialogue between Nandy's The intimate enemy and Dangarembga's Nervous conditions. *Postcolonial Studies* 21(2): 192–209.
De Castro, L.R. (2020). Otherness in me, otherness in others: Children's and youth's constructions of self and other. *Childhood* 11(4): 469–93.
Escobar, A. (2008). Beyond the third world: Imperial globality, global coloniality and anti-globalization social movements. *Third World Quarterly* 25(1): 207–30.
Finlay, L. (2002). Negotiating the swamp: The opportunity and challenge of reflexivity in research practice. *Qualitative Research* 2(2): 209–30.
Freeman, M. (1993). *Rewriting the Self: History, Memory, Narrative*. London, New York: Routledge.
Gandhi, L. (1998). *Postcolonial Theory: A Critical Introduction*. St. Leonards: Allen & Unwin.
Garfinkel, H. (1967). *Studies in Ethnomethodology*. Englewood Cliffs, NJ: Prentice-Hall.
Garfinkel, H. (1984). *Studies in Ethnomethodology*. Cambridge: Polity.
Government of India (2020). National Education Policy. New Delhi: Ministry of Human Resource Development.
Hart, M.A. (2010). Indigenous worldviews, knowledge, and research: The development of an indigenous research paradigm. *Journal of Indigenous Voices in Social Work* 1(1): 1–16.
International Institute for Population Sciences (IIPS) and ICF. (2021). National Family Health Survey (NFHS-5), 2019–21: India: Volume I. Mumbai: IIPS.

IWGIA (2020). *The Indigenous World*. Denmark: Danish Ministry of Foreign Affairs (DANIDA).

James, A., Jenks, C., and Prout, A. (1998). *Theorizing Childhood*. Cambridge: Polity.

Kirkness, V.J. and Barnhardt, R. (1991). First nations and higher education: The four R's – respect, relevance, reciprocity, responsibility. *Journal of American Indian Education* 30(3): 9–16.

Kumar. K. (2007). Education and culture: India's quest for secular policy. In Kumar, K. and Oesterheld, J. (eds) *Education and Social Change in South Asia*, pp. 196–217. Berlin: Orient Longman.

Kumar, K. and Oesterheld, J. (eds) (2007). *Education and Social Change in South Asia*. New Delhi: Orient Longman.

Lather, P. (1991). *Getting smart: Feminist research and pedagogy with/in the postmodern*. London: Routledge.

Liamputtong, P. (2010). *Performing Qualitative Cross-cultural Research*. Cambridge: Cambridge University Press.

Liamputtong, P. and Kurban, H. (2018). Health, social integration and social support: The lived experiences of young Middle Eastern refugees living in Melbourne, Australia. *Children and Youth Services Review* 85: 99–106.

Lynch, M. (2000). Against reflexivity as an academic virtue and source of privileged knowledge. *Theory, Culture and Society* 17(3): 26–54.

McGregor, H.E. and Marker, M. (2018). Reciprocity in indigenous educational research: Beyond compensation, towards decolonizing. *Anthropology & Education Quarterly* 49(3): 318–28.

McLaughlin, H. (2015). *Involving Children and Young People in Policy, Practice and Research*. London: National Children's Bureau.

Mascaro, J. (1965). *The Upanishads*. London, New York, Victoria, Ontario, New Delhi, Auckland, Rosebank: Penguin Books.

Ministry of Tribal Affairs (2010). *Annual Report 2020–21*. New Delhi: Government of India.

Nama, N. and Swartz, L. (2002). Ethical and social dilemmas in community-based controlled trials in situations of poverty: A view from a South African project. *Journal of Community & Applied Social Psychology* 12(4): 286–97.

Nandy, A. (1999/1987). *Traditions, Tyranny and Utopias: Essays in the Politics of Awareness*. New Delhi: Oxford University Press.

Nieuwenhuys, O. (2008). The ethics of children's rights. *Childhood* 15(1): 4–11.

Nieuwenhuys, O. (2009a). Is there an Indian childhood? *Childhood* 16(2): 147–53.

Nieuwenhuys, O. (2009b). How the poor develop (in spite of the rich): A commentary. *Journal of Health Management* 11(1): 243–50.

Nieuwenhuys, O. (2010). Keep asking: Why childhood? Why children? Why global? *Childhood* 17(3): 291–6.

Nieuwenhuys, O. (2013). Theorizing childhood(s): Why we need postcolonial perspectives. *Childhood* 20(1): 3–8.

Nsamenang, B.A. (2005). Educational development and knowledge flow: Local and global forces in human development in Africa. *Higher Education Policy* 18: 275–88.

Pal, B.C. (2010). *The Soul of India: A Constructive Study of Indian Thoughts and Ideals* (2nd edn). New Delhi: Rupa Co.

Pillow, W. (2003). Confession, catharsis, or cure? Rethinking the uses of reflexivity as methodological power in qualitative research. *International Journal of Qualitative Studies in Education* 16(2): 175–96.

Planning Commission Report (2005). *Schedule Tribes*. New Delhi: Government of India.

Registrar General and Census Commissioner (2011). Census of India: Report on post enumeration survey. New Delhi: Government of India.

Said, E.W. (1978). *Orientalism*. London and Henley: Routledge & Kegan Paul.

Santos, B. de S. (ed.). (2008). *Another Knowledge is Possible*. New York and London: Verso.

Santos, B. de S. (2018). *The End of the Cognitive Empire: The Coming of Age of Epistemologies of the South*. Durham, NC and London: Duke University Press.

Sinha, P. (2017). Listening ethically to indigenous children: Experiences from India. *International Journal of Inclusive Education* 21(3): 272–85.

Sircar, O. and Dutta, D. (2011). Beyond compassion: Children of sex workers in Kolkata's Sonagachi. *Childhood* 18(3): 333–349.

Smith, L.T. (2012). *Decolonising Methodologies: Research and Indigenous Peoples* (2nd edn). London and New York: Zed Books and New Zealand: University of Otago Press.

Spivak, G. (1998/1987). *In Other Worlds: Essays in Cultural Politics*. London and New York: Routledge.

Spivak, G. (1999). *A Critique of Post-Colonial Reason: Toward a History of the Vanishing Present*. Cambridge, MA: Harvard University Press.

Stephens, S. (1995). *Children and the Politics of Culture*. Princeton, NJ: Princeton University Press.

Swartz, S. (2011). 'Going deep' and 'giving back': Strategies for exceeding ethical expectations when researching amongst vulnerable youth. *Qualitative Research* 11(1): 47–68.

Valentine, G. (1996). Angels and devils: Moral landscapes of childhood. *Environment and Planning D: Society and Space* 14: 581–99.

Vanner, C. (2015). Positionality at the center: Constructing an epistemological and methodological approach for a western feminist doctoral candidate conducting research in the postcolonial. *International Journal of Qualitative Methods*, https://doi.org/10.1177%2F1609406915618094

Willis, P. (2000). *The Ethnographic Imagination*. Oxford: Polity Press.

4

Researching Children's Experiences in a Conflict Zone and a Red-light Area: Conducting Ethnographic Fieldwork in India and Kashmir[1]

Ayushi Rawat

Introduction

This chapter brings together key reflexive insights from two research studies – both attempting to research children's experience in sensitive contexts. The first research context is that of Budhwar Peth, a red-light area in India where I conducted research with the children of sex workers to understand their lifeworlds. The second research context is that of Indian-administered Kashmir, where I studied children's everyday experiences of conflict and resistance.

In the South Asian context, childhoods are multivariate and the extent of children's vulnerability is decided by their position on the axis of social identity. However, much of the available literature is written in the context of childhoods in the Global North. Yet there is an epistemic difference in the way childhoods are experienced in most South Asian countries. For instance, most of the methods I read about required children to express themselves through their art or stories. However, in a context where statements like 'Badon ke beech mein bache nahi bolte' [Kids shouldn't speak when adults are talking to each other] are a part of the cultural norm, children's voices are inevitably invisibilised. During my research in Kashmir, most of the children expressed that it was the first time in their lives that an adult had asked their opinion on political matters. Questions of privacy, space, dignity, and identity also have a different ontological construct in South Asia. Often young children in developing nations and from deprived backgrounds reflect the kind of emotional maturity that is expected of an adult or take up adult roles and responsibilities such as childcare for younger siblings and labour for contributing to family income.

As a researcher, stepping in to the environment of a red-light area to conduct my research was not only a question of my own safety as a woman, but also it was loaded with notions of societal morality. During my research process in Budhwar Peth, I was not able to tell my parents about where I was conducting my thesis project. I only told them after graduating. In the society that I come from, I would face opposition due to the stigma attached to the identity of a sex worker in mainstream India.

Similarly, during my study in Kashmir, I faced a lot of opposition from my relatives and extended family, who would warn my parents against 'allowing' me to go to Kashmir. Some of them even suggested that my father should force me to drop out of my PhD programme because they thought my life was at risk. I resisted and continued to do my work, but where I come from, the social ties among extended families are so strong that the 'elders' tend to impact the life decisions of the younger generation – especially women. Carrying on my work in both the studies, despite the pull of patriarchy, was not easy. This chapter reflexively explores some of my experiences in collecting data and highlights my perceptions of the success or otherwise of the methods chosen in these socially and politically sensitive areas. Initially the chapter provides a context through which the reader can situate the sensitivity of each research project but it begins with clarification of childhood as a social construction from a South Asian stance.

In the following section, I describe the emergence of the sociology of childhood within the Indian academic landscape. It points to the broader disciplinary framework within which I designed both the studies.

Finding the voice of children in the Indian sociological imagination

Although the origin of the study of children can be traced back to the work of Charles Darwin, sociological research with children gained popularity in India only post the 1980s. Significant work in the field has been done by Balagopalan (2002), who explores prevailing notions of Third World childhoods as constructed through the workings of colonialism. By acknowledging that 'culture is contingent', as well as 'culture as subject to the workings of power', we cannot fix a rigid identity to childhoods of the poor in the Third World, as distinct from the colonial meanings manifested in the cultures of childhood.

The research on the colonial notions of childhood and the post-colonial discourses on these notions claims that the agenda of the colonial project was to civilise the child, just like the colonial subject. This is reflected in our everyday cultures of communication as adults, where we make statements such as 'child-like', 'don't act like children', or 'are you a child?' (in a disapproving tone). In her editorial on the question of whether there can be a phenomenon that can be termed as an Indian childhood, Nieuwenhuys (2009) examines the conceptions of childhood in India drawing from the colonially constructed imagery to the modern day representations of childhood. She argues that this construction of Indian childhoods, which is also reflected in academic discourses on children, furthers the colonial heritage and the Euro-American-centric dominance of global academic research.

Bhadra (2014) brings to the forefront the lack of, and therefore the need for, a discourse on childhood and childhood studies in Indian sociology. Bhadra mentions how children's issues have so far only been raised, if at all, as part of policy discourses on child labour, street children, and education. However, an in-depth understanding and study of the concept of childhood within Indian sociological imagination is still missing. Even today in India, childhood studies is still a subject matter of the departments of education within universities (Bhadra, 2014). Bhadra identifies the study of children and childhood as Indian sociology's weakest link and reiterates the significance and urgency of sociological attention towards the everyday lives and the lived experiences of our children and their childhoods. This context setting is crucial in order to understand my struggle for finding culturally sensitive research tools for ethical research with children. In the following sections, I delineate some of the historical and socio-cultural specificities of both my research projects in sensitive contexts.

Contextualising the research universe
Budhwar Peth

Budhwar Peth is a red-light area in Pune, a city in the state of Maharashtra, India. Evidence highlights that Budhwar Peth served as a red-light area even at the time of the Peshwa rule in the 18th century (Apte, 2002). The area today stands in the middle of one of the busiest markets in the city and some of the most significant Ganesh temples.

Sex work in India suffers the contradiction of being culturally stigmatised, yet its existence is socially sanctioned. Mainstream society perceives sex work as a 'social evil' where monogamy is the norm, and for most social groups sexual relationships outside of marriage are considered immoral and taboo. However, members of the same society, mostly men, can be seen availing themselves of the sex workers' services. Sex workers are perceived as impure and immoral and are treated by society as outcasts. Sex workers have been depicted in the Indian media, films, and literature as mistresses and home breakers, who threaten the sanctity of the majoritarian monogamous Hindu marriage.

Sex work in India also has traditional moorings in the form of ritualised prostitution such as in the Devadasi system, which consisted of mostly Dalit women being tied to prostitution. Similarly, certain forms of prostitution were linked to caste-based occupations, as in the case of the Nats and the Bedia communities that relied on folk dance, singing, and theatre for their livelihood. Traditionally, most of the women in prostitution belonged to the Dalit community or tribal communities. This is still the case in most red-light areas in rural as well as urban areas in India. This points to the structural inequalities of the caste system in India, which pushes women into sex work due to circumstances.

Indian-administered Kashmir

The Princely State of Jammu and Kashmir was created in colonial India when, in 1846, the Dogras purchased rights to the Kashmir Valley from the British colonial rulers and signed the Treaty of Amritsar (Bamzai, 1994, p 666). Discrimination was experienced by the Muslim majority populace under the Dogra rule.[2] When the British left India in 1947, and erstwhile British India was partitioned into two nations, India and Pakistan, the British gave the then Princely States the choice to join either one of the nation-states or to remain independent. The decision of statehood was left to the 'autocratic rulers', and the Kashmiri people who were under the Dogra rule were not asked about their willingness to join either of the nation-states (Zutshi, 2003, p 300). The last Dogra ruler, Maharaja Hari Singh of Kashmir, a Hindu ruler in a majority Muslim state, kept delaying his decision to join either of the countries. Barely two months after India's independence, armed tribesmen from the north-west frontier of Pakistan entered Kashmir and joined forces with an internal armed rebellion (Ali et al, 2011). To quash this rebellion, the Maharaja Hari Singh asked for India's help and provisionally acceded to India. This accession was provisional because the then Indian Prime Minister Jawaharlal Nehru also signed an accord to conduct a plebiscite to discover what the people of Kashmir wanted, once the situation was under control. On 27 October 1947, Indian military forces were sent to Kashmir's Srinagar and the ensuing struggle resulted in the first Indo-Pak war. After mediation by the United Nations, the Indo-Pak war ended with a ceasefire on 1 January 1949. The ceasefire resolution was agreed upon by both the nation-states, along with an agreement to a plebiscite and withdrawal of armed forces behind the ceasefire line.

In 1950, India formalised its Constitution and Article 370 came into effect, which granted autonomous status to the state of Jammu and Kashmir. Indian administration and jurisdiction were to be limited to defence, foreign affairs, and communications with this accord. The period after 1950 saw a number of long, tense periods of conflict within the region; this led to the rise of militancy in Kashmir in the 1990s. The rebel groups stated an objective to liberate Indian-controlled Jammu and Kashmir (Bose, 2003). On 11 June 2010 Tufail Ahmed Mattoo, a 17-year-old boy from Rainawari, Kashmir, was killed when a tear gas shell that was directed at him from close range crushed his head. His killing led to mass protests that led to the first Intifada in Kashmir, breaking the 20-year period of peaceful protests.

My focus begins from 2016, when Burhan Wani, a popular young militant, was killed by the Indian armed forces on 8th July 2016. This was followed by the longest curfew in Kashmir's history up to that time, which lasted for about two to eight months in different parts of Kashmir. The curfew and *hartaal* period was eased around February 2017. I began my fieldwork for this study in April 2017. Tensions escalated again in Kashmir on 5 August 2019 as Article 370 of the Indian Constitution was revoked for Kashmir, dismissing the autonomous status that had been given to the state and its people. It was then converted into a union territory to be administered henceforth. Kashmir was under total shutdown following this decision.

With close to 950,000 security personnel deployed in Kashmir, including the army and the air force, as well as paramilitary forces and the special forces, it is the most militarised zone in the world today.

In the case of ethnographies that are being conducted where fieldwork is sensitive and risks are involved, for example conflict zones or red-light areas, the exercise of reflexivity takes centre stage. It extends beyond being a methodological framework to building an ethical purview. The questioning, interrogation, and reflection of one's own value systems as an ethnographer that we carry into our field becomes key.

Addressing reflexivity as ethics

In both the projects, I had what Pinto calls the 'the securing distance of a research agenda' (2014, p 12) while conducting emotionally intense research. In Kashmir, I was an outsider from the occupying nation with a Hindu name, making me eligible for state protection in case of an incidence of violence. In one instance, I was travelling with my hosts from Srinagar city to one of the villages in central Kashmir. Usually we avoided travelling after dark for security reasons, but on that particular day it was unavoidable and we had to be on the road after sunset. We were stopped by the army half-way to the village, our vehicle was thoroughly searched, and questions were asked of us. In that moment, I was scared for the safety of my hosts. The army checkpoint could have been attacked by militants and we could have been injured in the cross-fire. Such incidents were common at that time. Every moment waiting there as they checked our vehicle and documents, I feared for our safety. The army personnel could also have objected to my presence and entry into the village. In such a scenario, the army would have asked me to return to India but I was fearful of what might happen to my hosts. They did not have the same protection of statehood and identity. I could listen to stories and narratives of trauma of my respondents and feel emotional, yet at a distance; it was not my lived life but a research universe that I temporarily occupied.

One of the crucial requirements of ethical research with children is to acknowledge the power relationship that exists between the adult researcher and the child respondent. This relationship is also twofold: first, on account of being an adult and the cultural preconceived notions that adults and children have about each other; and secondly, the positionality of the researcher as an individual observing and asking questions about their lives and seeking their opinions on matters that, usually adults do not speak to children about. For the children, how much and how to share could be surprising and even confusing at times. I had thought my experience as a social worker with children in vulnerable contexts would help me to converse with children in a manner that was child friendly and could potentially minimize the adult–child power relationship. However, as some of the data presented here demonstrates, the distance between me and my participants was often explicit and insurmountable.

Self-reflexivity helped me explore, introspect, reflect on, and interrogate my own assumptions about children and childhood. My understanding of children's cultures and adult–child relationships from my previous research with children helped me foreground the methods for these projects. Among these, the 'presentation of the self as researcher' (Freeman and Mathison, 2009, p 58) is a significant practice. When I went into the field, I tried my best to assume the role of an 'incompetent adult' – which would put children around me at ease. Here again, the extent to which I was successful with my young participants was debatable.

In Budhwar Peth I met my participants at a day-care centre in the red-light area, which was run by an NGO. I was perceived as a volunteer who had come from 'outside' of Budhwar Peth. Without knowing much more about me in terms of my own caste identity, what the children here knew was how I was distinct from the people they met in their home environment. This understanding stemmed from the fact that I was meeting them at the day-care centre, instead of in the brothels or streets. The spatiality of that site was distinct and had the sense of a place where notions of safety were anchored. They got fed here and there was a television. They also identified it as a place where they got to play with the other children or on their own; some children who were bullied in school because of their mothers' identity regarded this as a safe space outside of their home environments. This contrasting space informed the older children's understandings: 'outside' is safe, 'outside' is where you develop and grow.

Most of these children had experienced trauma due to violence and abuse from their mothers' romantic and sexual partners as well as from the police. For the participants, my adult and inevitably distanced gaze was associated with notions of morality – they would be instructed by the NGO workers to be on their best behaviour when I arrived to speak to them because I was coming from 'outside'. Their past experiences with other 'volunteers' like me who came from exclusive spaces such as colleges in cities like Mumbai had also helped to develop their notions of me.

In Kashmir I was an outsider as a non-Kashmiri, non-Muslim adult – here the –insider-outsider equation played out on two levels. I was an outsider socially, culturally, and politically in my field, and I was an outsider, as an adult, in children's cultures, social worlds, and political subjectivities. My unfamiliarity with cultural practices and the local language made my position as a non-authoritarian adult very visible. The process of opening up also included curiosity from the children about my identity and wanting to attribute an identity that they could relate to. In one instance, an 11-year-old called Mahira asked me about my religious identity and the conversation went as follows:

Mahira:	Ma'm, I wanted to ask you something.
Researcher:	Yes, what is it?
Mahira:	You will feel bad … [hesitating]
Researcher:	No, I won't feel bad. Tell me?
Mahira:	Are you a Muslim?
Researcher:	No, I am not a Muslim. What happened?
Mahira:	No, first tell me if you are Muslim or not? [smiling shyly]
Researcher:	No, I am not.
Mahira:	Then what are you?
Researcher:	I am Hindu. Why do you ask?
Mahira:	No, I asked just like that.
Researcher:	What did you think I was?
Mahira:	I thought you are a Muslim.
Researcher:	Why did you think so?
Mahira:	Because you are dressed like us. You have covered your head with a *dupatta* like us. We do that in Islam.

I replied that I did this as a mark of respect to the people there, since I was their guest and it would make them happy to see that I was following the cultural codes of conduct even as an outsider. Appearing to hold cultural competence is also a necessary skill for ethnography, particularly in contexts of sensitivity or risk. I asked Mahira, "How do you feel about me covering my head?" to which she replied, "I really like it. It feels like you are one of us."

Figure 4.1: Free hand drawing by Anwar

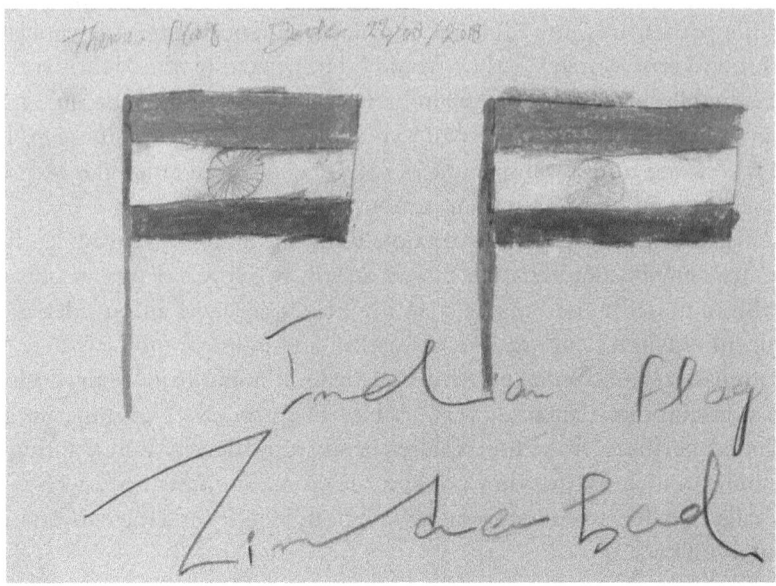

However, in the same group of children, Anwar, who was 13 years old, drew an image of the Indian flag (Figure 4.1). His explanation demonstrated to me the extent to which I remained on the outside of the worlds that these children occupy and that this distance was seen as a risk for them. In response, some sought to placate me and mediate this risk. I asked Anwar to describe the drawing and why he had drawn particularly an Indian flag. It is important to note that this drawing exercise was the first tool I used in each setting in order to further narrow down the sample.

Anwar: *Maine flag isliye banaya mujhko kyunki mujhko draw karna isko bahut hi acha lagta hai, isliye maine flag banaya hai.* (I have made a flag because I like drawing flags very much.)
Researcher: [Probing further]
Anwar: *Kyunki aaj kal Kashmir mein thodi haalat kharaab hai (while smiling) isliye maine thoda kuch likha hai aise.* (Because these days the situation in Kashmir is not good, that's why I have written something like this.)
Researcher: [Probing further]
Anwar: *Mujhe. ... mere mann mein ye aaya ki main flag banaun issey aapko bhi pata lagega Kashmiriyon mein Hindustan ka jazba hai ... Mujhko bahut acha lagta hai India flag banana.* (I ... I thought that I should make a flag, so that you

	will also get to know that Kashmiris also like India … I like drawing Indian flag very much.)
Researcher:	*Kyun pasand hai? Aisa kya hai usmein jo aapko pasand hai?* (Why do you like it? What do you like about it?)
Anwar:	*Mujhko full all country mujhe pasand hai, India country pasand hai mujhe. Isiliye maine ye banaya hai … Har koi, Indian team mujhe acha lagta hai, isliye maine banaya hai, Indian team acha lagta hai.* (I like the entire country, that's why I have drawn it. … I like everything, I like the Indian team also, that's why I have drawn it. … I like the Indian team.)

From this account, it is possible to argue that this boy drew an Indian flag because of my identity as an adult from India. He also mentioned that he liked the Indian cricket team. I tried to probe further and told him that he could speak to me in Kashmiri if he felt comfortable and that I could ask the coordinator to translate it for me later. He refused to participate further in this conversation, so I told him that it was alright and we could talk about this later. When I repeated his name to confirm for my own records, the tone of his voice changed and it was very evident that he was scared. Anwar did not return to the centre while I was there. Later on I learned from the coordinator that he became very scared and worried because I had told him that we would talk about his opinions later. He felt that he was being singled out and might have to face serious consequences for this. He felt that he had intended to please me by drawing the Indian flag and maybe felt interrogated. Moments like these made me aware and conscious of my own position of power in the field as an adult from Delhi. I spoke to the coordinator about this incident at length to find ways of addressing it. She assured me that she would talk to him individually and make him feel safe. She also said that when he interacted with the other children at the centre and they told him about their experiences with me, he might feel more at ease. The first relationship we need to build as researchers with children is the relationship of trust but, as evident in my experience with Anwar, this is not straightforward.

Reflections of an ethnographer

Both of these research experiences were extremely challenging for me as a young researcher. It was a constant mental battle of sticking to the research agenda and extending help wherever I could. The countless books and articles I had read in preparation seemed insignificant when I actually entered the field to conduct the studies. During my work at Budhwar Peth, I struggled with insomnia for weeks after the research process. Going to collect data every day, knowing that children were being abused, was jarring and difficult to live with. One of the conversations with a sex worker who had a three-year-old daughter at that time still haunts me. Since the daughter was too young, I had interviewed the mother for the purpose of my study. She sobbed mid-way through the interview as she described living with Type 1 Diabetes, which required her to take insulin injections she could not afford. A doctor had told her that at this rate, she only had a few months to live. She said that she could not imagine what would happen to her daughter after her death. Earlier, she used to work in the brothels of Kolkata where she got her insulin from the Missionaries of Charity, but since being brought to Pune's red-light area, she had been unable to find charity organisations that would donate insulin to her. I have lived with the same disability from ten years of age, so this particular connection, yet with distance from my participant, broke me in spirit.

In Kashmir there were attempts by the respondents, especially the adult respondents as my points of contact, to gauge my political standing on the Kashmir issue. I was asked this question very subtly in first-time encounters, and very directly in more comfortable settings. The respondents would often ask, "What is your opinion on the Kashmir issue as an outsider from *Hindustan*?" They would also ask if, and in what ways, my opinion on Kashmir changed after I actually visited and met the people. This conversation would be followed by the people telling me that Indian media coverage of Kashmir is negative and often biased.

Sometimes, my status as an unmarried woman also led to the women talking about marriage proposals. The elder men in the house would be concerned about my safety and would keep a track of where I was going and with whom; they also made arrangements to ensure that I was always accompanied by someone whenever I stepped out. In Lila Abu-Lughod's ([1986] 2016) words, I had become the 'guest-daughter'.

In the field, I made sure that I followed the dress code of the place that I was in. I covered my head with a *dupatta* every time I was living in the village. One reason for doing this was out of respect for the community and families who had given me access to their homes and private lives and had let an unknown guest live in their homes and consume their resources. This also helped me keep a low profile, which is necessary for fieldwork in spaces of conflict. I was often told by my hosts and my respondents that I looked like a Kashmiri because of my features and complexion, which also helped me blend in. Often I had strangers talking to me in Kashmiri, in public spaces, then I had to tell them that I was from 'outside'. I nurtured a deep sense of gratitude for the host families, but at the same time, I was harbouring constant guilt – the self-awareness of being associated with an identity that resonates with the pain of my respondents was very difficult. During the research process, there were times when I had to travel back to Delhi for a few days to support my mental health. My social and cultural distance from living in these environments, which posed such a challenge in the field for me as a researcher, was ultimately a benefit to my mental health. I could escape, a luxury my respondents did not have. It made me deeply aware of my position of privilege in the field and therefore it was even more important for me to write about this experience reflexively.

Tools of research with children in sensitive contexts
The mapping tool

The mapping tool was one of the most interesting tools that I developed and adapted to both the research contexts. It consists of different kinds of maps that can be used to locate children's geographies, children's social relationships, children's emotions and feelings, and many other aspects where direct questions cannot be asked. Maps may also help us understand and probe further into issues that children might not have been able to articulate with other tools.

With this tool, children were given a piece of paper and coloured pencils and crayons. They were asked to sit in a group and to draw a map from their home to a place that they regularly visited. So that it was easier for them to understand the activity, I first asked the children in a group to identify the places that they visited every day or regularly. Places that came up were: school, *darasgah* (madarsa), small local grocery shops, the field where they went to play, the areas where they went to work, and the institution that I was interviewing them at. I then asked them to draw a map from their home to any of these places of their choice. After they had drawn these maps, I asked each of them to describe their maps to me. Children's responses were very interesting and would often turn into stories about a certain day in their memory on a particular route or at a certain place, or, where something eventful had happened. It is interesting to note that in Budhwar Peth, the mapping tool was only successful with the boys.

In the image in Figure 4.2, one boy from Budhwar Peth drew a map from the police station to a restaurant in the locality. He described each of the places drawn inside the lanes of the red-light area. The maps boys drew were extensive and detailed. In contrast, the girls refused to participate. This unwillingness on the girls' part perhaps pointed to concerns about safety. Girls are prevented from leaving the brothels and exploring the area as easily as boys. Girls over the age of six to seven years were difficult to find in my recruitment, often being forcibly kept in brothels for sex work, and remaining hidden from public view because it is a crime. In some cases, mothers were able to send their daughters to extended families in the native villages to prevent them being forced into sex work. The absence of maps from the

Figure 4.2: Mapping activity – Budhwar Peth

girls provides insight into gender differences and their limited occupancy of the wider social sphere.

In Kashmir, gendered differences also emerged with regard to play, in accounts from girls aged between 12 and 16 years. The following conversation[3] is a discussion with 13-year-old Nazira about her map.

Researcher:	Do you go outside to play?
Nazira:	No, since I grew up ... it is like here, all the girls that are my age they don't go outside to play, little girls go outside the house to play.
Researcher:	Since when did you realise that you shouldn't go outside to play?
Nazira:	Umm ... when I came to the 7th std. Till 6th std. I used to go outside to play.
Researcher:	What happened at that time for you to stop?
Nazira:	No, it was like, my mother used to say, and now everyone says that here the situation should improve for us to be able to go out, these days the situation is not good here. Today, you never know, if you go out then the neighbours will talk ... even if we have some work and for that we have to leave the house, so the neighbours talk. They keep looking for negative things to say.

Figure 4.3: Mapping by Nazira

The perception here is that the current situation is different and relatively more unsafe today compared to past times, and that this change is related to the cultural shift that came with the onset of the conflict. Many of the respondents suggested that the social status and security of women having been jeopardised was one of the long-term effects of the conflict. The instances of increasing religious performativity and identity performance, whereby young college- and school-age girls were opting to wear the *burkha*, was also a result of the conflict.

In her map (Figure 4.3), Nazira drew a distinction between the boys in her own village and those from outside. She also indicated an element of fear about the boys from outside teasing her, suggesting that she would not be able make a complaint against them and that they would return to their villages, where no action could be taken against them. With boys from her own village, she felt able to address any issues by complaining to their parents. This insider/outsider distinction is crucial when we attempt to understand the fear and insecurity felt by girls and women due to the presence of the army, who are outsiders. Such boundaries can be extrapolated to the larger context of occupation and insecurity in this conflict zone and amplify gendered layers of experiences. However, it was not just the girls' maps that reflected places of danger.

Twelve-year-old Masood made a map from his home to school (Figure 4.4), and when I asked him if he felt scared when he took the route, he described it to me, saying:

Figure 4.4: Mapping activity – Kashmir

'This is the mosque, and this is my house, there is a tree here, and then there is the highway. And this is my school, there is a police station here. When we approach the police station, we hurry and pass it quickly. ... Because I am very scared of them ... because they fire guns. ... When we were playing on the ground one day, they came over there and they chased us away from there. I had gone there with the other children from the village to play. ... When there was hartaal [curfew], and when we used to pass by, there used to be people pelting stones and these people used to fire on them. That's why I am scared of them.'[4]

Masood remembers experiencing fear of the police when he saw them firing at the protesters in the shutdown in 2016. He also relates it to more recent experiences of fear of the police when they were chasing after him and his friends.

The self-portrait tool

Using this tool, I had asked children to draw themselves as they see themselves and used it to understand their aspirations. The self-portraits were linked to the question of adult employment. While the children in Budhwar Peth came up with some very creative illustrations, the children in Kashmir struggled with this task.

Figure 4.5: Self-portrait – Budhwar Peth

The drawing in Figure 4.5 by a respondent in Budhwar Peth shows the child portraying himself on the left hand side of the page as a police officer. The picture depicts him having caught an offender. We can see handcuffs being used. If we look carefully at the images of the 'officer' and the 'offender', we see that the officer is well built and wearing smart shoes and formal dress with stars on the shoulder, signifying his high rank, and a gun holster at his side. In contrast, the offender has crooked shoes, no specific dress code, and has a smaller figure than the officer. The officer has a smile on his face while the offender does not.

In Budhwar Peth, most children drew themselves as police officers. This was because for the children in the red-light area, the image of the police officer is that of an oppressor and abuser, but also of someone who has enormous power. Most of them had witnessed the police beating, raping, arresting, and verbally abusing their mothers and other significant adults in their lives. Some of the children had also suffered abuse at the hands of the police officers. So growing up to be police officers themselves seems to them a way in which they can take back some of their power.

In the picture in Figure 4.6, an 11-year-old boy in Budhwar Peth depicts himself as a scientist in the future. The figure on the extreme left hand side of the drawing is how the child sees himself at present; that on the extreme right is how the child will look when he becomes a scientist; and in the

Figure 4.6: Self-portrait II – Budhwar Peth

centre, the child has drawn the robot that he would make after becoming a scientist. When I probed further, asking him why he wanted to become a scientist, he said that he wanted to build a time machine. The conversation went as follows:

Researcher: *Kaay karsheel time machine madhe?* (What will you do with a time machine?)
Respondent: *Time machine madhe aplyala konti cheez, ashi hi apli cheezach nahi ahe, tikde lai swaste, tikde jaun ghyaychi.* (In the time machine, if there is anything that we are not getting or we don't have, there it will be cheaper, so we can go there and get it.)
Researcher: *Jasa kaay?* (Like what?)
Respondent: *Ata bagh, batate kiti mahaag astaat, tikde jaun kaay ek rupayala asel, don rupayala asel!* (Now see, potatoes are so expensive here, over there it would be only one rupee or two rupee a kilo!)

In the self-portrait in Figure 4.7 we see that a girl from Kashmir has drawn herself with a stethoscope in her ears, a hijab on her head, and a medicine bottle in one hand and an injection syringe in the other. She is situating herself as a practising Muslim girl who has become a doctor. The

Figure 4.7: Self-portrait – Kashmir

experience invoked here is the aspiration of becoming a successful doctor in her community. The child's aspirations to become a doctor and practise her religion are both enmeshed in the identity of the 'ideal child' that is constructed by the society around her. Academic performance and career aspirations are valued in that medical sciences are considered a socially celebrated choice of career. This is also apparent in the context of conflict, where doctors play a significant role in times of crisis. She expresses that living in vulnerable circumstances makes her angry at the state of affairs, and her self-portrait then becomes a way of projecting the ideal that she imagines for herself, which will help her to survive in this context of violent political conflict.

Conclusion

Two key features emerge from these research projects. The first feature is the relationship between the research context and methods chosen to elicit the data. The second is the co-production and multiplicity of identities required in the field.

Part of this discussion aimed to present and evaluate the tools used to elicit the voices of children unused to being asked their views. Furthermore, both research projects were sensitive in their nature. Conflict and sex work are two topics not usually explored with children, though there are of course exceptions (see Chapter 9). How to do this sensitively, in these challenging fields, was key to the success of both projects. Map making within the context of the sex workers' community failed to capture data from young girls but did highlight the geographical constraints surrounding them based on their gender. Maps drawn by boys demonstrated their fear of places and of those in uniform. The drawings of future selves revealed a desire to transcend the constraints of both these research contexts. However, using each of these methods revealed the importance of selecting the right tool in each research context. It is not sufficient to just think about the characteristics of our respondents or the topic; the social context, too, is important to understand when selecting a method.

My interactions with respondents in these research projects required varying attributes of my identity to be central. On occasion I was required to behave as a guest-daughter, performing this role to build and maintain good relations with my hosts in the field. As a former social worker, my desire to intervene shaped how I perceived the prevalent abuse of children. Disclosure of my religious identity became necessary at times, and dressing in accordance with the identity of a member of the community to both fit in and show respect was also necessary. On one occasion it was my identity as a diabetic that shaped my connection with a respondent. My gendered identity was relevant in every interaction, from choosing to hide my research from members of my own family to being able to recognise the extent to which gender shapes the lives and risks of many of my respondents. Ultimately, I recognise my identity as an outsider and inevitably separate from those whose lives I briefly glimpsed; distanced as an Indian citizen rather than Kashmiri in one context, and distinct as an educated woman from Deli rather than a sex-worker trapped by the structures of an unequal caste system.

Notes

[1] The title of this chapter maintains a distinction in the geographical regions of India and Indian-administered Kashmir. The author's study in Kashmir was conducted before the revocation of Article 370 of the Indian Constitution, which removed Kashmir's autonomous status. Following the revocation Kashmir lost its statehood and has been brought under direct rule of the central government as a union territory. Crucial to note in this context is that the revocation is unpopular with the people of Kashmir. Most Kashmiris see this revocation as a historic wrong and reject it in spirit.
[2] A more detailed understanding of Kashmir's pre-1947 history has been documented by scholars such as Mridu Rai and Chitralekha Zutshi, among others (Rai, 2014; Zutshi, 2003).
[3] Translated into English from the original conversation in Hindustani.
[4] Translated into English from the original conversation in Hindustani.

References

Abu-Lughod, L. ([1986] 2016). *Veiled Sentiments: Honor and Poetry in a Bedouin Society*. Berkeley, CA: University of California Press.

Ali, T., Bhatt, H., Chatterji, A.P., Khatun, H., Mishra, P. and Roy, A. (2011). *Kashmir: The Case for Freedom*. London: Verso.

Apte, A. (2002). *Punyatil Veshyavyavasaay: Sarvekshan 1998*. Pune: Vilas Chaphekar, Vipul Prakashan.

Balagopalan, S. (2002). Constructing indigenous childhoods: Colonialism, vocational education and the working child. *Childhood* 9(1): 19–34.

Balagopalan, S. (2011). Children's lives and the Indian context. *Childhood* 18(3): 291–97.

Bamzai, P.N.K. (1994). *Culture and Political History of Kashmir*. New Delhi: M.D. Publications Pvt. Ltd.

Bhadra, B. ed. (2014). *Sociology of Childhood and Youth*. New Delhi: Sage.

Bose, S. (2003). *Kashmir – Roots of Conflict, Paths to Peace*. London: Harvard University Press.

Freeman, M. and Mathison, S. (2009). *Researching Children's Experiences*. New York: Guilford Press.

Nieuwenhuys, O. (2009). Is there an Indian childhood? *Childhood* 16(2): 147–53.

Pinto, S. (2014). *Daughters of Parvati: Women and Madness in Contemporary India*. Philadelphia, PA: University of Pennsylvania.

Rai, M. (2014). *Hindu Rulers, Muslim Subjects: Islam, Rights and the History of Kashmir*. Ranikhet: Permanent Black.

Zutshi, C. (2003). *Languages of Belonging: Islam, Regional Identity and the Making of Kashmir*. New Delhi: Permanent Black.

5

Capturing Narratives: Adopting a Reflexive Approach to Research with Disabled Young People

Marianna Stella and Allison Boggis

Introduction

Historically, notions of disability have been underpinned by administrative measures, diagnostic categories, and traditional practices within regulated systems. Knowledge generated within disciplines such as medical sociology, philosophy, and psychology have shaped our knowledge and understanding of disability and impairment (Richards and Clark, 2018). Categories of disability and normality emerged through these disciplines, resulting in the separation of what constitutes normal/abnormal, typical/atypical. This academic and medical knowledge has informed social perceptions and understanding, resulting in the separation, marginalisation, and 'othering' of people with disabilities. Thanks, in part, to political campaigns and academic activism, which called for greater equality and rights for the disabled, these perceptions and categorisations have been challenged, and a more critical, flexible, and interdisciplinary perspective of disability has emerged (Goodley, 2017). Disabled people's experiences, views, and opinions have begun to be incorporated into policymaking, practice, research, and academic literature, engendering a more inclusive perspective, and one that values diversity and difference.

Notwithstanding these changes, there is clearly some way to go before inclusion and acceptance become commonplace, and it remains notable that the position of disabled young people within research and academic literature remains marginalised (Shakespeare and Watson, 1997; 2001). This absence is evident in the lack of first-person accounts from disabled young people themselves, researchers possibly preferring to talk on their behalf.

What is at the root of this exclusion? Perhaps assumptions of vulnerability and incompetence, which are so engrained in our everyday thinking that we assume such voices are too difficult to hear or even understand (Boggis, 2018). Conceivably there has been a deficit in the skills required to gather non-normative voices, and to subsequently navigate the academic barriers to including them in published works.

However, excluding populations from research and favouring voices that are easily sought or heard is highly problematic as it fails to recognise diversity, and limits our soundscapes (Richards et al, 2015). Therefore, we strongly believe it is no longer acceptable to exclude voices simply because they pose challenges to us as researchers, and the methods we use. Young disabled people are often constructed as passive, subordinate, and silent, and therefore we argue that encouraging them to tell their stories and listening to what they say not only challenges the traditional, and often mythical, version of disabled reality, but also subverts the oppression of dominant ideologies and common mis/understandings of disability and impairment. Quite simply, we believe that young disabled people's voices should not only be sought and heard, but included in all aspects of everyday life. Demonstrating our commitment to this social change, we became involved in a small-scale research project entitled 'More Than ...', which involved disabled young people sharing their everyday life experiences through conversations with us. The project embraced strength-based perceptions of disabled young people as experts in their own lives (James and Prout, 1997), as active citizens with rights to participation and having their voices heard (United Nations, 1989) and by forefronting equity within the research process.

The purpose of this chapter, however, is not to retell the participants' stories, which can be found elsewhere, but rather to offer a reflexive account of the processes, practicalities, and pleasures that accompanied the storying of these five, young disabled people, and their perspectives on life. We share our experiences of the research and expose some of our ethical predicaments. We also highlight, rather than hide, some of the imperfections inherent within our endeavours. We do this as a form of encouragement, to illustrate the impact of reflexivity, not only on and throughout this research, but also on ourselves, our personal growth as researchers, and equally on the participants and their responses. We acknowledge the presence of our own values, personal identities, positions in the field, and the impact of our individual subjectivities on this project. We therefore offer up a reflexive account of our experiences during this research, its methods, and the design used to capture the narratives of participants. We also interrogate some of the emotions we experienced as we listened to participants' stories, recognising the potential impact that emotional work can have on researchers and on the process itself. Finally, we close the chapter with an evaluation and reflection on the dilemmas we faced and decisions we made about publishing our work and disseminating the findings.

Reflexivity as part of ethical processes

Ethics and ethical approval contain well-established principles within research and are positioned at the heart of every research journey; this project is no exception. However, as researchers we often neglect to consider and reflect upon these principles within our own research, rather taking them at face value. Here, we demonstrate some of the twists and turns in our own thoughts and actions in relation to this. Guillemin and Gillam (2004) suggest that the notion of reflexivity is useful here; it acts as an ongoing process throughout the research as it helps us to contemplate and gain a deeper understanding of our influences, practices, and actions. Or, as Haynes (2012, p 73) suggests, 'reflexivity involves thinking about how our thinking came to be, how our pre-existing understanding is constantly revised in the light of new understandings and how this in turn effects our research'.

From the outset of this project, our thinking and values led us to focus primarily on three well-established key principles that we regarded as central to our understanding of the project and the care of our participants. The principles were those of anonymity, informed consent, and the participants' right to withdraw. However, it soon became clear, as often in research, that these well-trodden ideals were so much more than the ethical hoops often identified but rather, highly complex unknowns that changed and shifted our application of these standards.

We suggest that it is important for researchers to acknowledge, at the stage of applying for ethical approval, that there may be potential unknowns about their proposed research, which through the ongoing process of reflexivity may lead to alterations in thinking, planning, and practice. In the case of this project, while we outline our initial ideas and indicate potential ethical issues that could arise from this research, the impossibility to predict every issue and every scenario and find appropriate resolutions is also highlighted. These considerations and reflections are clearly emphasised from the outset and, to our minds, demonstrate thorough consideration and a duty of care to our participants. While our developing research skills and past experiences allowed us to demonstrate what we believed to be very good understandings of the potential ethical dilemmas that may arise when researching with young disabled people, we needed to show that we were mindful of ethical predicaments that could impact on the research as a whole. We acknowledge, however, that while some might view reflexive admissions, such as these, within research practices, application bids, and published work to be ethical weakness, we continue to hope that others would consider them as strengths.

For us, upholding the anonymity of our participants began as a perplexing key concern. Here we map our changing perspectives, demonstrating how the power of reflexivity can be used to support the embodying of research principles (Guillemin and Gillam, 2004). Keeping personal information and data confidential was our initial starting point, but this proved to be the most challenging of principles to uphold. As part of our responsibility towards our participants we had to ensure that they had access to 'trusted adults', who would work alongside them in case further support was required. Consequently, it was clear that the participants' stories would be shared not only with us, but also with other professionals. In addition, the chosen research design adopted visually recorded conversations as the data collection method, making the idea of full anonymity impractical. Although this method was ideal for this participant group to effectively elicit their stories, it potentially compromised their anonymity. With all this in mind, we deliberated at length and decided that as young disabled people's stories were central to this research project and our own values, promising total anonymity was not possible and furthermore would have defeated the purpose of seeking and projecting voices. We realised that our core conviction, that disabled young people's voices should not be ignored, was playing a significant role in our decision making here. Our awareness that disabled people and their voices remain invisible to many in both societal and political spheres encouraged us to bring the spotlight onto the voices and identities of our participants, rather than hide them away. This reflexive understanding of our position superseded the initial desire for anonymity. We therefore, when advising participants about the requirements of the project, particularly emphasised the personal information they might share, how they might share it, and the potential for their anonymity to be compromised in favour of sharing their unique stories of everyday life.

These considerations led to further challenges around our second key principle of gaining informed consent. Clearly in all types of research participants should be provided with detailed information about what the study involves in a way that is accessible to each individual. However, the key dilemma we encountered was how to fully inform participants of the aims of the study without influencing their responses, and/or the stories they chose to share with us. At first, we attempted to address this challenge by customising/personalising the information to each individual participant and thereby varying the levels/amount of information we provided on a case-by-case basis. However, we were never truly happy with this as a solution as we continued to hold fast to the belief that all participants should have access to the same information. Notwithstanding all our deliberations, we considered and reconsidered this as potentially the most inclusive approach to take, even though it remained a dilemma that was never entirely resolved.

The third ethical principle required a heightened awareness of, and duty to ensure, participants' right to withdraw. Again, applying this principle in practice raised some dilemmas for us, and again reflexivity helped us to think about and question 'our ways of doing things' (Haynes, 2012, p 73). Clearly, once the individual conversations were captured on film and pieced together in preparation for viewing, it would be highly challenging to remove individual snippets, and/or whole conversations should the participants decide to withdraw. It was also of central importance to consider how participants might want to express their decision to withdraw from the study. In practice, we reminded participants of their right to withdraw before the start of each conversation and were mindful throughout the conversations of any verbal, facial, or physical cues that might express either a reluctance to respond to a particular question or a desire to discontinue their involvement in the study. As Boggis (2018) has previously argued, many young disabled people are primed to acquiesce and therefore remain silent rather than displease researchers by withdrawing their consent. This clearly poses a number of important issues relating to power and positionality that we, as researchers, felt needed further consideration and reflection, and therefore we will explore these in the following section.

Reflexivity as an embedded research process

As discussed previously, the primary focus of this project was to hear the stories told by the participants themselves. However, our conviction that knowledge is situated, that it is produced in specific circumstances, which shape it in some way (see Rose, 1997 for a more detailed explanation), demanded the consideration of our own position/s and situated knowledge as part of this research. This interrogation of ourselves, both within the research and within our everyday lives, illustrated our potential to impact on the research itself. Being reflexive of our multiple positions as researchers, teachers, women, and academics within this field helped us to acknowledge how much they informed the way we made our decisions throughout the project, from its first conception to the dissemination of the young people's stories. By engaging reflexively, we were able to consider the strengths and influences of our positions, while equally recognising our positions as non-disabled people.

Becoming consciously reflexive in this way necessitated that we regularly took some time to distance ourselves from the study, thus providing us with the opportunity to look back on our processes, practices, and selves with fresh eyes. This reflexive time allowed us to more thoroughly and sensitively examine our approaches and actions, check our notes and choices, and make sure we were still happy with these, while also reflecting on previously rejected ideas to ensure that we were still engaging with our aims for the project. Not only did this 'time out' seem sensible because it gave us space and time to think and discuss, but we also felt it provided further insights into our work and added an additional layer of critical scrutiny to the research process and own motivations.

That said, adopting a reflexive approach calls upon us to identify that the knowledge made depends on who its makers are. Therefore, we interrogated our varying levels of research experience in this field, our frames of reference, and both our personal and professional involvement with disabled young people, as formative aspects of this research. We equally acknowledged our perceptions of the ways in which the voices of disabled young people are largely ignored by society and how these personal insights, sensitivities, and assessments influenced the conducting of this research project. This not only shed light on the research decisions and processes that we made and would choose to make, but also made our work more visible and transparent.

We felt strongly that the challenges and possibilities of adopting reflexivity as a central tenet of our work resonated with, and encapsulated, our experiences throughout the various stages of this study. Reflexivity provided us with ways to further consider how researchers' and participants' individualities and backgrounds influence interpretations (Berger, 2015; Townsend and Cushion, 2020), We regarded it as a valuable tool to use in this study, and in disability studies more generally, as it recognises that while there are some shared commonalities between individuals, they should not be grouped together homogeneously (Goethals et al, 2015). This was made further evident through the stories we were hearing; while common patterns, events, and experiences were evident, each participant shared these in their own unique way and expressed individual emotions to a variety of situations.

During this research journey, we became more closely aware of the reciprocal connection between reflexivity, positionality, and ethics, in that it allows us, as researchers, to be actively engaged in the research processes, while at the same time calling for the application of in-depth scrutiny. This is what Guillemin and Gillam (2004) argue reflects the research process as a whole, whereby an overview of the researchers and participants involved, the data, and the wider context of the research should be included. As Katz (1992) argues, when actively adopting a reflexive approach, neither the researcher nor the researched position or agency should be masked, and both should be sensitive to the intersection of power that accompanies the privileged position of the researcher. However, as the discussions within this chapter will reveal, having an intellectual and academic understanding of reflexivity and acknowledging the importance of adopting a reflexive methodological stance is one thing, but applying and defending it can be extraordinarily difficult and at times, easier said than done!

Reflexivity in research design and method

We considered the flexible and fluid aspects of qualitative enquiry to be well suited to this project because, as Liamputtong (2007) suggests, they enable situated understanding of meanings, interpretations, and subjective experiences of vulnerable groups. We hoped that by providing opportunities to hear the voices of these young people, creating relaxed and friendly spaces for listening, and actively engaging with groups who are often marginalised and rendered silent, we would encourage our participants to express their feelings and experiences in and on their own terms and through their own perspectives. Choosing the appropriate research design and method was a challenging process, during which time we had to consider our own experiences of various methodologies and methods, as well as our aims for this project. Therefore, being reflexive was essential at this stage as we wanted to remain true to the inclusive aims that we set for this project, while also ensuring that we were comfortable with and confident in our research skills to proceed in a new and – by us – previously unexplored direction.

A commitment to listening became essential to the principles of our research, and so we turned our attention towards engaging with storytelling as our research method. Our own experiences with this method were limited but nevertheless we felt it would be a great fit for the project. The principles of reflexivity allowed us to explore the ideas, values, and application of this method to our study, and equally to make it our own through change and adaptation; essentially, as Haynes (2012, p 87) argues, providing us with the benefits of 'thinking about our thinking'. Storytelling and the collection of narratives generated through research conversations have become valuable methods of data collection, involving the interactions between a teller, a coaxer, and a wider audience (Plummer, 1995). Reflection allowed us to develop our thinking further and shape our method to involve the combined characteristics of collecting stories, a semi-structured style, in the comfort and ease of conversations.

Using storytelling as a research method has been criticised because the very definition of 'story' is tricky and imprecise. Each story takes on an original form, and, according to Frank (2010), the positioning of stories is fragile and open to 'narrative ambush', whereby they hitch a ride on other stories and the characteristics of the audience. We became increasingly conscious of the challenges presented in terms of 'narrative ambush' by ourselves as the researchers/listeners of these stories, as even our follow-up questions could lead participants and their stories down a different path from the one that originally might have been taken. Having been so focused on collecting individual stories, we also uncovered communal stories that were created in the interactions between the researcher and the researched. Telling personal stories in this way can result in feelings of satisfaction, validation, fulfilment, affirmation, belonging, and a shared sense of identity; or, conversely, they can disrupt, trouble, and distress. During the conversations, we saw that participants were re-experiencing emotions they had felt during the situations they were describing. This was something that resonated with us and will be discussed later in the chapter. However, we found ourselves at times laughing along with our participants but also empathising with them when they described situations that were not so positive, thus reinforcing the notion that the sharing of stories is highly relational.

The role stories play is complex; while some appear to maintain dominant orders, others resist them. One feature of stories that cannot be overlooked, however, is the power they have; the personal power of individuals to voice or withhold their story, and the overarching social power that closes down or opens up spaces for stories to be told. During the research, and the conversations with our participants, we noted this compelling relationship and the powerful role we held as researchers within it. In order to acknowledge this powerful interplay, we spent time at the beginning of each conversation making sure our participants were comfortable and confident, both with ourselves and the video recording equipment. We highlighted their choices as central to participation; that they could ask us to start and stop the recording whenever they wanted, that they could express themselves in ways that were most convenient to them, that it was in fact their voices and stories that were of such meaning and interest to us. It was also interesting that towards the end of the conversations, participants were keen to share their thoughts about the dissemination of the stories. We felt this was important and part of a continuous process of empowerment, rather than us deciding, on the participants' behalf, how the stories would be shared.

Feminist methodological approaches encourage researchers to become involved and interconnected with their participants' worlds, and we felt that this project enabled us to be, even in a small way, part of the lives of this group of disabled young people. Sharing stories of their experiences, inviting conversations, and listening intently to them enabled familiarisation and afforded an otherwise perhaps unobtainable 'inside' view of their lives. Some of the stories were long and convoluted, some were happy and funny, some sad and heart wrenching, but all were compelling, precious, and unique, steeped in passion, humour, and integrity offering insights into the lives and worlds of these five young people.

Utilising and incorporating reflexivity as a 'set of mutually interrelated processes and practices involving the reflexive thinking, doing and evaluating of qualitative research' (Corlett and Mavin, 2018, p 377) allowed us to consider and more critically understand our choice of design and methods, from qualitative and feminist approaches to the listening and telling of stories. We began to unravel how our values, beliefs, and positions in the world merged with our research practices, and in turn shaped the knowledge we produced. Being reflexive in this way meant being constantly vigilant about our approaches to the research and our responses to the young people; were we asking questions at the right time, were we inadvertently guiding the stories in a particular direction or restricting the responses, (for further examples of this, see also Mactavish et al, 2000; Aldridge, 2007; Wickenden and Kembhavi-Tam, 2014), how much were we influencing this knowledge?

Having now reflexively explored some of the ethical principles, the research design and method, our final thoughts turned to capturing and disseminating the findings. We chose to capture these stories on video and project them onto a digital platform to share with a wider audience. The individual films were sent to each participant for approval and then collated. All participants were invited to come together, watch the recordings, and share their individual stories. We felt that by watching the recordings, the participants would be able to express their views about what they had decided to share (see also the work of Aldridge, 2007; Wickenden and Kembhavi-Tam, 2014). In addition, the opinions of the participants were sought in relation to the research process as a whole and any issues they wanted to raise. These interactions between participants were invaluable as they were able to see how other disabled people view life and express their interests. Additionally, it offered an opportunity for us to reflect back on the tools used, consider our choices and positions, and, as Guillemin and Gillam (2004, p 274) suggest, engage with reflexivity as a process that 'saturates every stage of the research'. With the participants' permission, the conversations and an unabridged collection of the stories were professionally collated as a film, and played continuously as an installation, captivating audiences of academics and professionals during a Storytelling Conference at the University of Suffolk in July 2018.[1]

Research as emotional work

Researching with humans is often complicated and rarely straightforward. The practicalities of collecting 'human documents' (See Blumer, 1979 for a more expansive analysis), or in this case, human stories, was multifaceted. For this project, we took on board Bourdieu and Wacquant's (1992) recommendation that we should be mindful of three main reflexive concerns – personal identity, location within the field, and scholastic fallacy – as these were likely to impact on interpretations of the social world that we produced through the collective unconscious of a particular academic field (Kenway and McLeod, 2004).

However, when reflecting on our journey throughout this project, we became aware that the three separate main concerns that Bourdieu and Wacquant (1992) write about in detail were actually inextricably linked for us. We found them to be entangled and inseparable, becoming what

Dickson-Smith et al (2009, p 61) term as an 'embodied experience', one where researchers are emotionally affected by the work they do (see also Davidson, 2011; Woodby et al, 2011; Liddiard, 2013). More specifically, as part of the project, we found that due to our direct involvement with our participants from the recruitment stage to the sharing of their stories as a film, we were deeply immersed in and connected with the stories that these disabled young people shared with us. Our personal identities and experiences very much affected how we responded and what feelings we experienced while listening to their stories. We were congruent in the way that we accepted our participants as unique individuals and we reflected regularly on the emotions that we were experiencing and how these affected our decisions for this project after the completion of the conversations, especially around dissemination of findings.

Almost by default, we began to realise the enormity of the emotion that was embedded in the research work of the project. On further investigation, we found that the emotional aspect of humanistic research is seldom theoretically or empirically investigated (Woodby et al, 2011). It became clear that the impact of emotional experiences within qualitative research has been underestimated. The purpose of raising this issue here is not to disregard the work of Bourdieu and Wacquant (1992) in relation to the three reflexive concerns of identity, location, and scholastic fallacy, but to make more visible the emotional aspect of the research process by offering a critical and reflexive reconsideration of the process behind the finished product.

The human engagement required by the researcher to gain the trust of the participants in order for them to feel comfortable to share their stories and reduce the researcher/participant power hierarchy was all-consuming and steeped in emotional investment. Many participants expressed their gratitude for being given the opportunity to share their life stories, in some cases for the first time. The emotions of the participants reinforced that research is emotional for both participants and researchers. This awareness affected us significantly, but instead of trying to remove these feelings from the process, we instead accepted them and shared them with each other. Listening to tales of participants' isolation, confusion, physical exhaustion, instances of bullying, and exclusion was overwhelming, and the participants' pain that surfaced through storytelling was hard to hear. Although we were aware of our own thoughts and feelings and arrived prepared for the emotional work that this project required, perhaps we did not anticipate that such a significant emotional load would arise from listening to the disabled young people's experiences. Working through all the stories multiple times brought back our feelings of worry, fear, and anxiety for our participants' lived experiences but also for their future. We were able to support each other through this process by being open and sharing our thoughts and feelings, but there is clearly a need for the accompaniment of self-care practices within research of this type. In the case of this project, the life-affirming stories about friendships and the humorous anecdotes lightened the emotional load somewhat, and keeping personal research journals, as well as organising informal reflexive chats over coffee, served as valuable self-help strategies in that they provided space to make sense of the shared stories.

To publish or not to publish

Turning research into academic literature to be published, discussed, and scrutinised was an expected and 'desirable outcome' of this project. Alongside the privilege of working with the young participants and hearing their stories first-hand came the responsibility of editing, interpreting, and sharing them with a wider audience. We had to reflect on the possibilities, benefits, and consequences of publishing these stories. As researchers, we felt a weight of responsibility in sharing findings, but this seemed to be going against our responsibility towards the disabled young people we spoke with and their stories.

Judging the extent to which the stories should be shaped and moulded to 'fit' the research brief, while staying true to the original voices, words, and storylines proved to be excruciatingly difficult. Apart from the dilemma about publishing the stories, we had to reflect and consider the medium or channel through which we could share the stories without changing them to 'fit' the structure and format of academic publications in the traditional sense. An initial idea of publishing the stories as an anthology was considered but rejected upon further reflection, as we felt that we would still be affecting the participants' original voices by transcribing them into written language. Editing seemed to be intruding on the words and potentially undermining the meanings of the disabled young people. We eventually decided on sharing the conversations as an unabridged collection of the stories as a film, which we felt was the best way to ensure that the disabled young people's stories remain intact.

Conclusion

In the conclusion we would like to iterate the importance of two key claims. The first is the importance of highlighting the messiness, complexity, and dilemmas that come with every research encounter, which are seldom presented in published accounts. The second is the responsibility of disseminating our research in ways that hold true to the aims and aspirations of the research.

As the messiness and granularity of research is something that might not always be given enough of the spotlight in public arenas and within published academic work, we felt compelled to write a chapter that reflected some of the dilemmas we experienced and those that challenged us. Before we started out, it would have been valuable to find examples of researchers speaking reflexively about issues and dilemmas in research, as they do in this volume. However, we only found documented accounts of studies that followed linear trajectories and well-trodden pathways. Those with imperfections are mostly unrecorded and unnoticed, as if the flaws they bear have no impact on the overall research process or are perhaps too challenging for researchers to reveal and still be credited as 'good' researchers. Therefore, this chapter has offered an open account of our own research journey. This is not a naval-gazing exercise, but rather offers fellow researchers some insight into the processes we experienced and reinforces that upholding scrutiny and transparency within and of research itself is a very necessary part of the overall process.

The second claim is for researchers to consider how and where they disseminate their research in relation to the aims and aspirations of the research and the desires of the participants. We are pleased that we chose an accessible method of data collection that complemented the overall aims of the study. In addition, the unabridged version of the video conversations used for the installation highlighted the to-ing and fro-ing of the research conversations that took place. We were therefore confident that the complete and unedited filmed stories matched our belief that disabled young people's voices should be heard. The desire to reach wider audiences and share the findings from the 'More Than …' project was strong, but institutional audit cultures that shoe-horn academic writers into placing their work in the high-prestige, secret realm of specialised journals (Back, 2007) raised an intellectual and moral predicament for us.

Whose stories were they, and to whom did they belong, the teller, the social researcher, both? Since these stories were generated through an open channel of dialogue and exploration, this made it so much more difficult for us to untangle and distinguish the effect we had on these stories while they were shared by our participants. While it is widely known that the publication of work to satisfy institutional and departmental requirements is part and parcel of the everyday pressures of being an academic, the compromise of authenticity of voice was considered too great, and while the research process that we engaged with has been offered up within this chapter, the stories have remained unpublished in the traditional sense.

We would like to thank the five participants who shared their stories with us. It was a privilege to work alongside you and learn from you.

Note
[1] https://www.youtube.com/watch?v=7paLOl-PNgQ&feature=youtu.be

References
Aldridge, J. (2007). Picture this: The use of participatory photographic research methods with people with learning disabilities. *Disability & Society* 22(1): 1–17.

Back, L. (2007). *The Art of Listening*. Oxford: Berg.

Berger, R. (2015). Now I see it, now I don't: Researcher's position and reflexivity in qualitative research. *Qualitative Research* 15(2): 219–34.

Blumer, H. (1979). *Critiques of Research in Social Sciences: An Appraisal of Thomas and Znanieck's The Polish Peasant in Europe and America*. New York: Social Science Research Council.

Boggis, A. ed. (2018). *Dis/abled Childhoods?* Cham: Palgrave Macmillan. https://doi.org/10.1007/978-3-319-65175-0_7

Bourdieu, P. and Wacquant, L. (1992). *An Invitation to Reflexive Sociology*. Chicago, IL: University of Chicago Press.

Corlett, S. and Mavin, S. (2018). Reflexivity and researcher positionality. In Cassell, C., Cunliffe, A., and Grandy, G. (eds) *The Sage Handbook of Qualitative Business and Management Research Methods* (pp 377–99). London: Sage.

Davidson, D. (2011). Reflections on doing feminist research grounded in my experience of perinatal loss: From auto/biography to autoethnography. *Sociological Research Online* 16(1): article 6. http://www.socresonline.org.uk/16/1/16.hml

Dickson-Smith, V., James, E.L., Kippen, S., and Liamputtong, P. (2009). Researching sensitive topics: Qualitative research as emotion work. *Qualitative Research* 9(10): 61–79.

Frank, A.W. (2010). *Letting stories breathe. A socio-narratology*. Chicago, IL and London: University of Chicago Press.

Goethals, T., De Schauwer, E., and Van Hove, G. (2015). Weaving intersectionality into disability studies research: Inclusion, reflexivity and anti-essentialism. *Journal of Diversity and Gender Studies* 2(1–2): 75–94.

Goodley, D. (2017). *Disability Studies: An Interdisciplinary Introduction* (2nd edn). London: Sage.

Guillemin, M. and Gillam, L. (2004). Ethics, reflexivity, and 'ethically important moments' in research. *Qualitative Inquiry* 10(2): 261–80.

Haynes, K. (2012). Reflexivity in qualitative research. In Symon, G. and Cassell, C. (eds) *Qualitative Organisational Research: Core Methods and Current Challenges* (pp 72–89). London: Sage.

James, A. and Prout, A. (1997). Re-presenting childhood: Time and transition in the study of childhood. In James, A. and Prout, A. (eds) *Constructing and Reconstructing Childhood* (pp 230–50). London: Falmer Press.

Katz, C. (1992). All the world is staged: Intellectuals and the projects of ethnography. *Environment and Planning: Society and Space* 10(5): 495–510.

Kenway, J. and McLeod, J. (2004). Bourdieu's reflexive sociology and 'spaces of points of view': Whose reflexivity, which perspective? *British Journal of Sociology of Education* 25(4): 525–44.

Liamputtong, P. (2007). *Researching the Vulnerable*. London: Sage.

Liddiard, K. (2013). Reflections on the process of researching disabled people's sexual lives. *Sociological Research Online* 18(3): 10. http://www.socresonline.org.uk/18/3/10.html

Mactavish, J.B., Mahon, M.J., and Lutfiyya, Z.M. (2000). 'I can speak for myself': Involving individuals with intellectual disabilities as research participants. *Mental Retardation* 38(3): 216–27.

Plummer, K. (1995). *Telling Sexual Stories: Power, Change and Social Worlds*. London: Routledge.

Richards, S. and Clark, J. (2018). Research with disabled children: Tracing the past, present and future. In Boggis, A. (ed.) *Dis/abled Childhoods? A Transdisciplinary Approach* (pp 187–210). Cham: Palgrave Macmillan/Springer Nature.

Richards, S., Clark, J., and Boggis, A. (2015). *Ethical Research with Children. Untold Narratives and Taboos*. Basingstoke: Palgrave Macmillan.

Rose, G. (1997). Situating knowledge: Positionality, reflexivities and other tactics. *Progress in Human Geography* 211(3): 305–20.

Shakespeare, T. and Watson, N. (1997). Defending the social model. *Disability and Society* 12(2): 293–300.

Shakespeare, T. and Watson, N. (2001). The social model of disability: An outdated ideology? Exploring theories and expanding methodologies. *Research in Social Science and Disability* 2: 9–28.

Townsend, R.C. and Cushion, C.J. (2020). 'Put that in your fucking research': Reflexivity, ethnography and disability sport coaching. *Qualitative Research* 21(2): 251–67. https://doi.org/10.1177/1468794120931349

United Nations (1989). *Conventions on the Rights of the Child*. Geneva: United Nations.

Wickenden, M. and Kembhavi-Tam, G. (2014). Ask us too! Doing participatory research with disabled children in the global south. *Childhood* 21(3): 400–17.

Woodby, L., Williams, B.R., Wittich, A.R., and Burgio, K.L. (2011). Expanding the notion of researcher distress: The cumulative effects of coding. *Qualitative Health Research* 21(6): 830–8.

6

Youth Social Action: Shaping Communities, Driving Change

Katie Tyrrell

Introduction

In this chapter I join with others to think reflexively and critically about participation with children and young people both in research and practice. First, introducing the notion of agency and voice with regard to research with children and young people, I subsequently explore a critical approach to participation, outlining the potential areas for further clarification and questioning, alongside the potential opportunities for meaningful engagement and co-production with young people. I refer directly to my experience of carrying out explorative qualitative research alongside young people across Suffolk, a county in the East of England, conducted to explore young people's perceptions of opportunities within their communities, which was followed by a second study to unpick the notions of meaningful participation and 'voice' for both young people themselves, but also local civic leaders. I reflect on my experiences as a perhaps naive, early-career researcher, and the practicalities, conflicts, and realities of researching alongside young people. Utilising a reflexive approach in this instance not only facilitated my understanding positionality and the influence upon the research process itself, but also further highlighted the ethical complexities of participatory and co-production methodological approaches to researching with young people. As Graham et al (2016, p 86) suggest, 'reflexivity offers a means by which participatory methods can be analysed to reveal the ethical nuance inherent in the creative processes used to invite and engage children in the research'.

The term *young people* is used throughout to refer to individuals aged 11–25 years who participated in the research, acknowledging that this age bracket spans both childhood, as conventionally defined as under 18, and youth. Furthermore, when discussing participation, it is realised that with the age of 18 comes a democratic right to vote, which could alter dynamics and perceptions of participation in both communities and wider society (Walther et al, 2019). It is not my aim to make sweeping generalisations about individuals within this age bracket, as all young people will have individual socio-cultural contexts from which they draw experience, and subsequent acknowledgement of this diversity, as well as the shared perceptions, is important. Nonetheless, participants within the study frequently referred to themselves as young people, as opposed to children, youth, or young adults, and therefore this term has been adopted.

Since the introduction of the United Nations Convention on the Rights of the Child (UNCRC) (United Nations, 1989), within social science, particularly childhood studies, there has been a surge in interest and adoption of participatory research methods and practice, to align with the children's rights agenda, and more specifically Article 12 of the UNCRC, which states that the child has the 'right to express those views freely in all matters affecting the child, the views of the child being given due weight in accordance with the age and maturity of the child'. Subsequently, the way in which participation has been defined and understood has predominantly focused upon enabling children to have 'voice' in the research process by adopting child-centred methods (James and Prout, 1990). While facilitating young people's engagement in research to enhance the likelihood of 'authentic' voice is to be admired, I argue, along with many others (Percy-Smith, 2006), that we need to look beyond just listening and discussion of methods to working alongside young people to facilitate meaningful intergenerational and peer relationships, to further understanding of young people's socio-cultural contexts and subsequently what they regard as 'meaningful', and to facilitate their contribution to all aspects of their communities and beyond by providing choice and opportunities, as well as working collaboratively to challenge the structures they identify as restricting them.

Agency, voice, and participation

It is widely accepted that for many years young people have been denied opportunities to feed back on experiences that shape their everyday lives (Lansdown, 2011) due to concerns about maturity or an inability to see young people as 'active agents'. However, in recent years, children and young people have increasingly been identified as social actors in their own right (Fleming, 2013), therefore inclusion of their voice as agentic beings in shaping policy, practice, and research is one of moral reasoning but, more importantly, a matter of ethics (Carnevale, 2020). Increasingly, young people, although some requiring legal authorisation to access various aspects of social life (the right to vote, ability to consent to healthcare), are regarded as active in shaping and contributing to their immediate context as well as wider society, both regarding their own interests and the interests of others (Carnevale et al, 2021). Agency is conceptually complex, and some critical approaches to participation have questioned the need for narratives which focus on children as 'active', emphasising action, particularly that of a dichotomised individualised nature, in which someone is 'active' or 'inactive', with the former being perceived as socially desired (Hammersley, 2017). Instead, some others have suggested that agency instead falls on a continuum, dependent on circumstance, or is limited to predetermined options (Klocker, 2007; Robson et al, 2007), highlighting the importance of considering the contextual environments in which young people are situated. Furthermore, inactivity and passivity in participatory research have equally been questioned, with passivity rightfully being conceived as a form of agency. Subsequently, the 'agency' of young people in research and practice is one which requires constant reflexive thought, taking into consideration the structural barriers and facilitators within and outside of the institutions and communities in which they reside (Thomas, 2021).

The realisation of young people as social actors in their own right has increased the domination of 'voice' and 'listening to children' in discourse surrounding childhood and youth (Walther et al, 2019). The inclusion of young people's voice has predominantly been positioned as a positive, to both shaping services to meet the needs of children and young people, but also facilitating empowerment and capital and contributing to enhanced confidence and self-esteem (Sinclair and Franklin, 2000). However, there are suggestions that the inclusion of children's (and adults') voice is in accordance with neoliberalist ideals, by shaping young people to fulfil their roles as contributing members of society and facilitating consumerism (Raby, 2014). Therefore, critical reflection upon young people's voice and agency in relation to their sociocultural contexts within research and practice is necessary, to avoid the tokenistic inclusion of voice as a 'testament of ethical and empowered status for children' (Clark and Richards, 2017).

The actualisation of young people's agency and voice, alongside the children's rights agenda and a focus on wider consumer and user involvement (Sinclair, 2004) promoted a focus towards participatory approaches in research and service development. Participation, with regard to the lives of young people more specifically, has taken on several meanings and has been critiqued as being difficult to define (Gallagher, 2008; Farthing, 2012). Put simply, participation is described as 'taking part' or being 'actively involved in something, however it is recognised within multiple definitions of the term that participation with regard to children and young people's worlds is complex and multifaceted (Clark and Percy-Smith, 2006). Nonetheless, multiple definitions centre around involvement of young people, from consultation to high-level decision making, with participation being considered critical to citizenship (Hart, 1992; Percy-Smith and Thomas, 2009).

In discourse, participation has been positively interpreted as a means of enlightenment, focusing on the narratives of young people as experts in their own everyday lives, and empowerment, shifting power dynamics between adults, with more democratic rights and authority, and children (Warshak, 2003). Furthermore, participation has been linked to pedagogical and relational processes, in which a young person, through participation, is able to learn and develop skills for the future and build positive intergenerational relationships (Percy-Smith, 2006). Conversely, some have implied that instead of undergoing critical questioning, the notion of participation as a concept and process within children and young people's lives has been assumed as a positive and subsequently facilitated and embedded in practice, with a focus on 'how' as opposed to 'why' (Farthing, 2012).

The practice of participation has also been highly debated and developed, with several typologies adopted in shaping both research and practice approaches to working alongside young people, for example Hart's (1992) 'ladder of participation', Treseder's (1997) 'degrees of participation', and Shier's (2001) 'pathway to participation'. Such models have been adopted extensively in practice, as a means of developing and evaluating local and national participatory work with children and young people. However, these typologies have been criticised for limited practical information on how adults can support young people in participatory work, as well as limited consideration of the varying levels of 'empowerment' that children might experience (Kellett, 2011).

While these typologies are positive in highlighting the importance of thinking critically about the level and means of facilitating participation practically, some have, possibly unfairly, critiqued these models for unintentionally generating a hierarchy of methods and processes for engaging with young people (Lundy, 2019). For example, in the United Kingdom, involving children at the highest level, by enabling them to facilitate decision making, coordinate their own institutions, and discuss what matters to them, in the form of school councils and youth parliaments, is identified by educational and governmental institutions as facilitating 'voice', 'agency', and 'empowerment' of young people. While some such institutions may lead to change or enable development of skills for some young people, research has highlighted that these bodies are identified by other young people as being limited in their diversity and associated with a degree of scepticism (Borland et al, 2001; Wyse, 2001; Stafford et al, 2003). Others have also questioned these approaches to participation, suggesting that aiming to fit children and young people into adult structures and systems can potentially exacerbate exclusion further (Lundy, 2007). Tisdall and Davies

(2004) suggest that developing long-term dialogue and sharing power over decisions between young people and decision makers alongside inclusion of a diversity of young people's voices are crucial to increasing the likelihood of meaningful outcomes.

Similar concerns have been raised around the use of participatory methods with young people in research, some suggesting that the focus on the hierarchy of methods, with participation featuring as a 'gold standard' of research practice with children (Gallacher and Gallagher, 2008), can potentially lead to increased tokenism (Fleming, 2013). Nonetheless, since the introduction of the UNCRC, participatory research with young people has been adopted widely (Alderson and Morrow, 2004), and a multitude of creative and innovative methods to facilitate research 'with' young people, as opposed to 'on' young people, have been developed (Barker and Weller, 2003). Child-centred approaches to research, such as photography (Yamada-Rice, 2017), digital methods (Bond and Agnew, 2015; Livingood et al, 2017), and the inclusion of children as researchers themselves (Kellett, 2011), are developed to facilitate meaningful engagement with young people, providing opportunities to participate in ways that prevent further marginalisation (Cahill, 2004). For example, Bucknall (2012) suggests that children becoming researchers themselves and leading on projects provides both a sense of ownership and empowerment but also motivation to continue to engage for the project duration. Furthermore, some evidence suggests that children's involvement as co-researchers or researchers themselves has led to a direct influence upon decision making within various contexts locally, such as schools, but also at the national policy level (Raymond, 2001; Kellett, 2011). However, the practice of research by children has been critically evaluated, with questions around the influence of adults in the process, with the potential for children, instead of expressing their own views, taking on the epistemological views of adults (Kim, 2016).

The need for reflexivity and development of better theorisation of participation in research and practice has been acknowledged widely (Tisdall, 2013), moving from the 'how' to 'why' and in what context, with suggestions that more interdisciplinary international collaboration would benefit understanding of participation in different contexts (McMellon and Tisdall, 2020). More recent models of participation have moved away slightly from typologies, to consider the prerequisites and contextual factors that facilitate young people's participation. From a children's rights perspective, Lundy (2007) describes a broader conceptualisation of Article 12 of the UNCRC, and includes other articles, centring around four main concepts: space, voice, audience, and influence. While Lundy (2007) refers predominantly to educational institutions, such as schools, the concepts described can be replicated across any structure in which young people are present. She highlights the need for space, for young people to express their views safely, for opportunities to express voice in a way meaningful for them, and a listening audience, which leads to subsequent influence and action. Using ecological approaches, Johnson (2011) also developed 'Change-scape', a model to help in identifying the interactions between young people's identity, agency, and participation in different contexts. Contextual factors, including external (for example, policy, cultural, and institutional context) and internal (capacity and commitment of those involved) were identified as crucial in understanding how young people's participation in evaluation, and research, can be more meaningful and based on relational processes. Facilitating positive and meaningful intergenerational connections based on shared respect and decision making is crucial, both in research, such as participatory and action research, and practice (Johnson, 2017).

While some have directly evaluated the impact of young people's participation or critically reflected upon participatory research with young people, this is far less frequent than comments upon participation in practice, as outlined by Clark and Richards (2017): 'As academics and researchers, we are quick to pick up on the perceived tokenism of children's rights in practice; for example, the school council (Wyse, 2001; Robinson and Kellett, 2004), but this stance is less often addressed in our own research practices' (Clark and Richards, 2017, p 133).

The purpose of the remainder of this chapter is therefore to present a critical reflexive account of my experience conducting exploratory participatory research with young people living in Suffolk, from 2019 to 2020. The focus will be upon discussing the complexity of interactions between adults and young people (Percy-Smith, 2006; Johnson, 2011) and exploring agency, voice, and participation in practice and subsequent ethical implications. I hope that discussion of some of the challenges and barriers faced when conducting this research, alongside my reflections on the process, facilitates learning and discussion around ethics and provides further insight into the nuanced reality of researching with young people.

Exploring young people's perceptions of community and participation

While on the surface Suffolk appears to be an area of low deprivation, there are pockets in which advantage sits alongside disadvantage, producing a range of inequality and 'hidden need', particularly with regard to the life chances of young people (Smith and Dogaru, 2020). Ipswich, the county town of Suffolk, was one of 12 areas defined by the Department for Education (2017) as an 'Opportunity Area', recognised as having long-standing and significant educational underperformance, deprivation, and social immobility of young people. Prior research has revealed that young people in Ipswich have a vast array of concerns about their local communities (Tyrrell, 2018), in particular the existence of gang violence within their local areas (Andell and Pitts, 2017) having negative implications for their sense of safety and generating feelings of ostracisation and social exclusion from their local communities. Despite this, little had been achieved locally to find out from young people themselves what their communities meant to them, how they could be improved from their perspectives, and whether they would like to shape the solutions to local issues.

Being a 'young', enthusiastic researcher at the start of my journey, I considered myself as ready for the challenge of investigating young people's (aged 11–21 years) perceptions of their local community contexts in Ipswich, but also wider areas of Suffolk. The young people who participated in the project were from a diverse range of backgrounds, including young people working with charitable organisations, young people who were not in employment, education, or training, and young people at secondary schools. The aim of the first project (project A) was to build an understanding of young people's current experiences within and perceptions of their communities to shape local decision making around community assets and opportunities for young people. The project involved visiting young people within schools, youth clubs, and local organisations in Suffolk to engage with them via participatory methods, including mapping, drawing, and group discussion. The second project (project B) focused predominantly on understanding perceptions of youth participation and voice among local civic leaders, practitioners, and young people themselves, to understand facilitators of and barriers to young people's participation in Suffolk. In project B, focus groups were conducted by young people with experience of youth work within local charitable organisations, who were subsequently trained in research methods and ethics. Both projects were underpinned by a commitment to flexible and participatory methods; I had read all the literature and I felt prepared, perhaps somewhat naively. I would soon realise that no amount of reading can instinctively equip you for the realities and moral and ethical dilemmas of researching with young people.

Agency and 'voice' in practice

During data collection, instead of focusing on 'active' participation – a space in which young people could choose to participate or not – simply asking them to tell us about their communities, if they wished to do so, was facilitated. Although community can take on different meanings for different people, most young people spoke directly about the immediate area in which they lived, including the structures within it, such as school, college, or surrounding facilities. The sessions were held in the environments in which the young people were based, and facilitated by myself and a community youth worker trained in research methods. A flexible structure was adopted, based predominantly around discussion which was led by the young people themselves, with the addition of arts materials and mapping exercises to facilitate the sharing of ideas where required (Barker and Weller, 2003). I was committed to working with young people in a flexible, ethical way, ensuring they had options to engage by utilising a range of child-centred methods that I had read about in multiple resources on how to conduct research with young people.

Despite this, as we entered the contexts in which young people lived their everyday lives, such as schools or services, I soon realised that the dynamics of agency and consent did not begin at the start of the data collection process, they are navigated during the process of liaising with gatekeepers and understanding the information shared with young people ahead of fieldwork visits. It is well documented that gatekeepers have a key role to play in the facilitation of research, particularly with communities at the edges of society (Emmel et al, 2007), as well as offering key insights into the population of interest. As researchers, we are often reliant on gatekeepers, such as youth workers or teachers, to help us to reach participants, so much so that we forget at times to reflect upon the process in which young people may be informed of the activities they are being asked to participate in.

Typically, I aim to ensure that participants who engage in my research have access to information, directly or via gatekeepers, prior to data collection, to discuss the project with parents, guardians, or others in order to make informed decisions about whether they would like to participate. However, on a few occasions during this project I found that young people had been targeted, selected, given very little information as to why they were present at the session, and did not have parental or guardian consent to participate. This raised a number of concerns for me as a researcher, one being the potential to omit perspectives of young people who go 'unselected' for various reasons, but also concerns around deviating from written ethical protocol and the limited time available for young people to consider their participation.

In that moment, I had to decide whether to delay the session or refuse participation for those young people under the age of 18 who did not have parental or guardian consent. Although it could be argued that schools and organisations were acting *in loco parentis*, I felt it was not possible to control for possible power imbalances during the 'selection' process, to which I was not party, and the young people were being considered last in a long and complex chain of 'approvals', further contributing to the removal, or denial, of agency. In addition, would I be further contributing to a removal of young people's agency if I denied participation due to a lack of parental or guardian consent when that young person had provided informed consent? It is in these situations that researcher judgement is crucial, and it was important for me to ensure that those young people were aware of the research aims, processes, and implications; and with their informed and ongoing consent,

I was not going to deny those young people participation rights to share their voice. Facilitating additional time and direct contact between participant and researcher to consider and understand the implications of participation in research is sometimes difficult and may not always be possible in the context of working alongside young people, however I realise that if we are to think about young people as agentic beings in their own right, we need to ensure that they are treated in equal ways.

It subsequently occurred to me that there is often a moral dissonance between ethical protocols, enforced rightly to protect research participants, and the theoretical underpinnings of children and young people's agency and rights to participation underpinned by the sociology of childhood (James and James 2004; Prout, 2005). Classification of young people as 'passive', 'incapable', and 'unknowing' as opposed to 'becoming' and 'agentic beings' contributes to the othering of children and young people and subsequent powerlessness. Participation in research is only one example of how young people's voices can at times be muted and considered last in a line of approvals, as a means of protection as opposed to perhaps ethical practice. A more in-depth discussion of the implications of research ethics committees and protocols for research with children may be found in Richards et al (2015, pp 14–31). This is, perhaps, a moral dilemma faced by any researcher committed to participatory research with young people.

In addition, the possibility for gatekeepers to select, at times unintentionally, the young people to participate in research also contributed to feelings of unease. To consider agency meant to ensure that young people from a diverse range of backgrounds have the opportunity to participate and that a deliberate steer away from more conventional voices may be necessary (Richards et al, 2015). As a result, we made it a priority for the research to actively seek out and include young people from various backgrounds, including those who were not in any form of education, employment, or training (NEET). It was with these young people that the dynamics of agency, voice, and participation, and the importance of the researchers' actions, became increasingly apparent.

Navigating the ethics of perceived inaction

The fieldwork took place within an organisation working alongside NEET young people, and after numerous conversations with the gatekeeper I felt confident that, as with other fieldwork visits to schools and other organisations, I would be able to engage with the young people in a positive way. Unlike other groups however, it soon became apparent that while the group were informed about the visit and the session ahead of time and had returned consent forms, after I had explained the research, asked for consent once again, and started to build rapport, with initial broad questions and icebreaker activities, there began to be a lull in the room. I encouraged the young people to engage with the questions around their community, the positives, the negatives, and any suggested improvements, using the materials available to express themselves if required, however they started to talk among themselves. In an attempt to re-engage, I found myself automatically directing their attention back to the questions, encouraging the young people to use the materials available to draw or write responses in small groups. Despite this, the young people reverted to conversation as opposed to engaging with the more creative activities planned as part of the participatory approach. At the time, I felt slightly out of my depth and disheartened, but nonetheless continued, with less focus on any planned or suggested activities in order to facilitate the agency of the young people in directing the research process. On reflection, it is perhaps unsurprising that these methods were met with some resistance by young people, who were likely to have been let down by the educational system. As Waller and Bitou (2011) suggest, participatory methods have the potential to elicit pedagogical relationships. Furthermore, the opportunity to disengage from more participatory methods could reflect a shift in the power dynamics and agency (Ansell, 2001). As Gallagher (2008) suggests, not only are young people navigating power dynamics within the group, but they are also managing power dynamics with the researcher and external systems, likely leading to a continuous exchange of power. Therefore, as opposed to affording power to young people per se, engagement or disengagement with participatory methods may reflect acts of agency or liberatory tactics, within social, relational contexts, to resist domination (Gallagher, 2008).

This highlights the importance of understanding experience and the positionality of young people within socio-cultural contexts, upon voice and agency. As our conversation continued, it became clear to me that some of the resistance may be linked to prior instances in which young people had been consulted on matters, which had led to inaction, or lack of feedback as to how their voices had shaped policy or practice. There was a sense of inevitability and desensitisation among the group, that their participation would not lead to any change, no matter how significant.

Katie:	Can you describe what opportunities or activities are available to you in your local area?
Jake:	There's nothing really to do is there.
Preston:	We don't get told about them.
Jake:	Whoever owns the council and that, they need to let us young people know.
Preston:	Nothing is going to happen is it, in ten years' time they will then decide to do something.
Liam:	Ten years later our kids will be going through this, but worse init.

Jake: Anything we do say, it's not going to matter to them, this has happened so many times, it won't change.

The last comment made by Jake in this extract has stayed with me ever since, and it raised significant questions for me around responsibility. Was I committing 'academic voyeurism', utilising these young people's voices to investigate an area of interest without any clear plan as to how to implement action as a result? Was it my responsibility as a researcher to rally action on behalf of these young people? Was it the responsibility of the young people themselves, the local authority, the commissioners of the research, or was it a combination of all stakeholders? I started to feel uncomfortable, knowing that I, as a researcher, may not have the necessary power and resources to be able to bring about action on behalf of these young people. I was developing knowledge of their contexts and worldviews, however what mattered to them most were the real-world implications of sharing their 'voice', something I was not necessarily able to predict.

Clearly defining the benefits, risks, and limits of research is crucial and an ethical responsibility within any research project, yet when researching with children and young people I felt a tendency to feel the need to overcompensate, to view children and young people as 'vulnerable', in need of advocates. In this moment, when Jake expressed this view, a desire to over-promise suddenly dominated, to act in a way to protect and commiserate, to take on the world on behalf of these 'vulnerable' young people, directly contradicting epistemological values underpinning the sociology of childhood and parity of power. Instead, I was open and honest about the potential implications of the research, that any action as a result of the project would require resource, but I would endeavour to share the findings of the project widely and make suggestions to the project steering group, many of whom were local civic leaders. Furthermore, I highlighted my admiration for their questioning, for me, the apprehension represented agency itself. By, demonstrating a sense of uncertainty and fatigue in the inaction resulting from consultation, the young people contributed further to understanding how they felt about agency, their voice, and participation in local decision making and shaping communities.

Co-production: participation as relational

Making young people's participation in research meaningful and effective in influencing change involves moving beyond isolated instances of data collection to building relational connections (Sinclair, 2004). During the initial project I realised the ethical dilemma of researching with young people who had felt deflated by participation in local consultation with limited feedback or action, and was subsequently interested in how local individuals, organisations, and communities could work alongside young people more effectively towards shared, meaningful outcomes. Using co-production methodologies, the project sought to engage collaboratively with young people to explore previous research findings, develop ideas for future research and interventions, and collect primary data. Co-production is suggested to be a positive approach in bridging academic and non-academic worlds to facilitate knowledge construction intended for both academia and wider society (Campbell and Vanderhoven, 2016), and is a method typically utilised in service evaluation and development (Dixon et al, 2019).

> Co-production methodologies might be realistically conceived as ones in which fairer distributions of contribution, decision making, value and recognition are constantly strived for in research activities but may not always be successful in the ways we hope or intend. It requires us to be flexible in our expectations and to be open to a model of research where the majority of insights will emerge through the process of collaboration, rather than at the final destination. (Berriman et al, 2018, p 161)

As part of the project, young people from schools and organisations who participated in the original research were invited to attend a workshop of participatory activities, to engage with each other, the researchers, and gatekeepers, such as teachers and youth workers, to reflect upon the findings and what this might mean practically for opportunities and provision for young people in their communities. The workshop highlighted the importance of peers, alongside researchers and gatekeepers, in shaping decision making, with young people collaborating on deciding what constituted a 'safe space' to them, many drawing and developing hubs or centres for young people. The collaborative nature of these workshops was indicative of the distributive disposition of agency (Oswell, 2012; Berriman et al, 2018), with young people drawing ideas, advice, and encouragement from social networks. In addition, the young people who participated also reflected upon their influence in shaping provision, suggesting that, similarly to the original findings, they felt they were not consulted or involved in decision making regarding matters that influenced their lives. As a result of this consistent theme, I worked alongside local youth organisations to employ three young people (aged 18–25) as co-researchers, to conduct some follow-up research alongside myself. After research and ethics training, we went into the field, to conduct focus groups and lead community engagement events to understand young people's perceptions of participation and voice.

Shortly after beginning data collection, we started to realise that the narratives presented by young people centred predominantly around opportunity, support, empowerment, and respect. Similar to Lundy's (2007) suggestions of prerequisites and contextual factors influencing positive participation, all of the themes were related to the young people's wider networks, requiring peers and 'adults' to create and facilitate opportunities for participation, provide safe and supportive spaces, and empower young people to share perceptions and respect ideas. It was acknowledged by young people that the balance of power was not straightforward and that while they felt that they should have more opportunities to feed into or be directly involved in decision-making processes, they felt that in some instances they would prefer to have others, particularly other young people, as advocates on their behalf, or to 'have the option to not be involved' in some stages of a project or discussion. To them, this was not a symbol of disempowerment, but respect for their wishes, highlighting a challenge for co-production methodologies in which there is an expectation of equality at all stages of the research process, from conception to dissemination. Interestingly, when engaging in reflection, the co-researchers also shared this perspective, implying that the process of co-production in research and practice with young people is not static and is a continually evolving process of shared power and responsibility, which fluctuates within the interdependent relationships.

Subsequently, as others, such as Oswell (2012), Clark and Richards (2017), and Gallagher (2019), have suggested, instead of conceptualising agency as being about the individualised agentic being, perhaps participation, in which agency is a foundation, should be understood as relational, tied to social assemblages and networks. A more relational, co-creative, or co-productive approach to both understanding participation as a concept, but also reflecting upon research with children and young people would open interesting avenues for research and practice, focusing on how young people work collectively with peers or adults to facilitate social change. For example, here Luke and Sharanya describe their views on effective mechanisms to involve young people in sharing their ideas for local community development. To them, this is a combination of both 'adults' and 'young people' working together to shape the most effective outcomes based on young people's feedback.

Luke: Just putting it on every single platform, at least one page where we can text in, have a few people working there who are adults, looking at our opinions.

Sharanya: But then maybe even a few young people working along with them, just because they won't then select some ideas, but the youngsters might see a new perspective from that idea if that makes sense, more than the adult would.

It is recognised in social theory that relationships are crucial in securing a sense of safety in the world, of identity, and of basic trust in others within the social world (Jamieson and Milne, 2012). As White and Choudhury (2010) highlight, this is not to take away from the rights and agency of children and young people, but it is to acknowledge that similarly to adults, they are not completely autonomous beings and navigate the world of relationships and structures within various socio-cultural contexts. McMellon and Tisdall (2020) highlight that this conceptual change could influence how we think about supporting young people, looking instead at what steps can be taken to facilitate agency and participation. Not only this, but such a conceptual change to consider relational process in working alongside young people also influences how we reflect upon researching alongside them. Reflexivity is important in qualitative research, particularly for researchers adopting participatory or co-production methodologies, in which continual shifts in power exist and knowledge is shaped by multiple stakeholders. I felt that although my attempts at a neutral positionality while being an 'outsider' may, at times, have influenced young people's responses when discussing the need for local change due to a preformulated assumption of inaction based on prior experience, when adopting co-production methodologies with partner community organisations the boundaries between 'insider' and 'outsider' began to blur, with such fluid researcher positionality enhancing the research process (Canosa et al, 2018).

In the projects outlined in this chapter, young people were also invited to attend a session in which they could feed back on the findings of the research, to identify if they still resonated and reflected their views, and to help shape them further. It was from this session that a group of young people discussed the BikeStormz 'Bikes Up, Knives Down' movement and the local adaptation of this called 'Swerve Sunday', in which a local community group worked with young people in the area to support a series of social action events to raise awareness of tackling gang violence and knife crime among young people (Day, 2019). The young people, while showing us videos of bike tricks on Instagram, were passionate about their involvement in this national movement, facilitated via network effects through social media to local community groups investing in their ideas. In this example, young people's participation experience was developed via social networks, through their experience of relating to others online but also by identifying and collaborating with local communities of adults and young people who were passionate about reducing knife crime.

Increasingly, young people are becoming involved in activism (Earl et al, 2017), with individuals such as Greta Thunberg and Amanda Gorman using spoken word, poetry, and political action to deliver powerful messages to tackle global issues such as climate change and racism. Another local project, led and developed by young women with Volunteering Matters, called Women Against Sexual Exploitation and Violence Speak Up (WASSUP), is also an example of how participation in the form of collective social action can lead to positive changes to policy and practice (Mitchell, 2017). Both projects were supported by adults within community groups or charitable organisations; however, the ideas are organic and developed based on the young people's agendas, moving away from the idea of participation for young people as consumers of state provision (Shukra et al, 2012). In participatory research and practice, acknowledgement of the role of the relationships and social connections in shaping young people's participation, via the researcher, peers, or supporting adults, is important to developing further understanding of this interdependency and agency (Clark and Richards, 2017).

Conclusion

The identification and recognition of young people as social actors worthy of study is to be commended. Participatory research and practice can facilitate opportunities for young people to be involved directly in shaping knowledge, policy, and practice. Nonetheless, it is also important to think critically and reflexively about participative research, moving away from methods and typologies solely, to interpreting the messy and unpredictable nature of researching within children and young people (O'Farrelly, 2021), to investigating the collaborative practices, and how researchers, practitioners, and adults are involved in that process. Reflexivity is critical in moving towards a more participatory ideology, in encouraging reflection on positionality of the researcher, acknowledging the influence of relational processes in shaping research and facilitating iterative and responsive methodological and ethical approaches to working with young people. I hope that my reflections on experiences as an early-career researcher, on the context-dependent and temporal nature of agency, voice, and participation, offer opportunities for further discussion of the ethical and moral dilemmas afforded by participatory and co-produced methodologies with young people.

The research presented suggests that, as Lundy (2007) outlined, young people require safe spaces, opportunities to share their views and perceptions, an audience, and influencers to facilitate action. Co-produced research with young people, in addition to a reconceptualisation of agency as relational, could facilitate a movement towards more collaborative interpretations of participation.

Critics suggest that young people's participation is preparing them for a neoliberal culture of citizen-consumers (Farthing, 2012), however participation, in the form of co-produced practice or research, can also offer young people the opportunity to collectively challenge the structures and cultures that may act to oppress or exclude them. Article 12 of the UNCRC highlights that young people should have a voice in matters that directly impact their lives; however, as identified by Uprichard (2010), it is when we move beyond this, to enabling young people to develop collaborative co-produced narratives, not just what on impacts them, but what impacts us all, within our immediate communities as well as globally, that meaningful participation will be achieved. Viewing young people as part of the whole community, as opposed to separate entities, is important when striving towards a more participatory ideology (Beresford, 2021).

References

Alderson, P. and Morrow, V. (2004). *Ethics, Social Research and Consulting with Children and Young People*. Barkingside: Barnado's.

Andell, P. and Pitts, J. (2017). *County Lines Ipswich: Young People; Anti-Social Behaviour and Safeguarding*. https://www.suffolkscb.org.uk/assets/Safeguarding-Topics/Gangs/County-Lines-Final-Report-16-08-2017.pdf

Ansell, N. (2001). Producing knowledge about 'third world women': The politics of fieldwork in a Zimbabwean secondary school. *Ethics, Place & Environment* 4(2): 101–16.

Barker, J. and Weller, S. (2003). 'Is it fun?' Developing children centred research methods. *International Journal of Sociology and Social Policy* 23(1/2): 33–58. https://doi.org/10.1108/01443330310790435

Beresford, P. (2021). *Participatory Ideology: From Exclusion to Involvement*. Bristol: Policy Press.

Berriman, L., Howland, K., and Courage, F. (2018). Recipes for co-production with children and young people. In Thomson, R., Berriman, L., and Bragg, S. (eds) *Researching Everyday Childhoods: Time, Technology and Documentation in a Digital Age* (pp 139–162). London: Bloomsbury Academic. http://dx.doi.org/10.5040/9781350011779.ch-008

Bond, E. and Agnew, S. (2015). Using digital methods with young people: Methodological innovation or madness? In Hine, C., Morey, Y., Roberts, S., Snee, H., and Watson, H. (eds) *Digital Methods for Social Sciences: An Interdisciplinary Guide to Research Innovation* (pp 190–205). Basingstoke: Palgrave.

Borland, M., Hill, M., Laybourn, A., and Stafford, A. (2001). Improving consultation with children and young people in relevant aspects of policy making and legislation in Scotland. Commissioned by the Scottish Parliament Information Centre for the Education, Culture and Sport Committee. http://archive.scottish.parliament.uk/business/committees/historic/education/re ports-01/edconsultrep02.htm

Bucknall, S. (2012). *Children as Researchers in Primary Schools: Choice, Voice and Participation*. London and New York: Routledge.

Cahill, C. (2004). Defying gravity? Raising consciousness through collective research. *Children's Geographies* 2(2): 273–86.

Campbell, H.J. and Vanderhoven, D. (2016). Knowledge that matters: Realising the potential of co-production. Report. N8 Research Partnership, Manchester.

Canosa, A., Graham, A., and Wilson, E. (2018). Reflexivity and ethical mindfulness in participatory research with children: What does it really look like? *Childhood* 25(3): 400–15. https://doi.org/10.1177/0907568218769342

Carnevale, F.A. (2020). A 'thick' conception of children's voices: A hermeneutical framework for childhood research. *International Journal of Qualitative Methods* 19. https://doi.org/10.1177/1609406920933767

Carnevale, F.A., Collin-Vézina, D., Macdonald, M.E., Ménard, J.-F., Talwar, V., and Van Praagh, S. (2021). Childhood ethics: An ontological advancement for childhood studies. *Children and Society* 35(1): 110–24. https://doi.org/10.1111/chso.12406

Clark, A. and Percy-Smith, B. (2006). Beyond consultation: Participatory practices in everyday spaces. *Children Youth and Environments* 16(2): 1–9.

Clark, J. and Richards, S. (2017). The cherished conceits of research with children: Does seeking the agentic voice of the child through participatory methods deliver what it promises? In *Researching Children and Youth: Methodological Issues, Strategies, and Innovations* (pp 190–205). Bingley: Emerald Publishing Limited. Online. http://dx.doi.org/10.1108/S1537-466120180000022007

Day, S. (2019). YouTube BMX star meets fans to spread anti-knife message. *Ipswich Star*. https://www.ipswichstar.co.uk/news/you-tuber-ryan-taylor-at-swerve-sunday-in-ipswich-2852248

Department for Education (2017). Policy paper: Social mobility and opportunity areas. https://www.gov.uk/government/publications/social-mobility-and-opportunity-areas

Dixon, J., Ward, J., and Blower, S. (2019). 'They sat and actually listened to what we think about the care system': The use of participation, consultation, peer research and co-production to raise the voices of young people in and leaving care in England. *Child Care in Practice* 25(1): 6–21. https://doi.org/10.1080/13575279.2018.1521380

Earl, J., Maher, T.V., and Elliott, T. (2017). Youth, activism, and social movements. *Sociology Compass* 11(4): e12465. https://doi.org/10.1111/soc4.12465

Emmel, N., Hughes, K., Greenhalgh, J., and Sales, A. (2007). Accessing socially excluded people: Trust and the gatekeeper in the researcher-participant relationship. *Sociological Research Online* 12(2): 43–55.

Farthing, R. (2012). Why youth participation? Some justifications and critiques of youth participation using New Labour's youth policies as a case study. *Youth & Policy* 109: 71–97.

Fleming, J. (2013). Young people's participation – where next? *Children & Society* 27(6): 484–95.

Gallacher, L.A. and Gallagher, M. (2008). Methodological immaturity in childhood research? Thinking through participatory methods. *Childhood* 15(4): 499–516.

Gallagher, M. (2008). 'Power is not an evil': Rethinking power in participatory methods. *Children's Geographies* 6(2): 137–50. https://doi.org/10.1080/14733280801963045

Gallagher, M. (2019). Rethinking children's agency: Power, assemblages, freedom and materiality. *Global Studies of Childhood* 9(3): 188–99. https://doi.org/10.1177/2043610619860993

Graham, A., Powell, M.A., and Truscott, J. (2016). Exploring the nexus between participatory methods and ethics in early childhood research. *Australasian Journal of Early Childhood* 41(1): 82–9. https://doi.org/10.1177/183693911604100111

Hammersley, M. (2017). Childhood studies: A sustainable paradigm? *Childhood* 24(1): 113–27.

Hart, R. (1992). *Children's Participation: From Tokenism to Citizenship*. Florence: UNICEF.

James, A. and James, A. (2004). *Constructing Childhood: Theory, Policy and Social Practice*. Basingstoke: Palgrave.

James, A. and Prout, A. (1990). *Constructing and Reconstructing Childhood: New Directions in the Sociological Study of Childhood* (2nd edn 1997). Oxford: Routledge.

Jamieson, L. and Milne, S. (2012). Children and young people's relationships, relational processes and social change: Reading across worlds. *Children's Geographies* 10(3): 265–78.

Johnson, V. (2011). Conditions for change for children and young people's participation in evaluation: 'Change-scape'. *Child Indicators Research* 4(4): 577–96. https://doi.org/10.1007/s12187-010-9099-6

Johnson, V. (2017). Moving beyond voice in children and young people's participation. *Action Research* 15(1): 104–24. https://doi.org/10.1177/1476750317698025

Kellett, M. (2011). Empowering children and young people as researchers: Overcoming barriers and building capacity. *Child Indicator Research* 4: 205–19.

Kim, C.Y. (2016). Why research 'by' children? Rethinking the assumptions underlying the facilitation of children as researchers. *Children & Society* 30(3): 230–40.

Klocker, N. (2007). An example of thin agency: Child domestic workers in Tanzania. In: Panelli, R., Punch, S., and Robson, E. (eds) *Global Perspectives on Rural Childhood and Youth: Young Rural Lives* (pp 153–78). London: Routledge.

Lansdown, G. (2011). *Every child's right to be heard: A resource guide on the UN Committee on the Rights of the Child general comment no. 12*. https://resourcecentre.savethechildren.net/pdf/5259.pdf/

Livingood, W.C., Monticalvo, D., Bernhardt, J.M., Wells, K.T., Harris, T., Kee, K., and Woodhouse, L.D. (2017). Engaging adolescents through participatory and qualitative research methods to develop a digital communication intervention to reduce adolescent obesity. *Health Education & Behavior* 44(4): 570–80.

Lundy, L. (2007). 'Voice' is not enough: Conceptualising Article 12 of the United Nations Convention on the Rights of the Child. *British Educational Research Journal* 33(6): 947–52.

Lundy, L. (2019). In defence of tokenism? Implementing children's rights to participate in collective decision-making. *Childhood* 25(3): 340–54. https://doi.org/10.1177/0907568218777292

McMellon, C. and Tisdall, E.K.M. (2020). Children and young people's participation rights: Looking backwards and moving forwards. *The International Journal of Children's Rights* 28(1): 157–82.

Mitchell, G. (2017). Ipswich women's youth group WASSUP wins Crimebeat Award for work against violence and sexual exploitation. *Ipswich Star*. https://www.ipswichstar.co.uk/news/ipswich-women-s-youth-group-wassup-wins-crimebeat-award-for-2777590

O'Farrelly, C. (2021). Bringing young children's voices into programme development, randomized controlled trials and other unlikely places. *Children & Society* 35(1): 34–47.

Oswell, D. (2012). *The Agency of Children: From Family to Global Human Rights*. Cambridge: Cambridge University Press.

Percy-Smith, B. (2006). From consultation to social learning in community participation with young people. *Children Youth and Environments* 16(2): 153–79.

Percy-Smith, B. and Thomas, N. eds (2009). *A Handbook of Children and Young People's Participation: Perspectives from Theory and Practice*. London and New York: Routledge.

Prout, A. (2005). *Future of Childhood: Towards the Interdisciplinary Study of Children*. London: Routledge/Falmer.

Raby, R. (2014). Children's participation as neo-liberal governance? *Discourse: Studies in the Cultural Politics of Education* 35(1): 77–89. https://doi.org/10.1080/01596306.2012.739468

Raymond, L. (2001). Student involvement in school improvement: From data source to significant voice. *Forum* 43: 58–61.

Richards, S., Clark, J., and Boggis, A. (2015). *Ethical Research with Children: Untold Narratives and Taboos*. Basingstoke: Palgrave Macmillan.

Robinson, C., and Kellet, M. (2004). Power. In Fraser, S., Lewis, V., Ding, S., Kellet, M., and Robinson, C. (eds) *Doing Research with Children and Young People*. London: The Open University/Sage.

Robson, E., Bell, S., and Klocker, N. (2007). Conceptualizing agency in the lives and actions of rural young people. In Panelli, R., Punch, S., and Robson, E. (eds) *Global Perspectives on Rural Childhood and Youth: Young Rural Lives* (pp 72–86). London: Routledge.

Shier, H. (2001). Pathways to participation: Openings, opportunities and obligations. *Children & Society* 15(2): 107–17.

Shukra, K., Ball, M., and Brown, K. (2012). Participation and activism: Young people shaping their worlds. *Youth and Policy* 108: 36–54.

Sinclair, R. (2004). Participation in practice: Making it meaningful, effective and sustainable. *Children & Society* 18(2): 106–18.

Sinclair, R. and Franklin, A. (2000). 'Young People's Participation' Quality protects research briefing. https://lemosandcrane.co.uk/resources/DoH%20-%20Young%20Peoples%20participation.pdf

Smith, N. and Dogaru, C. (2020). Hidden needs in Suffolk: Taking the long view. https://www.suffolkcf.org.uk/wp-content/uploads/2020/11/Suffolk-Community-Foundation-Hidden-Needs-2020.pdf

Stafford, A., Laybourn, A., Hill, M., and Walker, M. (2003). 'Having a say': Children and young people talk about consultation. *Children & Society* 17(5): 361–73.

Thomas, N.P. (2021). Child-led research, children's rights, and childhood studies: A defence. *Childhood* 28(2): 186–99. https://doi.org/10.1177/0907568221996743

Tisdall, E.K.M. (2013). The transformation of participation? Exploring the potential of 'Transformative Participation' for theory and practice around children and young people's participation. *Global Studies of Childhood* 3(2): 183–93.

Tisdall, E.K.M. and Davis, J. (2004). Making a difference? Bringing children's and young people's views into policymaking. *Children & Society* 18(2): 131–42.

Treseder, P. (1997). *Empowering Children and Young People*. London: Save the Children.

Tyrrell, K. (2018). *Youth Engagement: Exploring Methods of Engagement and Feedback on the Ipswich Opportunity Area Delivery Plan with Young People*. Ipswich: University of Suffolk.

United Nations (1989). Convention on the Rights of the Child https://downloads.unicef.org.uk/wp-content/uploads/2010/05/UNCRC_united_nations_convention_on_the_rights_of_the_child.pdf?_adal_sd=www.unicef.org.uk.1619821693540&_adal_ca=so%3DGoogle%26me%3Dorganic%26ca%3D(not%2520set)%26co%3D(not%2520set)%26ke%3D(not%2520set).1619821693540&_adal_cw=1619700504230.1619821693540&_adal_id=2083995e-b23e-4a09-80f5-d059c7471b02.1619700504.3.1619821689.1619700504.4d825266-8e07-4f6b-829a-050d5e0aa58a.1619821693540&_ga=2.234097758.1989231875.1619821689-968360291.1619700504 [29/04/21]

Uprichard, E. (2010). Questioning research with children: Discrepancy between theory and practice? *Children & Society* 24(1): 3–13.

Waller, T. and Bitou, A. (2011). Research with children: Three challenges for participatory research in early childhood. *European Early Childhood Education Research* 19(1): 5–20.

Walther, A., Pohl, A., Loncle, P., and Thomas, N.P. (2019). Researching Youth Participation – theoretical and methodological reflections on limitations of existing research and innovative perspectives. In Walther, A., Batsleer, J., Loncle, P., and Axel, P. (eds) *Young People and the Struggle for Participation: Contested Practices, Power and Pedagogies in Public Spaces* (pp 15–33). Abingdon: Routledge.

Warshak, R. (2003). Payoffs and pitfalls of listening to children. *Family Relations* 52: 373–84.

White, S.C. and Choudhury, S.A. (2010). Children's participation in Bangladesh: Issues of agency and structure of violence. In Percy-Smith, B. and Thomas, N. (eds) *A Handbook of Children and Young People's Participation: Perspectives from Theory and Practice* (pp 39–50). London and New York: Routledge.

Wyse, D. (2001). Felt tip pens and school councils: Children's participation rights in four English schools. *Children & Society* 15(4): 209–18.

Yamada-Rice, D. (2017). Using visual and digital research methods with young children. In Christensen, P. and James, A. (eds) *Research with Children* (pp 71–86). London: Routledge.

7

A New Panorama of Child Voice in the Child Protection Context

Samia Michail

Introduction

This chapter uses reflexivity, the ability to reflect and recognise how individuals and their contexts connect with social and cultural understandings (Fook, 2004, p 18), to encourage a different view of child voice. It proposes that child voice within child protection processes is the product of a dynamic interplay of relationships that occurs within and outside of the child protection system. These relationships include those between children[1] subject to child protection interventions and child protection practitioners; child protection practitioners and the organisations who employ them, thus providing the institutional settings for child protection practice; and children and the state, both the state as guardian and in the state's role in providing resources to children and families (the welfare state). Both structural and cultural dimensions of relationships need to be analysed to recognise under which conditions children can express voice.

These relationships are centred on how opportunities for child voice within child protection are a policy and political choice. This politicisation of child voice needs to be articulated for a critical analysis of the complex variables that impact a child's capacity to represent themself and have their views respected and acted upon. Clarity about the conditions under which child voice may occur produces a realistic understanding of how the complex set of relationships, outside of the child's micro-system but *deeply related to it*, impact the implementation of children's participation in their own safety. More importantly, it paves the way to understanding how the system can move beyond children's voices just being heard.

The discussion of the various conditions needed for child voice, in the context of child protection, starts with three key observations. First, child voice is understood here as children having autonomy (the rights and conditions to self-govern) and agency (the capacity to act and create positive change in their lives), and that these are supported by the structures and processes of relevance to them, namely child protection processes and normative expectations around children and children's rights. Secondly, child voice is qualitatively different to child participation. Even when children are involved in decisions about their lives, this is not always necessarily child voice, which requires systems to acknowledge children's perspectives in a sustainable way. Thirdly, the social construction of child voice is limited in the child protection space because of the nature of child protection work.

This chapter is a critical reflection process that interrogates how the concept of child voice has been narrowly experienced and structurally created and/or applied within contemporary child protection discourse. Fook (2004, p 20) suggests that communication and dialogue are important for shared understandings to be created. The communication of child voice as a concept and practice may not receive as much attention as participation within child protection work because the work is intense, emotional, time pressured, and difficult. Yet the characteristics of practice can be challenged and changed if we are reflexive about child protection systems and participate in 'consciousness' raising about the facts (Fook, 2004, p 21). The use of reflexivity can extend and enhance practice options, beyond practice that identifies and manages 'risk' (D'Cruz and Gillingham, 2017). Reflexivity on the differences between child voice and child participation may be useful to child protection practitioners, who are often required to engage with children to hear their voice in decisions about their safety. Reflexivity requires the practitioner to recognise the influence of self (Fook and Gardner, 2007) and the capacity to reflect on their views and give equal weighting to children's views (Davis, 1998; Bruce, 2014; van Bijleveld, Bunders-Aelen, and Dedding, 2020).

To that end, this chapter presents a personal critical appraisal of the connections between theory, knowledge, and practice of child voice specifically when children need protection. It attempts to recognise the multiple influences on child voice that sit in the background of everyday practice. It goes beyond the causal links of micro-elements of supporting child participation. For example, the features of the practitioner and organisation, such as skills for working with children (building rapport, trauma-informed practice, group engagement methods and worker attitudes towards children's capacities) and workplace culture (worker turnover and resources to design creative methods of capturing children's views). A focus on these micro-elements presents a view that they are the only key determinants of children's participation. This is not, however, analogous to the barriers and enablers of child voice in child protection contexts. Attention to the way child protection is carried out and adherence to rights-based rhetoric limits our appreciation of the concept of child voice. It confines our thinking to the particularised and immediate context of the child. In turn, this leads to similarly limited practice, such as the popular child-centred approaches. Child-centred, child-aware, and child-inclusive practice approaches are important first steps in creating awareness of children's rights to decision making. They compel us to gaze intensely at the child's perspective. But, if we place our energies into only thinking about the single vista of the child's situation, it is at the cost of a more holistic panorama that situates the child in the reality of a more complex environment.

The confusion between child voice and children's participation is more a conflation of children's involvement as autonomy and agency (Dillon et al, 2016; Collins, 2017). The emphasis on eliciting children's views and their engagement in child protection decision making, has led to a plethora of practice tools and guides on children's participation. They aim to increase engagement with children in a prescribed time and place. Unfortunately, the popularity of these practice tools may have implied that an increase in children's participation will bring about the cultural and structural change which is required for child voice. Organisations and practitioners employ these tools to consult with children and document children's perspectives, and these tasks are important for children's views to be made known and influence decision making. Yet, this is not equivalent to a child's enduring capacity to act and make a difference to their own life. Structural and cultural changes that position children as essential to designing service provision embed their autonomy and agency in a sustained way. Children's participation tools and guides can be misleading to practitioners if they are used mechanically, without a more thorough agenda around how children's perspectives they elicit will be used to bring about change. The discussion here suggests the child is part of a range of other relationships of power that often child-centredness does not accommodate. The concept and practice of child voice may be better understood as political in nature, and as distinct from children's participation.

The political nature of child voice is not yet well defined. This chapter works to reimagine this politicisation, that is, the way child voice is related to relationships between the state, and key stakeholders involving the use of power in policy and practice. The chapter outlines the significant role of political structures, processes, relationships, and narratives (established, contemporary, and emerging) to clearly articulate the linkages between them, as well as the multiplicity of children's lived experience of autonomy and agency (or lack thereof). It does this using a conceptual framework that considers the complex arrangements through which child voice is configured, such as the political-structural influences on children's participation discourse and practice, contemporary ideologies (for example globalisation, individualisation), social and political agendas, the children's rights movement, international conventions, sector governance (for example managerialism), organisational policies and processes, and welfare sector orientations. The framework is designed to recognise that child voice requires not only relationship-based work with children, but also an understanding of the complex web of other stakeholder relationships beyond the child–adult dyad or triad of social worker, parent, and child (Cossar et al, 2014, p 103). The political relationships between stakeholders in the child protection system need to be articulated for a critical ecology of child voice.

The conceptual framework provides one way for practitioners to be reflexive on the less tangible, underlying political influences on their everyday work. It encourages questioning about why we should or should not become involved in listening to children, or why they should be involved in decision making, and the importance of being aware of political affinities and commitments. It is crucial to think about, but also beyond, our individual choices, organisational barriers, and policy limitations and towards recognising policy and practice choices as political preferences. We can then distinguish between what is needed for child voice and not just children's participation.

The framework

The conceptual framework presented here is made up of several component structures and relationships that exist in child protection work. It attempts to represent the interdependency of relevant components. An 'ecosystem of child voice' provides a suitable metaphor for the dynamics between culture, policies, practices, individuals, and structures, including any assumptions, beliefs, and discourse. Each component contributes a unique set of characteristics to the political ecosystem, which are continually changing based on people's lived experience. Therefore, the ecosystem of child voice itself is always changing. This framework offers a way of accounting for the array of variables that dictate where children might participate and when this might become child voice.

This broad picture encourages us to reflect on the real context of tensions, informal alliances, economic agreements, and power between children, policymakers, and practitioners. A fresh framework of child voice is needed because the literature suggests there are gaps in our conceptual knowledge of participation and in what we have included in our discussion of children's participation (McMellon and Tisdall, 2020) and because '[t]he tension between individual autonomy and dependence on social conditions is one of the most important aspects of children's agency' (Baraldi and Cockburn, 2018, p 12). Considering the socio-cultural aspects of participation, policymaking, and practice with children draws attention to the complexity of social conditions influencing children's capacity to exercise voice. Single contextual elements that influence child voice, in isolation, provide a limited appreciation of why children continue to be excluded from decision making about their own lives. For example, the difference in power between children and adults is often cited as an important element in children's participation, so we then focus on improving the child–practitioner relationship. Nevertheless, this framework extends our thinking beyond a single relationship to an 'ecosystem' of relationships within environments and asks 'what other systemic elements are influential and shape this relationship?'

The dynamics in this conceptual framework occur between a whole series of component structures and individuals. For example, the child–practitioner relationship within child protection canvasses a few kinds of work, depending on the child protection system, from the work involved in initial assessments related to risk of harm, through to ongoing case work to support children and families. The key element of this approach involves direct work between the child and practitioner. It allows children to receive and give information, be part of dialogue about the implications of decisions and options available to them (Toros, 2020). The child–practitioner relationship is pivotal to the ecosystem because this is where the child interfaces with the child protection system. The relationship between practitioner and their workplace is the central site for the development of a culture that endorses relationship-based practice skills. The connections between the practitioner and the larger organisation in which they work is the juncture between instinctive work habits and the assumptions and beliefs about children and child voice embedded in social work. The associations between practitioners from across different agencies in the ecosystem tests collaboration with different disciplines that take different approaches to child voice. The practitioner and state governing bodies define how policies are taken up by individual practitioners and either impede or promote child voice. The dynamics between organisations and governing bodies give us data on the impact of economics on child voice despite its distance from direct practice with children. The way statutory child protection services and government interact draws attention to tensions stemming from competing agendas that can undermine the capacity of practitioners to commit to child voice. Finally, the links between national policy trends and local practice are arguably some of the most important key influences in terms of bringing the concept of child voice into the child protection arena. The component relationships of the framework are now outlined in more detail in the next section. They contain some of the everyday issues of child protection work. However, this critical reflection is a way of developing 'our understandings of ourselves as knowers' so we can 'make the connections between ourselves as individuals and our broader social, cultural and structural environments' (Fook, 2004, p 19).

The child–practitioner relationship

The child–practitioner relationship is considered a key determinant of genuine children's participation because it can foster trust. This trust encourages a child to be confident and express their views. The trust relationship facilitates the exchange of information, the child's understanding of child protection intervention processes, and stimulates dialogue between the child and adult, allowing an exploration of children's needs and engagement in decision making (Cossar et al, 2014; Toros, 2020). Research shows how central the child–adult relationship is to best practice in formal child protection processes (Cossar et al, 2014, p 113; Goh and Baruch, 2018; Vosz et al, 2020). Children themselves say meaningful relationships with their caseworkers are important to them (van Bijleveld et al, 2015; Mason and Fattore, 2021). A large portion of this discourse is about the skills of the practitioner to work with children and, in particular, their individual characteristics, described as the 'professional habitus' or unconscious day-to-day practices that can limit children's participation if effective connections with children are not developed (Winter, 2011). Relationship-based practice stems largely from the attitudes of practitioners and their personal emotional capacity to reinforce children's rights (Bruce, 2014; van Bijleveld, de Vetten, and Dedding, 2020). Practitioners need both the attitudes and emotional capacity to be reflexive for professional purposes (assessing the grounds of our own beliefs) but also reflexivity, looking inwards and outwards to the environments in which we live and work (Fook, 2004, p 17; Watts, 2019). Therefore, this child–adult relationship is influenced by other relationships outside of the child–practitioner interaction.

Practitioner and organisation relationship

The relationship between practitioner and their employing organisation is important, as is their connection to the wider field of welfare. The immediate workplace conditions of the practitioner can facilitate and support relationship-based work, as captured in research on the impact of work environment on caseworker practice (Vis and Fossum, 2015; Alfandari, 2017; Diaz et al, 2018; Harkin et al, 2020; van Bijleveld et al, 2020). Culture, resources, and service orientation have a significant effect on the capacity of practitioners to engage with children and reinforce their rights in everyday tasks. Similarly, caseload, quality of professional supervision (Lefevre et al, 2019), practice approaches encouraged by managers (van Bijleveld et al, 2020), and styles of teamwork can be strong internal influences on individual practitioner skills and attitudes. Supervision, collaborative teamwork, and resources that support practitioner reflexivity, where they can articulate and share their experiences with colleagues, can counteract feelings of disempowerment to enact change in a complex child protection system (Fook, 2004, p 22).

Additionally, external influences, such as the nature of the practitioner's employing organisation and the field of social work, contribute to practitioner 'professional habitus', 'the taken-for-granted practices – or habits – of social workers formed in response to the pressures of the broader organizational context of the social work profession' (Winter, 2011). Organisations' mission, availability, level and type of funding for social programmes, human resources, and administration can all dictate the physical and metaphorical space in which practitioners function. For example, a focus on parental issues, or faith-based philosophies that might underpin service delivery, can impact children's participation directly (Zell, 2006; Raby, 2014; Diaz, 2018; Harkin et al, 2020).

Organisational characteristics can impede the building of meaningful relationships with children and therefore inhibit children's participation (Winter, 2011, p 55). The CREATE organisation in Australia recognises that paternalistic attitudes are barriers to child voice and therefore proactively supports young people to lead their research and advocacy work (McDowall, 2016). The type of service provision may predict children's participation (see, for example, the work by Vis and Fossum (2015) on differences in children's participation in residential care compared to foster care).

Practitioners employed in safeguarding organisations are faced with the competing demands of their core statutory work and social work principles of self-determination, the encouragement of client involvement, and use of relational skills and emotional intelligence (Lefevre et al, 2019). Furthermore, managerialist approaches to social work aim to produce regulated and standardised responses to children and do not support the complexity of relationship-based practice (Middel et al, 2020), for example understanding children's emotions and their need to be seen as subjective collaborators in child protection assessment processes (Arbeiter and Toros, 2017) or the way children's participation is intertwined with parent and practitioner relationships (Oppenheim-Weller et al, 2017). Participation work is messy and difficult to conduct in a regulated way, so bureaucratic environments that value the use of sociometric tools can impede children's participation. There are a variety of welfare service types, which all have unique organisational cultures that practitioners engage with.

Practitioner and other agencies in the field

Children involved with the child protection system are usually involved with many professionals who are simultaneously responsible for their care. These professionals function in different service contexts unique to their area of expertise, for example healthcare (Lewkowicz and Tayebjee, 2019), education, juvenile justice, but also childcare, family support services, and advocacy bodies. Practitioners from different disciplines, providing different services, can become gatekeepers of the children they see if they are not willing to work across organisational boundaries, for example being selective about the referrals they accept (Scott, 2010, p 81). It is prudent to consider these relationships as involving potential for collaboration and competition between organisations (Todd, 2014, p 792). Interagency guidelines are seen as a mechanism for better communication skills between agencies and to clarify ways of working collaboratively. They can be improved by providing a shared definition of children's participation (as distinct from child voice, which is rarely considered in such guidelines) to facilitate dialogue about different expectations of engaging children. As noted earlier, social change requires communication of shared understandings and can be fostered through reflexive processes. For example, the Crossover Youth Practice Model (CYPM), developed by Georgetown University, found that there were different practitioner experiences of child participation between the child welfare system and the juvenile justice system:

> Team members also viewed the initiative as doing something different from the status quo of juvenile justice, particularly by allowing the youth to have 'a voice' by telling the team about the event that brought them to the attention of authorities (e.g., what led up to their misbehavior, why they misbehaved, etc.). (Wright et al, 2017, p 487)

Interagency work, which operates at a macro level, can build child voice if it distinguishes between what is required for child voice, as separate from children's participation. We know that close inter-professional cooperation can encourage and support children to contribute to decisions about their life (Todd, 2014; Schwartz, 2017). The Nordic Barnahus Model is an example of a multi-professional approach where 'law enforcement, child welfare services and health care' come to the child and come together to consult to provide the most appropriate service provision for the child. This model 'takes shape in relation to – and operates within – the distinct child welfare and criminal justice systems of the Nordic countries' (Johansson et al, 2017, pp 5 and 8). Here we see the necessity of larger system characteristics to promote child voice, addressed in the next section.

Practitioner and state governing bodies

Links between the practitioner and the state governing body are not often identified as central to children's participation. Yet, practitioners are often aware of their organisation's funding arrangements (Lohvansuu and Emond,

2020). They can take on views represented in the media. For example, the stereotypical view of western child protection systems is that they are 'broken' (Daly et al, 2016). Negative undertones about the system they work in may lead practitioners to feel uncomfortable about the inaction of state governing bodies. They may sense reservations about the capacity of their organisation to implement policies set by the state and statutory bodies (Zuchowski, 2019). Practitioners can personally shoulder the burden of meeting children's needs, as in the case of Finnish and Scottish practitioners in the age of austerity (Lohvansuu and Emond, 2020).

Generally, the individual practitioner needs time, training, and ongoing material and expressive support in their role of protecting children. Simple engagement with individual children is often easier than the structural work of child voice. Structural and cultural determinants are difficult to address because, first, there are competing demands between regulatory responsibilities, and the immediacy of direct personal engagement with children, often in times of crisis. Second, there are pressures from a child protection system governed by a liberal state that endorses individualism and a view of child abuse as an individual pathology, rather than the product of social equality (Qvortrup, 1997). Thirdly, the mass prevalence and use of system-supported practice tools promote an understanding of child safety through psychological and developmental lenses, as opposed to promoting professional judgement within structural issues that maintain social inequality (Gillingham, 2011).

Organisations and state governing bodies

It may seem we have exhausted the list of possible relationships that influence a child protection practitioner, but to tap into the transformative effects of reflexivity, we would need to deconstruct some of the connections between organisations and the relevant state governing bodies which have an indirect, yet significant, bearing on child voice. For example, in the United Kingdom and Australia there is usually an economically driven relationship where a non-government organisation, providing child protection, support, or advocacy services, is accountable to a state funding body, against a set of tightly regulated funding agreement criteria (Murphy, 2006). This relationship between service delivery organisations and funders (who are often the leading statutory body in child protection) is delicate and requires ongoing attention. There is a political need to maintain a working relationship with government where 'the community might benefit from positioning itself as part of a broader public system of welfare, rather than in opposition to government' (Andrew, 2006, p 323). Service delivery organisations need to be strategic to protect their own independence and viability to maintain the quality and reach of their services. The pressure to survive as an efficient service can get in the way of child-centred work because children's participation is resource intensive and might cost more than funding allows.

Moreover, service providers, funders, and the state take up different roles in the social protection of children, which need to be negotiated for them to work cohesively. Political and economic negotiations are carried out by key senior decision makers who are somewhat removed from the child–practitioner practice on the ground. Hence, this dynamic relationship, while even further removed from the direct practice with children, is an element just as central to their participation in decision making.

State statutory child protection services and state/national government

The way statutory state services and state/national government work together is not easily defined publicly, but the quality of this component relationship becomes evident when statutory services are required to respond to royal inquiries, commissions, and external policy reform. Their interactions are visible when there are recommendations to be implemented that change policy and practice with children. Government changes to service provision require negotiation about the financial and human resources needed to implement the changes. Statutory services play a large role in reinforcing or resisting government priorities and in time frames for policy change. They may have different perspectives on the positioning of children in terms of their safety and rights to participate while unsafe (Powell et al, 2021). The potentially competing agendas can impact practitioners directly although this is rarely discussed in relation to children's participation or voice.

Connections between statutory services and governments play out in discrepancies between expected professional standards of practice and employment conditions. An illustrative example is the high turnover of staff in child protection roles, related to both inadequate staff support to deal with moral dilemmas and the lack of preparation for intense emotional work (Healy et al, 2009). The stress experienced by staff might be exacerbated if they need to meet certain outcomes for children to comply with legislation, stringent programme criteria, or policy recommendations, but do not have enough resources or encouragement for relationship-based work with children. In considering these variable tensions, it becomes evident that the child protection practitioner is regularly inundated with political decisions that may undermine their ability to engage in anything except piecemeal and tokenistic forms of engagement with children. Once again, a practitioner who can narrate their practice struggles through a critical reflection process can have their experience validated and be recognised for their expertise (Fook, 2004, p 27) on how to improve child protection work to hear children. There are other intangible components of the child protection ecosystem that can be included in the critical reflection process.

National and global policy trends

Children, practitioners, non-government organisations, state statutory governing bodies, and governments are all influenced by the way other states and countries conceptualise and practice welfare. At the time of writing, the COVID-19 pandemic has necessitated new discourse on child protection and introduced new forms of international coordination on keeping children safe. Globalisation circulates neoliberal thinking so that social work takes a 'glocal' approach to practice, and there is pressure on local and state organisations to conform to remain relevant (Briskman et al, 2013). Consequently, local and state organisations can have less control over practice.

Kaufman et al (2002) discuss the influence of the human rights movement on children's participation, where international values are transmitted to nation-states through the United Nations Convention on the Rights of the Child (UNCROC) principles, which are key to child protection legislation (Duffy and Collins, 2010). Two international trends from the anglosphere demonstrate this influence. The first is the sway of individualism that promotes a focus on individual opportunities and not collective well-being, where the individual child is viewed as a 'consumer' of public services. The second is non-government sector advocacy for children's participation as a resistance to managerialism. This is a bid to push against an increase in non-government service provision so government can reduce its involvement and expenditure on social welfare (Thompson and Wadley, 2018). Social, economic, and cultural changes directly and indirectly impact children and can work counter to relationship-based practice, which is necessary for both children's participation and child voice. A case in point are those associated with the corporatisation of human services, whereby a regime of contractual obligation, strict accountability measures, and competitive funding are used as mechanisms to achieve 'quality outcomes' (Trevithick, 2014).

Child protection services cannot avoid national and global influences or the relationship between nation states and may unintentionally prioritise children's participation in ways that support neoliberal thinking. Children's participation can be used by governments to progress neoliberal socio-political agendas (Hyslop and Keddell, 2018), or alternatively the principles of children's participation can be used to promote child-centred child protection work (Moore, 2017). What might seem like work on children's rights may actually hide the lack of effort being put into creating child voice at a *structural level*, where children are believed to be more than just consumers but valued citizens (Raby, 2014).

Moreover, individual statutory child protection systems in different countries engage with each other, and elements of governance in one system can behave as impetus for local, state, or even national policy and practice change. For example, there are policy initiatives and academic research comparing national child protection systems as a means of understanding how to improve child outcomes (see, for example, Kojan and Lonne, 2012; Berrick et al, 2015).

Connected and dynamic component relationships

The various component relationships discussed so far need to be brought together in a framework to understand the complexity that shapes child voice. The complexity is visually represented by utilising the ecological theory of nested systems developed by Urie Bronfenbrenner in 1977 (and further in 1994), but for which there is limited research examining meso systems (Ashiabi and O'Neal, 2015). The diagram in Figure 7.1 attempts to magnify the 'meso system' connected in various ways to the macro and micro systems. In this framework, the meso system is defined as the space experienced by the practitioner in the child protection system, while the diagram remains child centric. The diagram includes the structures (circles) and relationships (arrows) together as a conceptual tool, where relationships between structures both impact, and are impacted, as indicated by the thick double-ended arrows. The relationships less articulated in discourse on child voice are represented by the thin, smaller, double-ended arrows, that largely occur within the 'messy meso' section of the child protection field. Ideally, this diagram would exist as a moving panorama, where the component structures and processes are not connected in linear ways but in a complex system of relationships that overlap and straddle other systems. These relationships fall into the middle layer of the diagram and are the junctures that can offer data on how structures and processes impact child voice. It is this 'messy meso' layer which is not often the subject of literature on children's participation or child voice because the child itself is not present or privy to those associations. These junctures are important because if what occurs between them is excluded, any strategies for cultural change required for child voice will be politically inadequate.

Discourse and research on the micro and macro systems provide essential insights into child voice. Discourse on children's participation largely focuses on relationships within the micro-system of the child, where people come into direct contact with the child – leading to concepts of child-centred practice and associated child-centred practice tools. What is missing is critical discussion about how the relationships that lie in between these layers relate to the issues in both the micro and macro systems. This framework shows what areas of the ecosystem intersect and can be assessed to elicit

Figure 7.1: Component structures and relationships in child protection

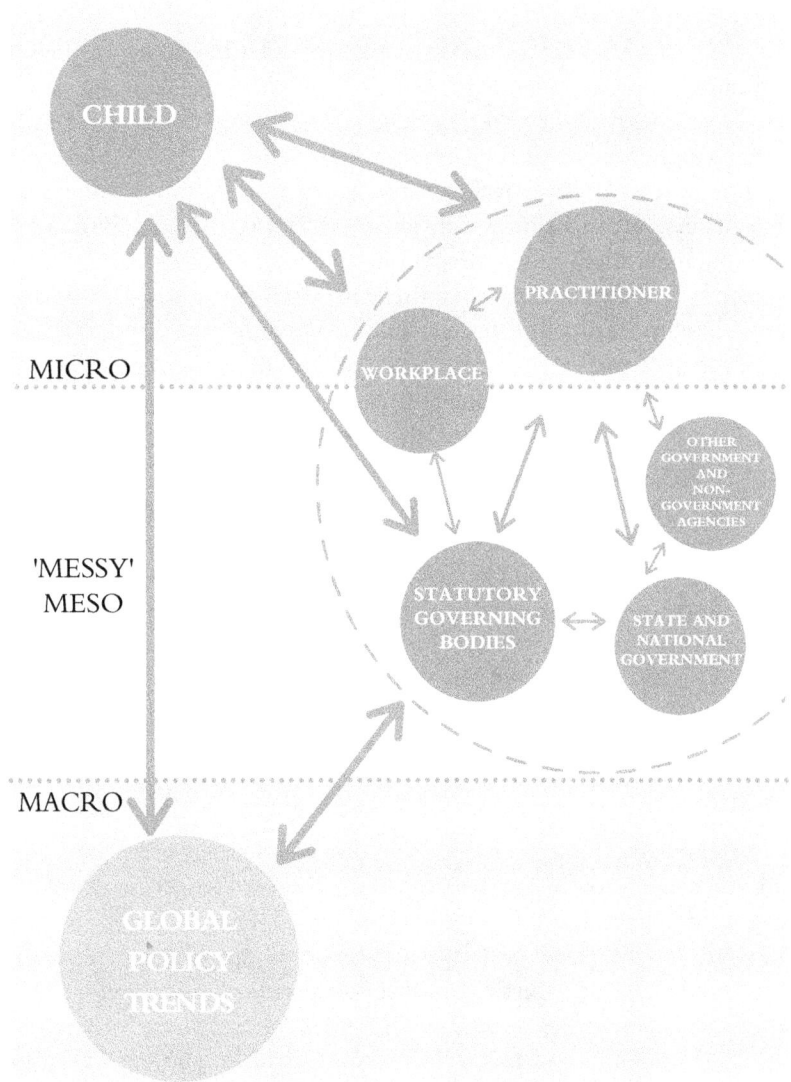

Source: Samia Michail, 2021

data in terms of impact on child voice. We can query whether structures and processes align or misalign in their interpretation, appreciation, and endeavours towards child voice. For example, in explaining the lack of interconnection between protection and participation rights, as the rights-based debate has acknowledged (Collins et al, 2021), we might identify the dissonance between funder reporting requirements on child outcomes to satisfy a managerial approach to service delivery and service provision based on a rights perspective of social work – what does this mean for relationship-based practice? This '[s]tructural insight is fundamental to social work and it has unavoidable political and ideological implications' (Hyslop and Keddell, 2018, p 8). We can use this framework to describe the ecosystem of child voice at any point in time.

This conceptual framework has manifold uses. It is useful as a heuristic tool for researchers to further develop knowledge on child voice, or by governments to analyse alternative approaches to child protection systems. Policymakers, organisations, and practitioners can increase awareness of what influences children's participation and promote child voice in child protection. It can yield data when there are significant social changes, such as periods of government election, funding agreement renewals, a crisis in child placement, state legislation change, periods of unmanageable high staff turnover, child protection policy reform, findings of a Royal Commission, and so on. Component relationships become more influential at different times of social change and the framework can encourage dialogue around the level of influence of each at these times. The framework can accommodate the continual flux in the ecosystem. Therefore, the framework is useful to understand what is needed for child voice, using an ongoing evaluation of the dynamics of relevant system components at time. Most of all, it can inform a reconstruction of identities, by first naming the 'identity politics' (Fook, 2004, p 27) embedded in the child protection system, asking what the political interests of each group are and how they work together.

Discussion

This reflexive interrogation has led to a discussion about the way in which child voice is narrowly constructed (both personally and structurally) as engagement and not children's autonomy and agency in child protection work. Models of child participation in child protection have largely constructed children's participation as occurring at the level of child–practitioner relationships (Cossar et al, 2014; Goh and Baruch, 2018; Vosz et al, 2020). While important, this conceptualisation ignores other factors critical to children being able to participate in child protection processes, including relationships between the practitioner and their employing organisation, other agencies they interact with in the welfare field, and state governing bodies, as well as relationships between organisations and statutory governing bodies, state and national governments alongside national and global policy trends, as outlined in this chapter. Moreover, it has been argued that a deeper form of engagement is possible, that of child voice, which is children having autonomy (the rights and conditions to self-govern) and agency (the capacity to act and create positive change in their lives). For this deeper engagement to be realised, we must consider the broader dimensions which impact child protection work, beyond the child–practitioner relationship.

Hartung (2017, p 54) applauds the recognition of children's participation that has come out of humanistic thinking so dominant in welfare but cautions that it can ignore 'contextual complexities and the dynamic and multi-levelled connections between subjects and social structures', and that is the greater challenge to sustained ways of working with children. The focus on the role of the practitioner seems warranted because this is the interface of the child with the child protection system and the manifestation of the relationship between the child and the state. However, addressing the structural and cultural determinants of disadvantage to build child voice involves change in the many relationships of the ecosystem, as has been described. Hyslop and Keddell (2018, p 106) refer to this as the 'big and small picture of social life'. Children's participation and child voice can be supported by practitioners and socio-political structures, in equal measure, if the basis is knowledge and practice that addresses the political nature of child voice. The junctures in the meso level explain how 'child protection professionals become enculturated into professional systems of thought and employ the discourses and conceptual tools that are available to them' (Duncan, 2018, p 9). This framework is one such conceptual tool, which provides a comprehensive approach to articulating the inherent tensions and incongruities in the ecosystem to which practitioners are exposed. It can help identify what is needed for cultural and structural change.

Critical reflection processes such as reflexivity and reflective practice are proactive strategies for considering our connections to social and cultural aspects of our work environments. They are not easy processes and require climates of trust, openness, and non-judgementalism (Fook, 2004, p 22) and a level of practitioner confidence (D'Cruz et al, 2019) to 'go beyond individual work to account for structure and culture' (Watts, 2019, p 17).

The restructuring of welfare agendas is complex, 'never wholly predictable, linear and unproblematic' and '[i]nterventions designed to transform working practices meet with ongoing social struggles and are translated in numerous ways' (Amoore, 2002, p 162). Concepts such as the child's best interests, child voice, and child participation are often included in policy but not implemented in practice and remain rhetoric. They can stem from mismatches between policy on best practice and organisational practice constraints, from individuals' motivation and limited resources, from organisational core objectives and the politics of direct experience of children, staff, management, and/or governance.

The framework introduced in this chapter offers a way for us to reflect on the structural and cultural changes that are needed to sustain not only child-centred approaches that engage children in decisions in an ad hoc way, but ways to systemically embed them as essential elements of service provision. It represents the ecosystem of tangible and intangible elements of child voice. It supports the idea that children make decisions influenced by the structures in which they live and not independently of them (Hartung, 2017, p 53). Children can be encouraged to participate in decisions but excluded from varying the structures and processes in key systemic political landscapes that define the decisions they may be invited to make. We need to reimagine what we know about children's participation and child voice as essentially political in nature.

Note

[1] The terms child and children are used throughout this chapter to respectfully refer to both children and young people.

References

Alfandari, R. (2017). Systemic barriers to effective utilization of decision making tools in child protection practice. *Child Abuse & Neglect* 67: 207–15. https://doi.org/10.1016/j.chiabu.2017.02.030

Amoore, L. (2002). *Globalisation Contested: An International Political Economy of Work*. Manchester: Manchester University Press.

Andrew, M. (2006). Learning to love (the state) again? Money, legitimacy and community sector politics. *Australian Journal of Social Issues* 41(3): 313–26. http://dx.doi.org/10.1002/j.1839-4655.2006.tb00018.x

Arbeiter, E. and Toros, K. (2017). Participatory discourse: Engagement in the context of child protection assessment practices from the perspectives of child protection workers, parents and children. *Children and Youth Services Review* 74: 17–27. https://doi.org/10.1016/j.childyouth.2017.01.020

Ashiabi, G.S. and O'Neal, K.K. (2015). Child social development in context: An examination of some propositions in Bronfenbrenner's bioecological theory. *SAGE Open* 5(2): 1–14. https://doi.org/10.1016/j.childyouth.2017.01.02010.1177/2158244015590840

Baraldi, C. and Cockburn, T. (2018). Introduction: Lived citizenship, rights and participation in contemporary Europe. In Baraldi, C. and Cockburn, T. (eds) *Theorising Childhood: Citizenship, Rights and Participation*. London: Palgrave Macmillan.

Berrick, J.D., Dickens, J., Pösö, T., and Skivenes, M. (2015). Children's involvement in care order decision-making: A cross-country analysis. *Child Abuse & Neglect* 49: 128–41. https://doi.org/10.1016/j.chiabu.2015.07.001

Briskman, L., Jarema, A., Kuek, S., and Martin, J. (2013). Without borders: Fostering development studies in social work. *Policy & Practice (Centre for Global Education)* 17: 70–89.

Bruce, M. (2014). The voice of the child in child protection: Whose voice? *Social Sciences (Basel)* 3(3): 514–26. https://doi.org/10.3390/socsci3030514

Collins, T.M. (2017). A child's right to participate: Implications for international child protection. *International Journal of Human Rights* 21(1): 14–46. https://doi.org/10.1080/13642987.2016.1248122

Collins, T.M., Rizzini, I., and Mayhew, A. (2021). Fostering global dialogue: Conceptualisations of children's rights to participation and protection. *Children & Society* 35(2): 295–310. https://doi.org/10.1111/chso.12437

Cossar, J., Brandon, M., and Jordan, P. (2014). 'You've got to trust her and she's got to trust you': Children's views on participation in the child protection system. *Child and Family Social Work* 21(1): 103–12. https://doi.org/10.1111/cfs.12115

D'Cruz, H. and Gillingham, P. (2017). Participatory research ideals and practice experience: Reflections and analysis. *Journal of Social Work* 17(4): 434–52. https://doi.org/10.1177/1468017316644704

D'Cruz, H., Gillingham, P., and Melendez, S. (2019). Reflexivity. *Critical Social Work* 8(1). https://doi.org/10.22329/csw.v8i1.5744

Daly, N., James, F., Bennett, R., Hunter, N., and Noble, K. (2016). *Royal Commission: Juvenile Justice: The Northern Territory Youth Detention Royal Commission has been told community solutions are needed to fix a broken child protection system*. ABC1 Darwin, 2016. Film.

Davis, J.M. (1998). Understanding the meanings of children: A reflexive process. *Children & Society* 12(5): 325–35. https://doi.org/10.1111/j.1099-0860.1998.tb00089.x

Diaz, C. (2018). *A Study into Children and Young People's Participation in Their Child in Care Reviews*. PhD thesis, Cardiff University.

Diaz, C., Pert, H., and Thomas, N. (2018). 'Just another person in the room': Young people's views on their participation in child in care reviews. *Adoption & Fostering* 42(4): 369–82. https://doi.org/10.1177/0308575918801663

Dillon, J., Greenop, D., and Hills, M. (2016). Participation in child protection: A small-scale qualitative study. *Qualitative Social Work* 15(1): 70–85. https://doi.org/10.1177/1473325015578946

Duffy, J. and Collins, M.E. (2010). Macro impacts on caseworker decision-making in child welfare: A cross-national comparison. *European Journal of Social Work* 13(1): 35–54. https://doi.org/10.1080/13691450903135618

Duncan, M. (2018). *Participation in Child Protection: Theorizing Children's Perspectives*. Basingstoke: Palgrave Macmillan.

Fook, J. (2004). Critical reflection and transformative possibilities. In Davies, L. and Leonard, P. (eds) *Social Work in a Corporate Era: Practices of Power and Resistance* (pp 85–92). London: Routledge.

Fook, J. and Gardner, F. (2007). *Practising Critical Reflection: A Resource Handbook*. Maidenhead: Open University Press.

Gillingham, P. (2011). Decision-making tools and the development of expertise in child protection practitioners: Are we 'just breeding workers who are good at ticking boxes'? *Child & Family Social Work* 16(4): 412–21. https://doi.org/10.1111/j.1365-2206.2011.00756.x

Goh, E.C.L. and Baruch, H. (2018). Young persons as epistemological agents in social work assessment and intervention. *Children and Youth Services Review* 88: 88–95. https://doi.org/10.1016/j.childyouth.2018.02.027

Harkin, J.A., Stafford, L., and Leggatt-Cook, C. (2020). Influences on children's voices in family support services: Practitioner perspectives. *Child & Family Social Work* 25(4): 955–63. https://doi.org/10.1111/cfs.12781

Hartung, C. (2017). *Conditional Citizens, Rethinking Children and Young People's Participation.* Singapore: Springer.

Healy, K., Meagher, G., and Cullin, J. (2009). Retaining novices to become expert child protection practitioners: Creating career pathways in direct practice. *The British Journal of Social Work* 39(2): 299–317. http://www.jstor.org.ezproxy.uws.edu.au/stable/23724700

Hyslop, I. and Keddell, E. (2018). Outing the elephants: Exploring a new paradigm for child protection social work. *Social Sciences* 7(7): 105. https://www.mdpi.com/2076-0760/7/7/105

Johansson, S., Stefansen, K., Bakketeig, E., and Kaldal, A. (2017). Implementing the Nordic Barnahus model: Characteristics and local adaptions. In Johansson, S., Stefansen, K., Bakketeig, E., and Kaldal, A. (eds) *Collaborating Against Child Abuse: Exploring the Nordic Barnahus Model* (pp 67–90). Cham: Springer International Publishing.

Kaufman, N., Rizzinin, I., Wilson, K., and Bush, M. (2002). The impact of global economic, political, and social transformations on the lives of children: A framework for analysis. In Kaufman, N. and Rizzinin, I. (eds) *Globalization and Children: Exploring Potentials for Enhancing Opportunities in the Lives of Children and Youth* (pp 3–18). New York: Kluwer Academic/Plenum Publishers.

Kojan, B.H. and Lonne, B. (2012). A comparison of systems and outcomes for safeguarding children in Australia and Norway. *Child & Family Social Work* 17(1): 96–107. https://doi.org/10.1111/j.1365-2206.2011.00776.x

Lefevre, M., Hickle, K., and Luckock, B. (2019). 'Both/and' not 'either/or': Reconciling rights to protection and participation in working with child sexual exploitation. *British Journal of Social Work* 49(7): 1837–55. https://doi.org/10.1093/bjsw/bcy106

Lewkowicz, D. and Tayebjee, Z. (2019). Creating a collaborative working culture across health and child protection to support vulnerable pregnant women. *International Journal of Integrated Care* 19(4): 92. https://doi.org/10.5334/ijic.s3092

Lohvansuu, J. and Emond, R. (2020). 'Everyday' Scottish and Finnish child protection work in an age of austerity: A practitioner perspective. *Child & Family Social Work* 25(3): 576–84. https://doi.org/10.1111/cfs.12729

Mason, J. and Fattore, T. (2021). Child protection and child participation. In Fernandez, E. and Delfabbro, P. (eds) *Child Protection and the Care Continuum* (pp 271–88). London: Routledge Taylor and Francis Group.

McDowall, J.J. (2016). Are we listening? The need to facilitate participation in decision-making by children and young people in out-of-home care. *Developing Practice: The Child, Youth and Family Work Journal* 44(April): 77–93. https://create.org.au/wp-content/uploads/2017/03/2016-McDowall-DP.pdf

McMellon, C. and Tisdall, E.K.M. (2020). Children and young people's participation rights: Looking backwards and moving forwards. *The International Journal of Children's Rights* 28(1): 157–82. https://doi.org/10.1163/15718182-02801002

Middel, F., Post, W., López López, M., and Grietens, H. (2020). Participation of children involved in the child protection system – Validation of the Meaningful Participation Assessment Tool (MPAT). *Child Indicators Research* 14: 713–35. https://doi.org/10.1007/s12187-020-09772-2

Moore, T. (2017). *Protection Through Participation: Involving Children in Child-safe Organisations*. Australia: Australian Institute of Family Studies. https://aifs.gov.au/cfca/publications/protection-through-participation

Murphy, J. (2006). The other welfare state non-government agencies and the mixed economy of welfare in Australia. *History Australia* 3(2): 44.1–44.15. https://doi.org/10.2104/ha060044

Oppenheim-Weller, S., Schwartz, E., and Ben-Arieh, A. (2017). Child involvement in treatment planning and assessment in Israel. *Child and Family Social Work* 22(3): 1302–12. https://doi.org/10.1111/cfs.12347

Powell, M.A., Graham, A., Canosa, A., Anderson, D., Taylor, N., Robinson, S., Moore, T., and Thomas, N.P. (2021). Children and safety in Australian policy: Implications for organisations and practitioners. *Australian Journal of Social Issues* 56(1): 17–41. https://doi.org/10.1002/ajs4.134

Qvortrup, J. (1997). Review essay – Children, individualism and community. *Childhood* 4: 359–68.

Raby, R. (2014). Children's participation as neo-liberal governance? *Discourse: Studies in the Cultural Politics of Education* 35(1): 77–89. https://doi.org/10.1080/01596306.2012.739468

Schwartz, I. (2017). Putting the child at the centre of inter-professional cooperation in out-of-home care. *Child & Family Social Work* 22(2): 992–9. https://doi.org/10.1111/cfs.12319

Scott, D. (2010). Working within and between organisations. In Scott, D. and Arney, F. (eds) *Working With Vulnerable Families: A Partnership Approach* (pp 53–76). Cambridge: Cambridge University Press.

Thompson, L.J. and Wadley, D.A. (2018). Countering globalisation and managerialism: Relationist ethics in social work. *International Social Work* 61(5): 706–23. https://doi.org/10.1177/0020872816655867

Todd, L. (2014). Inter-agency working and special education: Beyond 'virtuous' ideas of partnership towards alternative frameworks for collaborative work with children. In L. Florian (ed.) *The SAGE Handbook of Special Education: Two Volume Set* (2nd Edition). London: Sage.

Toros, K. (2020). A systematic review of children's participation in child protection decision-making: Tokenistic presence or not? *Children & Society* 35(3): 395–411. https://doi.org/10.1111/chso.12418

Trevithick, P. (2014). Humanising managerialism: Reclaiming emotional reasoning, intuition, the relationship, and knowledge and skills in social work. *Journal of Social Work Practice* 28(3): 287–311. https://doi.org/10.1080/02650533.2014.926868

van Bijleveld, G.G., Dedding, C.W.M., and Bunders-Aelen, J.G.F. (2015). Children's and young people's participation within child welfare and child protection services: A state-of-the-art review. *Child & Family Social Work* 20(2): 129–38. https://doi.org/10.1111/cfs.12082

van Bijleveld, G.G., Bunders-Aelen, J.F.G., and Dedding, C.W.M. (2020). Exploring the essence of enabling child participation within child protection services. *Child & Family Social Work* 25(2): 286–93. https://doi.org/10.1111/cfs.12684

van Bijleveld, G.G., de Vetten, M., and Dedding, C.W. (2020). Co-creating participation tools with children within child protection services: What lessons we can learn from the children. *Action Research* 19(4): 693–709. https://doi.org/10.1177/1476750319899715

Vis, S.A. and Fossum, S. (2015). Organizational factors and child participation in decision-making: Differences between two child welfare organizations. *Child and Family Social Work* 20(3): 277–87. https://doi.org/10.1111/cfs.12076

Vosz, M., Keevers, S., Williams, D., withheld, B., withheld, B., and withheld, N. (2020). *Through our eyes: Giving due weight to the views of children and young people in policy making*. Better Care Network. https://bettercarenetwork.org/library/principles-of-good-care-practices/child-participation/through-our-eyes-giving-due-weight-to-the-views-of-children-and-young-people-in-policy-making.

Watts, L. (2019). Reflective practice, reflexivity, and critical reflection in social work education in Australia. *Australian Social Work* 72(1): 8–20. https://doi.org/10.1080/0312407X.2018.1521856

Winter, K. (2011). *Building Relationships and Communicating with Young Children: A Practical Guide for Social Workers*. London: Routledge.

Wright, E.M., Spohn, R., Chenane, J., and Juliano, N. (2017). The importance of interagency collaboration for crossover youth: A research note. *Youth Violence and Juvenile Justice* 15(4): 481–91. https://doi.org/10.1177/1541204016686663

Zell, M.C. (2006). Child welfare workers: Who they are and how they view the child welfare system. *Child Welfare* 85(1): 83–103.

Zuchowski, I. (2019). Five years after Carmody: Practitioners' views of changes, challenges and research in child protection. *Children Australia* 44(3): 146–53. https://doi.org/10.1017/cha.2019.14

8

A Bump on the Head in the Graveyard: Palimpsests of Death, Selves, Care, and Touch

Sarah Coombs and Sarah Richards

Introduction

In this chapter we reflexively consider the emotional labour involved in engaging young children in participatory research through feminist ideals, which embed the researcher within, rather than remove them from, the research. This discussion is drawn from our experiences in conducting a qualitative study that explored children's perceptions of their playground space incorporating a graveyard, complete with gravestones, alter tombs, and coped stones. We explore the emotional labour of maintaining young children's well-being as they navigate what constitutes a 'sensitive' topic in research with children. We borrow from feminist methodology, an ethic of care, positionality, and recognition of emotional labour, to strengthen our child-focused approach. Here we reflexively address the challenges of conducting sensitive research with young children and highlight the ways in which our 'other' selves, beyond the identity of researcher, were exposed. We highlight our anxiety about assuming our subjective positions and explore their potential conflict with contemporary discourses of childhood, whereby supporting the emotional well-being of young children through the researcher's proximity or touch is constructed as taboo. Ultimately, we argue that just as the graveyard runs like a palimpsest in the playground so too do our other selves in this fieldwork.

Setting the context for children, play, and death

The association between children and play is surely one of the most cherished and natural perspectives on children and childhoods that exists in contemporary western society, with childhood being positioned as utterly distinguishable from adulthood through the child's lack of responsibility and time to play (Wyness, 2018). One of the most appropriate contexts for this activity is the school playground, a familiar and friendly landscape of climbing frames and games marked out on the floor. In saying this we fully recognise the contested status of these assumptions and are aware of the school playground also as a potential site of rules, hierarchy, and bullying.

However, bearing this treasured evocation of childhood in mind, what happens when the school play area is a disused graveyard, with all the remaining accoutrements of death (gravestones and memorials), and therefore your playmates just happen to be the dead of long ago or supernatural creatures associated with the un-dead? This question was, to begin with, the main focus of our study. From a contemporary western viewpoint, children's relationship with death can only be considered when deemed absolutely necessary, and certainly not within the context of the school playground. Paradoxically, over the centuries, the relationship between death and children has been close and intimate. Gillis (1997) notes that prior to the 19th century, children in western countries were introduced to death early; death was as familiar to children as to adults, children played death games, built pretend coffins, and were conspicuous in their involvement with funerals, wakes, and deathbed scenes. Similarly, Ariès ([1981] 2008, p 167) describes how, in the mid-17th century, children from Paris orphanages, foundling homes, and charity schools were used to escort the funeral processions of the wealthy and were described as 'specialists in death'.

The following collected standpoints present some of the dynamic and shifting arguments and tensions that surround adults, children, and death in western society from both historical and contemporary perspectives. Exploring both death and childhood through socially constructed ideas, a binary picture emerges of two opposingly different elements that should not be allowed to transgress their boundaries: light and dark, good and evil, sacred and profane. Yet, these supposedly incompatible strangers, death and childhood, quite literally and happily occupy this same space, playing together on a daily basis, despite the concerns of the adult world.

Holt (1975) argues that childhood is situated within a safe and protected 'walled garden', where the child is secure and kept well away from the knowledge or worries of the adult world. Faulkner (2011, pp 8–9) portrays this garden as more perfect than God's Eden, and Taylor (2011, p 420) calls to mind a utopian 'Neverland' to describe 'that idealized and timeless childhood place of perfect harmony'. Taylor further argues that the continuation of such nostalgic and romantic notions of childhood promotes a protectionist stance, alongside which Faulkner (2011, pp 78–79) alludes to a state of 'carefully crafted ignorance'. This deliberately fashioned child is characterised by innocence, dependence, vulnerability, and a lack of knowledge, particularly pertaining to death. Wyness (2019) contends that this child is obliged to be happy, have fun, and be free from responsibility and does not and cannot play with death. This child is sacred to life.

Death is situated differently to the sacred child, constructed in opposition as the profane provider of all that is dark, corrupt, and contaminating. Berger and Luckmann ([1966] 1991, p 119) propose that death 'posits the most terrifying threat to the taken-for-granted realities of everyday life'; Becker (1973, p xvii) that the fear of death is universal, it 'haunts the human animal like nothing else'; Howarth (2007, p 15) that 'death raises the problem of meaning for human beings'; and Yalom (2008, p 1) that 'mortality has haunted us from the beginning of history'. Death is therefore situated in a context of fear, denial, sequestration, and notions of the taboo.

In contrast, however, there is clear evidence that death is not always such a hidden secret. Berridge (2002, p 26) argues that death has moved from the margins to the mainstream, death is 'becoming social not anti-social, public not private, fashionable not fearful, death is the focus of a new permissiveness. Death is in.' Exposure to death is highly evident in the mass media, literature, film, art, celebrity deaths, and the rise of the internet and new technologies. Walter et al (2011) argue that through our social networks and mobile devices the dead are literally becoming part of our everyday lives once again. It seems inappropriate, therefore, to denounce death as taboo for adults or children. However, there is one area where proclaiming this assertion is more problematic, and that is in the field of childhood (Coombs, 2017). Although we might argue that neither childhood nor death are taboo topics, the dividing line, the oppositional binary, like many others in childhood, remains stubbornly in place. If adults are challenged by their own understanding of mortality, then death and childhood are encouraged to maintain an unfriendly and silent relationship, leaving us to question if they can ever coexist. The discursive tensions are clear.

As a consequence, Kastenbaum and Fox (2007) suggest that adults assume children do not, cannot, and should not think about death. Berridge (2002, p 4) proposes that 'death is the first big lie parents tell children, a close second to Father Christmas'. More recently, Beit-Hallahmi (2011, p 42) implies that we live in a time which arguably goes to 'extraordinary efforts to hide the reality of death from children'. Under such circumstances, 'the child had become the favourite symbol of life' (Gillis, 1997, p 210).

Notwithstanding the earlier discourse, Bluebond-Langer and DeCicco (2006, pp 85–6) highlight the 'sophisticated understanding of death' demonstrated by some young people, in comparison with the 'childish notions' of some adults. McCormick (2011) equally questions the notion of a 'mature' construct of death, agreeing that adults are often as confused about death as children arguably are.

To ascertain children's understanding of death in ordinary contexts, such as the playground, we must create opportunities to listen (Coombs, 2017). These occasions reveal how children engage with mortality in creative, vibrant, and imaginative ways (Coombs, 2014). While it is not surprising that society/adults have problems with the emotionality and challenges that bringing youth and death together brings, if we do not do it, children will continue to play happily in this sphere, while adults remain in the dark.

Methodology

Researching topics related to mortality is never going to be the most straightforward, and prevailing assumptions reveal that examining this topic, in any form, must inevitably be 'sensitive'. Additionally, children are constructed as a 'frail population' within research (Martins et al, 2018, p 459) due to their perceived vulnerability. Considering this double jeopardy, alongside the controversies revealed in the literature referred to earlier, challenges become apparent and it is incumbent on researchers to tread softly into this arena. The potential for emotionality is clear, and responsibility for the emotional well-being of participants of ultimate importance.

There is no straightforward response to the question, what is a sensitive topic? While almost any issue can be judged sensitive, certain topics are deemed more 'sensitive' than others and death is clearly one of these. Therefore, a focus on children and aspects relating to end of life, whatever the context, is going to raise eyebrows and anxieties, as adults traditionally seek to protect children from this knowledge. Notions of what constructs sensitivity within research is not universally defined and ranges from material that can be intrusive, threatening, and deeply personal (Renzetti and Lee, 1993) to positioning sensitivity within relational circumstances. Hydén (2008) suggests that intimate and sensitive topics can be discussed within close relationships, such as family and friends, or within 'special relationships', such as between doctor and patient. Such relationships have the potential to strip away some of the intimacy of the topic. However, it was certainly not our intention to strip away this intimacy, rather to develop a research relationship, informed by warmth, friendship, and fun, in which the children were unmistakably experts in knowing and understanding their own unique playground 'deathscape' (Maddrell and Sidaway, 2010).

Qualitative methodologies have often been associated with sensitive research (Lee, 1993; Dickson-Swift et al, 2008) and equally with children (Greig et al, 2007). Such research is exploratory in nature, thus gaining insights into areas in which little is known, and searches for multiple truths and realities rather than one. Despite our passion for child-focused research, it is feminist methodologies that align well with these ideals in their promotion of non-hierarchical relationships, building trust and rapport, care and concern for participants, and a flexible form of enquiry that gives voice to everyday experience.

The central methodological values in this research involved a feminist ethic of care, the positionality of the researchers, and the emotional labour involved in conducting research with very young children on a topic construed as highly sensitive. We examine how the sensitivities and emotionality of the topic merge within the deathscape of the playground and the personalities of the researchers and participants to create an encounter based on care, feminist principles, and 'who we are'.

As qualitative researchers we have always acknowledged and celebrated the intricacies of being present in our research and that our positionality and subjectivities shape our research encounters and analysis. However, what was challenging here was that the position of researcher became secondary to our other personal biographical characteristics such as teacher, nurse, mother. Christensen and James (2008) position a reflexive approach of this nature as crucial to highlighting the relationship between the researchers' identities and previous experience, alongside their academic knowledge and understanding. Who we are ran through this research and our responses to the participants, as clearly as death ran underneath this playground, evoking the notion of the palimpsest.

The palimpsest conjures images of ancient texts or works of art, in which previous writing/painting has either been removed, covered, or replaced, only to be rediscovered through intense scholarship. A palimpsest of death was unmistakeable in the children's playground. The graveyard was visible and tangible, but new layers, archaeologies of life, are now more obviously discernible. However, the palimpsest of 'ourselves' was initially less recognisable. It was this [re]discovery and connection to these perhaps forgotten aspects and facets of self that developed through our methodological approach and re-emerged in our thoughts, acts, and writing as the emergent script of emotional labour.

Tronto (2009, p 98) suggests that the world would look a very different place if care were more central to human life. The value of care is a fundamental tenet underpinning our methodological approach. We argue that we live in a society where care and caring are undervalued and underappreciated, and that furthermore this has an impact on how care is regarded within the research encounter. Although Tronto (2009, p 104) contends that care is a concern of everyday living, and 'both a practice and a disposition', she locates an 'ethic of care' as a 'moral choice' and a 'serious ethical idea' (2009, p 125) and not just a trite invocation of women's presumed, natural, instinctive, and caring morality.

Bergmark (2020, p 341) highlights togetherness, valuing, and learning from each other, and importantly 'giving care specified to needs based on a particular situation' as key to working with an ethic of care. Moreover, Bergmark (2020, p 334) points to how '[a]ctions are not motivated by reasons and principles – but instead by the needs of and the responsibility for others', a perspective which marries well with our application of emotional labour and the events of the afternoon in question.

Bearing in mind the exploration of an ethic of care, its proclivity to expose what we might like to conceal, and the struggles and dilemmas of revealing such experiences, it was necessary to reflect further on our position/s within this research. Vanner (2015, p 3) expresses how our values, opinions, beliefs, and social backgrounds accompany us into our research. We cannot, under such circumstances, be neutral and stand aside, nor would we want to. Indeed, Halse and Honey (2005) argue there is no neutral research and that we, as subjective selves, shape our research. However, while we readily acknowledged some of our positions almost as a matter of course, others were hardly considered. Yet, it was these standings, as carers, mothers, teachers, and nurses, that were brought to the fore and informed our relational responses. We might allude to these as more mundane positions, those we take for granted in everyday life, and therefore not initially noteworthy. However, on reflection, it was these neglected, and perhaps unacknowledged, aspects of self that often led and shaped our interactions.

Clearly, then, emotions and feelings are a central part of social research and while we were mindful of the potential for emotion from the children, we considered, less fully, ourselves and our responses. As Carroll (2012, p 557) argues, '[r]ather than *estrangement* from emotion, the emotional labour involved in some sensitive, reflexive and feminist research can result in the *foregrounding* of a researcher's own biological, emotional and social identities' (emphasis in the original). As researchers, academics, and professionals we are encouraged not to show our emotions or act in an overtly responsive way, and yet, to ensure the well-being of our participants it was important to demonstrate our care of and for them. As Dickson-Swift et al (2008) suggest, if we accept that qualitative research can be emotional then we must also accept the embodied nature of it and the use of our bodies as mechanisms of emotion, and perhaps here we might equally suggest, instruments of comfort through proximity and touch. However, this becomes uncomfortable and challenging to consider and admit to, especially in the context of research with children, where overriding discourses of safeguarding abound.

Remaining true to our methodological underpinnings brought us into contention with these debates, in particular the appropriateness of providing comfort through touch, although clearly, children can, and often do, need embodied and emotional comfort from the adults around them. The topic and context of this research can be construed as highly sensitive, and therefore it demanded of us, as researchers, to develop relationships of trust and care, and required us to be emotionally and physically available and willing to engage and provide for our participants' welfare. Not to have done so would have been to deny our methodological foundations.

In carrying out research on sensitive topics with children we are already inhabiting a space of potential emotionality. Dickson-Swift et al (2008, p 42) explore the value of touching, offering support, showing emotion, and generally 'being with' the participants during the research encounter. They highlight researchers' feelings in speaking out about 'the need to be human and not scared to show human emotions … [as] good research practice'. Using our embodied selves is an interactive process, which for us involved acts of care, being supportive, showing, and on occasion hiding, our emotions. The expressions and denials of emotions, rapport building, and our application of an ethic of care constitute Hochschild's (2003) and Carroll's (2012) definitions of emotional labour.

Carroll (2012, p 556) argues that the impact of emotional labour is mediated through our subjective life experiences and positionalities. Such identity positions, or, as Carroll describes them, 'our past ghostly selves' (2012, p 557) can and do emerge in fieldwork that foregrounds the importance of relational practices and privileging the well-being of participants.

Our methodological values were influenced by the need to be reflexive about the centrality of the human being, both participant and researcher, and to embrace the socially active and competent, yet potentially vulnerable child. Guba and Lincoln (2008, p 27) argue that this type of reflexivity is important for the researcher/s to come to terms not only with the research itself and the 'discovery of the subject', but also the 'discovery of self'. Holmes (2010) extends this stance on reflexivity by arguing that emotional reflexivity can not only encompass the emotions of the researched and the researcher, but also challenge the notion of either identity being a fixed personhood.

We entered this fieldwork purposefully, assuming identities that would not only provide support and care throughout discussions of a potentially sensitive topic, but also that would encourage, privilege, and elicit data from our young participants. One of our first steps was to separate ourselves from other normative, formalised adult roles in school by asking the children to call us by our first names. This simple act was complicated by our having the same name, which generated giggles and loud whispers. As we led the children from their classroom, they speculated on why we were both called Sarah, with one child concluding that we "must be sisters". We giggled with them as we shepherded them carefully, holding their hands and speaking to them encouragingly with light voices and smiles through the school corridors, one Sarah at the front of the line and one at the back. Our focus on the children's welfare and well-being was already at the forefront of our actions as we made our way to the playground; our emotional labour already hard at work.

Vignette 1: Entering the field – children, researchers, and other personas

Captured here are the first few minutes of entering the field. The scenario highlights the initial emotional intensity of attempting to interact through an ethic of care. The afternoon was very hot but the opportunity for the children to take us on a guided tour of their play area, draw pictures with us, and be out of the classroom was before of us. As the children initially gathered around us in the graveyard play area, we attempted to assure ourselves of, and reiterate, ongoing informed consent. We asked the children, "Can you remember why we're here this afternoon?" Immediately, a small girl (Sophie) replied that it was because "we don't speak English good". Somewhat taken aback by the response, we both sought to reassure Sophie, disconcerted by the thought that our best-laid plans of providing information and gaining consent were already in disarray. We offered firm assurances that this was definitely not the case, and strongly re-enforced the point that it was because she, and all the other children, had knowledge about this place that we did not, and we wanted to learn from them.

The acknowledgement of Sophie's need for reassurance at this point, although not articulated directly, was recognised by us and manifestly cared about. Our ethic of care was to accept and respond to Sophie's need, by encouraging her, and all the children, to feel confident, secure, and positive about themselves and their participation. The ongoing context of our research encounter, therefore, was underpinned by promoting their capabilities rather than their deficits.

In this scenario, previous and continuing roles emerged unbidden, first that of primary school teacher. This persona responded by reassuring and encouraging Sophie to recognise her contribution and be positive about her participation. Similarly, the role of mother arose from both researchers; nurturance and responsiveness came to the fore, taking responsibility for Sophie's insecurity by offering alternative ideas about herself.

Through this scenario we found other, unanticipated, levels of understanding within this space. Unbeknown to us, this place was where the children were often taken for 'extra' lessons and support with their language skills or other aspects of the curriculum. Although the children recognised this, we did not. Not only was this a space of death, which we assumed would be sensitive, but also a place that the children associated with extra learning support. This knowledge heightened our responsibility to the children and our emotional labour towards them, as we juggled the double concerns of death and assumed learning deficits by some of the children.

While, to some extent, we hid the fact that we were worried about informed consent when the children appeared unsure why they were there, we reassured them by smiling, using encouraging words, and exchanging any less than positive notions the children articulated with positive affirmations of their presence in this place.

Vignette 2: Losing/(re)gaining control

Research with children is often situated within a context of promoting agency, autonomy, and decision making, and attempts at shifting the balance of power within the research encounter. As researchers we embraced this often espoused set of values but soon realised the challenges this represents. This space was clearly associated with play, where children are positioned as more agentic than in other places in school. Our friendly approach encouraged a more relaxed engagement with us than with other adults in this setting. Our chosen method was designed to place the children in charge of leading us through their space. All these strategies speak to contemporary, participatory research with children. In the practice of this, however, we both experienced unanticipated unease, while recognising that the children had in fact embraced this approach wholeheartedly. We were faced with 15 exuberant and enthusiastic five-year-olds all wanting our attention simultaneously.

Our first activity was a guided tour, the children taking the lead as they showed us around their play area and chatting with us about all the objects in the space and how they interacted with them. It all began in an orderly procession around the graveyard with discussions about angels, the undead, and long dead people under the ground. However, it soon became clear that we could not control this procession, and children began to drift away and have conversations between themselves, and the quietness of the space was filled with loud discourse. At this point, we realised that we had been successful in shifting the power to such an extent that we could not retrieve it without going into 'teacher mode' and thus risking the autonomy and agency we sought to promote. In the transcript we note the words "Sarah, we're losing control", as the situation around us became increasingly led by the children. We adapted to this change by separating, so that we could literally cover more ground, rather than leaving some children unattended, and retain the appearance, if not the reality, of control. We were aware of the potential scrutiny from the school building, with its many open windows and panopticon views onto and into the playground. The competing discourses of children's agency in research versus the expected, controlled behaviour found in schools collided in this space with its palimpsest of expected reverence associated with the graveyard. We became aware of how this scene might be interpreted by others watching and it was this that caused a sense of unease and insecurity in a situation that would normally be very comfortable. We hid these feelings from the children but simultaneously were very conscious of how our performance might be being viewed by the professionals in the building.

We had inadvertently created a situation where we felt uncomfortable with the shift of power and thus began to view the scene as teachers rather than researchers and felt the need to reassert our control. The need to re-establish normative adult/child relationships in this situation was totally unexpected and disconcerting. This was the children's space, not ours, and yet their control of it made us uneasy.

At this point, due to our unease, we encouraged the children to come together in a cool and shady spot, where lessons often take place, to carry out a drawing activity. This activity reasserted a teacher/pupil type relationship and reconstituted a classroom agenda. The power balance restored, we settled into the roles of researcher and teacher by saying encouraging things and having positive conversations about what the children were drawing. This scene restored our anxieties around the potential for an adverse gaze from the school yet also re-established an equilibrium with the children that we did not want. The role of teacher became a dominant identity trait pushed to the forefront of our interactions, as the children settled into a 'schooled' role by sitting at tables with adults standing over them and commenting on their work.

We had encouraged the children to take part in the research on their terms, but when the agenda was led by them, we felt a need to reclaim our control rather than continue to promote their agency in the playground. This revealed to us that the ideals and values promoted in research with children can be less liberating and revolutionary than is at first perceived, and that adult control runs through our research interactions and relationships like a palimpsest of power.

Vignette 3: Talking death

For the children the graveyard play area was a secure space that they were familiar with, and the school had very much constructed it as associated with life, nature, growth, and vibrancy. This was the only green space in the playground, the trees provided shade, and vegetables grew perhaps disconcertingly close to the actual graves and bones below. The palimpsest of the graveyard was tangible through the light and dark spaces, the proximity of life and death, and the presence of youth and decay.

As we stood among the gravestones the children showed us the ladybirds and bugs they found, they talked excitedly about the vegetables they were growing, and pointed out their interactive display board about the changing seasons. Amongst all this life, we were well aware that we had come to talk about death to the social group most distanced from it.

We were aware that we did not want to divest our ideas about death onto the children, but rather listen to what they had to say. As researchers, we wanted to validate, support, and encourage all the different views related to death that the children might espouse and not prioritise one truth above another. For example, while Sophie told us about how Jesus returned from the dead, James talked excitedly about vampires living under the graves and coming out to play in the dark. We felt responsible to respond appropriately to a variety of children's understandings of death. This called on us to mask our own perceptions of this topic as we listened to children's contrasting ideas on orthodox Christian beliefs, zombies, vampires, and dinosaurs. Our obligation, within an ethic of care, was to manage each child's emotional welfare to feel their knowledge was legitimate, expert, and authentic, while hearing contrasting ideas to their own.

An additional emotional burden was our responsibility to the children who were perhaps hearing for the first time about Jesus or zombies, or what the stones in the playground were. We wanted to capture these stories but not at the expense of undermining the well-being of children who only saw this space as their playground and did not associate the artefacts with death. Here there was also an element of self-preservation as we did not want children returning to the classroom or home upset and anxious about what they had heard and telling stories about the dead contrary to family beliefs. We wanted the children who knew about death to talk freely, while not disrupting the inexperience of others. Our emotional task was to research the proximity of children and death whilst simultaneously maintaining the dominant discourse of distance between childhood and death.

Such emotional entanglements were imposed on us from a variety of directions, our ethic of care, the child-centred methodology, the taboo topic, and the graveyard space. We found ourselves in the unlikely position of supporting the discourse around children and death rather than challenging it. We entered the graveyard expecting to confront entrenched orthodoxies but found ourselves shoring them up by re-emphasising this space as one of life and for the living.

Vignette 4: A bump on the head

As the drawing activity came to a close, we told the children that the new pens we had used were to be a present, to say thank you for helping us with the research. As we tidied away, the children played together excitedly, some balancing on the coped stones, perhaps sensing that the fun was ending, and it would soon be time to return to lessons.

These particular gravestones were laid in parallel to each other and offered great opportunities to demonstrate balancing skills as they were low to the ground and pointed in shape. While the children were focused on demonstrating their physical prowess there was a sudden commotion. A child began to cry quite loudly, claiming that he had fallen off the coped stones and bumped his head. The persona of both nurse and mother came to the fore as a visibly, hot, tearful Jack rubbed his head and cried loudly. Sarah(i) scooped him up and sat on the nearby bench, placing Jack on her lap in order to offer both comfort and to check the bump. The persona of nurse arose unbidden, in which physically assessing Jack's head became paramount. The process of sitting Jack across her knee, holding his head and body to provide care and control was instinctive and almost instantaneously calmed the situation. The reassuring words, "I'm just going to check your head Jack" were followed by "Oh that's good, I can't see anything too much, I think you're fine." At this point Sarah(ii), observing the scene, recognised how the scenario might be viewed by others. Behind us, a sea of windows, which overlooked the play area, watched on and metaphorically began to question our moves as transgressors of appropriate behaviour towards children, where touch is taboo.

As childhood researchers and adults more generally, we all find ourselves in an environment where touching children is considered highly problematic and should not happen. Today's climate espouses the view that before you have access to children a certificate (DBS) is needed, in order to demonstrate no previous harm has been done. This discourse ensures that adults must be very circumspect about their interactions with children, with touch being censured. Sitting a child on your lap in certain contexts, even while distressed, falls outside of what is now considered appropriate behaviour with children. We became explicitly aware of how this scene might be perceived by teachers and staff within the building behind us. The conflict comes, therefore, when our methodology of care, which promotes nurturance, sensitivity, emotional well-being, and connection, collides with the hegemonic discourse of contemporary safeguarding. Within this, all adults are seen as a potential threat to children but they also need to safeguard themselves against accusations of inappropriate behaviour.

Returning to the scene, we see Sarah(i), as the nurse, seeking to check for any physical injury and its extent. Equally visible is the identity of mother, here providing a place of comfort and reassurance, whereby the lap is recognised as a place of warmth, where children can receive solace and adults can provide it. The emotional labour of both these positions was manifestly focused on the child. Sarah(ii), however, was able to view the scene from alternative perspectives, those of researcher and teacher, and was thereby situated within the dominant discourse of safeguarding, where touching children is off limits. Our recognition of this act of transgression was instantaneous and solidified in the following exchange …

Sarah(ii) [in a questioning voice]:   Sarah?
Sarah(i) [lifting Jack off her lap]:   I know.

This incident took no longer than a minute to unfold but immediately demonstrated to each of us the embedded and profound conflict between our methodology, our positionalities, and the boundaries of contemporary safeguarding practice. Jack fell, hurt himself, and received the attention he needed from the adults he looked to for care, but the adults were left with the emotional labour of wondering if they had done the right thing. Providing this care brought us into conflict with current thinking around safeguarding practice and induced emotional angst. We felt we had done the right thing by Jack but would a professional looking on through the sea of windows behind us feel the same?

Vignette 5: Exiting the field

We gathered the children together and encouraged them to form a line, in a very familiar 'school-type' way. We walked across the playground and into the school building with its rules and the traditional relationship between adult and child. We hushed our conversations, encouraged walking not running, and passed by classrooms quietly. Internally we both felt anxious about Jack's fall and what we were going to say. On entering the classroom, Sarah(ii) explained that Jack had tumbled and had bumped his head. She identified that Sarah(i) was a nurse, had checked him over and that he now appeared to be fine. We asked if the teacher would like us to complete any paperwork to describe the incident, an accident form for instance, but this was dismissed, and Jack told to "go and sit down". We said our goodbyes and left. On the walk home, this incident was all we discussed. We had prepared for the death taboo but not the taboo of touch.

Discussion

As Dickson-Swift et al (2008, p 33) suggest, we, as researchers, are 'entering the lives of others', sharing ourselves as part of reciprocal relationships, caring and responding as embodied human beings. Therefore, in embracing our research context with all its underlying emotionality (the graveyard playground); caring for our young and, yes, despite all our methodological claims, potentially vulnerable participants (the children); acknowledging the situations that arose during that hot July afternoon (a bump on the head); and, most significantly perhaps, responding reflexively to the actions we took (comforting a child); we revealed ourselves not only in the moment, but also parts of ourselves we considered long since left behind. The boundaries between life and death, researcher and participant, comfort and distress, were crossed, and not without feelings of guilt and personal cost.

As researchers we had encouraged children to participate in this study; we asked them to talk to us and share their understanding of the space in which they play, we invited them to take us on a guided tour, draw pictures, and share the afternoon together. Therefore, when a child fell and bumped their head, it was not possible, in that moment, to stand back from the upset and tears. Indeed, what would all our ethical and academic musings mean if we did not step forward to offer physical comfort at that point. While it might be argued that the care shown was an inbuilt human reaction, particularly from one steeped in the 'caring profession', conversely, and with the benefit of hindsight, it can be viewed as impulsive, unthinking, and ill considered. Therefore, the following discussions will interrogate such arguments, engaging with our subsequent emotional labour and our consideration of the taboo of touch.

Constanti and Gibbs (2004, p 243) argue that professionals in education must hide their feelings to be successful, so that '[p]erforming emotional labour is required both for a successful delivery of service to customers, but also as a strategy for coping with the need to conceal feelings'. This can be applied to our own emotional labour in the graveyard. As researchers we sought to present calm, friendly, approachable, empathetic figures to our young participants. To the children we exhibited as open, both physically and emotionally. Yet on occasion, when the children were at the height of their power, the need for us to claw it back was palpable. To the teachers we appeared as professionals with authority, expertise, and control. However, staring past Sarah(i) with a crying child on her lap, to rows of blank, black, window spaces, induced feelings of panic that had to be shut down and saved for later consumption. These emotional performances were contradictory and not indicative of our feelings in any given moment. Suspending our actual emotions became even more 'effort intensive' (Stienberg and Figart, 1999), as the taboo of touch emerged unwanted and unexpected from the graveyard.

We had entered this research focused on, and ready to challenge, the taboo of death and childhood but instead found ourselves confronted by a more profane taboo, that of touch and childhood. Touch, like death before it, has come to represent everything ambivalent, unsure, and undecided about childhood. While Coombs (2017) has previously argued that childhood and death might be conflated as the final taboo, this was prior to encountering a potentially more controversial and unsettling boundary, that of childhood and touch. At the start of this chapter, we were presented with the cherished evocation of childhood innocence, the child at play, the persistent representation of childhood. It was in this 'walled garden' (Holt, 1975) that these children played. Yet, this was no Eden, the palimpsests of death and touch materialised.

Childhood and touch have been viewed from multiple perspectives, some of which profess touch to be necessary for good emotional outcomes, some of which position touch as healing, and some of which equate touch with confusion and sexual predation. Drawing on research that highlights the benefits of touch to children, Johansson et al (2021) argue that touch and bodily contact are important. First, they highlight touch as significant to children's physical, emotional, and psychological well-being, and in creating and communicating close, caring, and trusting social relationships between caregivers and children. Similarly, from the perspective of the nursing profession, Davin et al (2019, p 559) argue that 'the appropriate use of touch is central to effective and compassionate care' and that touch can be seen as appropriate and beneficial when conducting physical examination and providing comfort. Benner (2004) identifies a 'disclosive space' as one where solace, trust, and reassurance are enacted between patient and professional, in which touch is comforting and safe.

However, even under circumstances where touch is positioned as offering benefits to children, Piper et al (2013) argue that teachers are increasingly confused and worried about touch, claiming that established guidelines and policies have led to the institutionalisation of non-touch. Jones (2004, p 53) suggests that we are currently experiencing 'a time when the need for "safety from sexual abuse" defines every act of child-adult touch as suspicious' resulting in proximity between the two being strictly governed, and furthermore is characterised by 'anxiety, fear and contradictions' (Johansson et al 2021, p 290). Yet, their study with newly graduated preschool teachers demonstrates how most participants would comfort a crying child by either holding the child or putting the child on their lap. Notwithstanding this point, Piper et al (2013) emphasise that if a child needs comfort in this way, the presence of another professional is welcomed and encouraged. Jones (2004) argues that this visibility acts as a mechanism of control as well as safety for teachers and is positively desired.

In a society where 'all adult-child touch and even adult-child proximity is an object of anxiety and suspicion, the network of visibility that teachers believe is their protection can act in unpredictable ways' (Jones, 2004). The onlooker, so desired by teachers, the witness of no misdemeanours, acts as both protector and accuser. The sea of school windows behind the graveyard served to witness either the power of healing through touch or the spectre of inappropriate touch, rising from the graveyard.

This event became the site of our anxiety, the focus of this chapter, and the intensity of our emotional labour. The focus had shifted from protecting children from death to protecting children from ourselves, and the ghosts of our former selves. How had helping and comforting a distressed child changed from an act of human care to one of harm? The safe space we had worked so hard to achieve for the children in this challenging context was changed, becoming potentially unsafe and risky for us. Researching human beings, perhaps very young ones in particular, can be especially challenging, and opens researchers up to unexpected events. It is in how we respond to them that we reveal ourselves. As Montgomery suggests (see Chapter 9), we must 'own our mistakes', and perhaps touching this child was a mistake. This will remain one of those incidents in our research that stays with us forever. On the one hand, and in the present context of 'do not touch children', yes, this can be owned as a mistake; on the other hand, no, this was the unseen and unbidden culmination of our methodological approach and ourselves. What would be the point of espousing this philosophical 'ethic of care' if we had not been prepared to touch?

Conclusion

The distinctive space we had chosen for our research was, prior to our arrival, already underpinned with layers of history, meaning, and feelings. This living, vibrant deathscape mingled with the children's excitement and their understanding of what one child termed "the most specialest place". The emotions and emotionality of this place were already here, running through the graveyard playground as palimpsests of life, death, childhood, and our multiple selves as centrally and fundamentally human, while, equally and pivotally, researchers.

As researchers into sensitive topics in childhood, particularly death and childhood, we had considered ourselves more than capable and experienced to deal with taboo topics and unexpected events. However, the emergence of, and our subsequent engagement with, a taboo more unshakeable than perhaps death itself, resulted in immersive reflections and the emotional responses evidenced here.

Researching with children calls for closeness and encourages emotional engagement through the development of trusting relationships and the building of warm rapport and connectedness. Under such circumstances, the spaces between researcher and participant become naturally less defined, more intimate, and less easily controlled. What is clear is that the methodological underpinnings of this research; an ethic of care and embracing emotion as a central part of the journey were well placed to meet the emotional well-being of our young participants. However, the challenge of caring for the children's emotional well-being, presenting ourselves as researchers both to children and to their teachers, while also hiding our actual emotions and anxieties, was labour intensive and beyond what we had expected.

As researchers, the necessity to reflect on the emotional labour and our actions of that afternoon culminated in a need to write this chapter. Revealing the events of this fieldwork is not without anxieties, both on a personal and professional level, but also in relation to how our reflections of this incident and reactions to it will be received. However, as our chosen methodology requires recognition of our emotional labour it also necessitates reflexivity on the decisions we made in the moment, even the uncomfortable ones that we might hesitate to share.

On a hot July afternoon, when having lots of fun, and showing these 'not-teacher' adults how to balance on a coped stone, a child falls and bumps their head. It is these unforeseen and uncontrollable events in research, and how we respond to them, which throw light on who we are as researchers, as well as who we are, have been, and will be in everyday life.

References

Ariès, P. ([1981] 2008). *The Hour of our Death* (2nd edn). New York: Vintage.

Becker, E. (1973). *The Denial of Death*. New York: Free Press.

Beit-Hallahmi, B. (2011). Ambivalent teaching and painful learning: Mastering the facts of life (?) In Talwar, V., Harris, P., and Schleifer, M. (eds) *Children's Understanding of Death: From Biological to Religious Conceptions* (pp 41–60). New York: Cambridge University Press.

Benner, P. (2004). Relational ethics of comfort, touch and solace – Endangered arts? *American Journal of Critical Care* 13(4): 346–9.

Berger, P. and Luckman, T. ([1966] 1991). *The Social Construction of Reality: A Treatise in the Sociology of Knowledge*. Harmondsworth: Penguin.

Bergmark, U. (2020). Rethinking researcher-teacher roles and relationships in educational action research through the use of Nel Noddings' ethics of care. *Educational Action Research* 28(3): 331–44.

Berridge, K. (2002). *Vigor Mortis*. London: Profile Books.

Bluebond-Langer, M. and DeCicco, A. (2006). Children's views of death. In Goldman, A., Hain, R., and Liben, S. (eds) *The Oxford Textbook of Palliative Care for Children* (2nd edn) (pp 68–77). Oxford: Oxford University Press.

Carroll, K. (2012). Infertile? The emotional labour of sensitive and feminist research methodologies. *Qualitative Research* 13(5): 546–61.

Christensen, P. and James, A. eds (2008). *Research with Children: Perspectives and Practices* (2nd edn). Abingdon: Routledge.

Constanti, P. and Gibbs, P. (2004). Higher education teachers and emotional labour. *International Journal of Educational Management* 18(4): 243–9.

Coombs, S. (2014). Death wears a T-shirt – Listening to young people talk about death. *Mortality* 19(3): 284–302.

Coombs, S. (2017). *Young People's Perspectives on End-of-life: Death, Culture and the Everyday*. Cham: Palgrave Macmillan.

Davin, L., Thistlethwaite, J., Bartle, E., and Russel, K. (2019). Touch in health professional practice: A review. *The Clinical Teacher* 16(6): 559–64.

Dickson-Swift, V., James, E.L., and Liamputtong, P. (2008). *Undertaking Sensitive Research in the Health and Social Sciences: Managing Boundaries, Emotions and Risk*. Cambridge: Cambridge University Press.

Faulkner, J. (2011). *The Importance of Being Innocent: Why We Worry about Children*. Cambridge: Cambridge University Press.

Gillis, J.R. (1997). *A World of Their Own Making: Myth, Ritual, and the Quest for Family Values*. Cambridge, MA: Harvard University Press.

Greig, A., Taylor, J., and MacKay, T. (2007). *Doing Research with Children* (2nd edn). London: Sage.

Guba, E. and Lincoln, Y. (2008). Paradigmatic controversies, contradictions, and emerging confluences. In Denzin, N. and Lincoln, Y. (eds) *The Landscape of Qualitative Research*. London: Sage.

Halse, C. and Honey, A. (2005). Unravelling ethics: Illuminating the moral dilemmas of research ethics. *Signs: Journal of Women in Culture and Society* 30: 2141–65.

Hochschild, A.R. ([1983] 2003). *The Managed Heart: Commercialization of Human Feeling* (20th anniversary edn). Berkley, CA: University of California Press.

Holmes, M. (2010). The emotionalization of reflexivity. *Sociology* 44(1): 139–54.

Holt, J. (1975). *Escape from Childhood: The Needs and Rights of Children*. Harmondsworth: Penguin.

Howarth, G. (2007). *Death and Dying: A Sociological Introduction*. Cambridge: Polity.

Hydén, M. (2008). Narrating sensitive topics. In Andrews, M., Squire, C., and Tamboukou, M. (eds) *Doing Narrative Research*. London: Sage.

Johansson, C., Aberg, M., and Hedlin, M. (2021). Touch the children, or please don't – Preschool teachers' approach to touch. *Scandinavian Journal of Educational Research* 65(2): 288–301.

Jones, A. (2004). Social anxiety, sex, surveillance, and the safe teacher. *British Journal of Sociology of Education* 25(1): 53–66.

Kastenbaum, R. and Fox, L. (2007). Do imaginary companions die? An exploratory study. *Omega – Journal of Death and Dying* 56(2): 123–52.

Lee, R.M. (1993). *Doing Research on Sensitive Topics*. London: Sage.

Maddrell, A. and Sidaway, J.D. (2010). *Deathscapes: Spaces for Death, Dying, Mourning and Remembrance*. Farnham: Ashgate.

Martins, P.C., Oliveira, V.H., and Tendai, I. (2018). Research with children and young people on sensitive topics – The case of poverty and delinquency. *Childhood* 25(4): 458–72.

McCormick, M. (2011). Responsible believing. In Talwar, V., Harris, P.L., and Schleifer, M. (eds) *Children's Understanding of Death*. New York: Cambridge University Press.

Piper, H., Garratt, D., and Taylor, B. (2013). Hands off! The practice and politics of touch in physical education and sports coaching. *Sport, Education and Society* 18(5): 575–82.

Renzetti, C.M. and Lee, R.M. (1993). *Researching Sensitive Topics*. London: Sage.

Stienbery, R.J. and Figart, D.M. (1999). Emotional labor since The Managed Heart. *The American Academy of Political and Social Science* 561(1): 8–26.

Taylor, A. (2011). Reconceptualizing the 'nature' of childhood. *Childhood* 18(4): 420–33.

Tronto, J.C. ([1993] 2009). *Moral Boundaries: A Political Argument for an Ethic of Care*. London: Routledge.

Vanner, C. (2015). Positionality at the center: Constructing an epistemological and methodological approach for a western feminist doctoral candidate conducting research in the postcolonial. *International Journal of Qualitative Methods* 1–12.

Walter, T., Hourizi, R., Moncur, W., and Pitsillides, S. (2011). Does the internet change how we die and mourn? Overview and analysis. *Omega – Journal of Death and Dying* 64(4): 275–302.

Wyness, M. (2018). *Childhood, Culture and Society: In a Global Context*. London: Sage.

Wyness, M. (2019). *Childhood and Society* (3rd edn). London: Red Globe Press.

Yalom, I.D. (2008). *Staring at the Sun: Overcoming the Dread of Death*. London: Piatkus Books.

9

Owning Our Mistakes: Confessions of an Unethical Researcher

Heather Montgomery

Introduction

When I started my PhD in social anthropology my fellow students had pinned a cartoon to the wall with the title 'The Post-Modern Anthropologist'. It was a picture of an old-school anthropologist, in a pith-helmet, talking to an informant. Under the title there was a speech bubble coming out of his mouth, which read 'That's enough about you, let's talk about me.' It rather neatly encapsulated some of the dilemmas of doing fieldwork at that time. On the one hand there was a welcome reflexive turn within the discipline where the role and the responsibilities of the researcher were called into question, yet, on the other, a worry that this sort of reflection could lead to insularity and navel gazing and a greater concern with the anthropologist's own feelings and experiences than those of informants.

I had chosen to do my PhD research on child prostitutes in Thailand, a topic which, with the naiveté and sense of invincibility that comes with beginning a project in your early 20s, I thought I could 'sort out'. I believed that with the right methods, and indeed the right attitude, I could shed new light on the problem, change perceptions of how to intervene, and influence national and international policy. Backed up with an interest, and sincerely held belief, in children's rights, what could go wrong? And indeed, in many ways it was a success. I found a small group of children relatively easily who were happy to let me spend time with them. I moved in with a wonderful NGO led by inspirational leaders who gave the children practical and emotional support and looked after me as well. Four years later I received my PhD and, as I got older, got scholarships, jobs, and promotions based, in part, on this initial work and my analyses of it.

Yet there was much I left unsaid and unexplored and which only now, with the benefit of long hindsight (and cynics might say with the benefit of a secure university post) that I have started to rethink and explore. The longer I am away from fieldwork, and the older I have become, the more doubts and dilemmas I have about the ethics of this fieldwork and the less certain I am about my interpretations and ideas about the children I encountered there. This chapter therefore will not be a triumphal account of how my mistakes turned out to be blessings in disguise or how I found redemption through practical action. I did not discover a 'magic methods' key that unlocked the possibilities of truly understanding children's lives. Instead it is about the errors I made: the things that went wrong, the mistakes that were not learning opportunities, the problems that never became challenges but just remained problems. It is about research that says the wrong things and comes up with the wrong findings and where listening to children also means ignoring what they say. It is less about overcoming ethical dilemmas and more about acknowledging the intractability of some problems and the difficulties that undertaking research with children involves, and the way it can have far-reaching impacts on one's personal and professional identity. I deliberately offer no solutions to the ethical dilemmas I raise because to me they are still a work in progress. I believe, however, an honest account of these difficulties can pave the way for a fuller discussion of the ways in which researchers and other practitioners think about ethical issues arising during research with children. I hope it is self-reflective rather than self-centred or self-indulgent. I do not want to be *that* Post-Modern Anthropologist.

In the beginning

In 1992 I embarked on a four-year PhD in social anthropology. In doing so I was heavily influenced by the 'New Social Studies of Childhood' and new ways of theorising and working with children that had come to prominence throughout the social sciences in the 1980s (see James and Prout, 1997; Mayall, 2013). Researchers working in this framework had made concerted attempts to focus more directly on children and young people, their own experiences and explanations, and had acknowledged age as an important organising principle in society, as worthy of study as gender or ethnicity. They argued for more child-centred, or child-focused, forms of research, based on the assumption that children themselves were the best informants about their own lives. For me, this new theorisation was radical and exciting. Furthermore, it was rooted in concepts and ideas about children's rights and children's agency. Children should be consulted and asked to participate as informants not only because they were the experts on their lives, but also because they had a *right* to participation. This necessitated a shift in power relations and a need for researchers to engage with children on their own terms, take what they said seriously, and understand the world through their eyes.

Inspired by this new way of thinking I started to research child labour in Thailand. Although it appeared that there was a problem of children working in sweatshops, the most pressing concern seemed to be the numbers of children who were working in the sex trade, particularly those selling sex (or being forced to sell sex) to foreign men. In the mid-1990s both the international and English-language media in Thailand were full of stories of western men travelling to South East Asia, particularly Thailand and the Philippines if they wanted young girls, or Sri Lanka if they wanted young boys, and buying sex. There seemed to be no repercussions and, on the rare occasions they were caught, they were often able to leave the country without penalties. The injustice of this and the obvious violation of the rights of the children involved drew me to the topic along with the belief that my work could somehow change the situation. I felt instinctively that long-term fieldwork could offer a very different narrative to the one presented in the newspapers and that in order to know how best to help these young people it would be important to know more precisely about their lives and experiences. I assumed that by showing the realities of their lives I would be able to change policy and show the world the 'truth' about these children's lives.

Today, university ethics committees provide guidance and restraint on researchers going into the field to undertake work with difficult, dangerous, or vulnerable people. There are also a variety of books on ethics and methods on how to work with such groups, especially children, and on how to conduct ethical and appropriate research (see, for example, Alderson and Morrow, 2020). Thirty years ago there was no such guidelines or advice – it sounds shocking now but I made no application to an ethics committee, we had little training in fieldwork methods or working with human subjects, there were no checks on what we going to do and no checks on our own safety. There was a sense that fieldwork should be a rite of passage, if not an ordeal, and that surviving it was a mark of success and the mark of a 'true' researcher. Despite, or because, of this, I set off to Thailand in 1993 as a naive, and probably rather arrogant, 23-year-old. I knew the anthropological theories of participant observation, of the importance of using children as informants, of listening to their voices, and of ethical engagement. In theory at least: the realities, as I found, were very different.

The practical realities

Doing such research was never going to be easy and the initial difficulty was finding children whom I could talk to and who would be prepared to talk to me. Conducting participant observation or ethnographic interviews among children doing any form of illegal or dangerous work, whether as prostitutes, in illegal sweatshops, or begging on the streets, is always going to be difficult to do (although there have been some superb monographs based on excellent fieldwork in the most difficult of circumstances, such as those done in Haiti by Christopher Kovats-Bernat (2008) or the contributors to Allerton (2016). Such children have a well-founded suspicion of outsiders, and of adults, and they are aware that talking to a foreigner will attract unwelcome attention.

It took me three months before I found a slum community near a tourist resort where children regularly sold sex to foreigners. I made contact with this community through a small, church-based NGO whose practitioners worked with young prostitutes and street children, as well as with adult sex workers, and who were prepared to let me work with them as long as I gave them assurances that I would not name the organisation, its workers, any of the children I worked with, or indeed the town I worked in. The community where I was based for the next 15 months was called Baan Nua (this is a pseudonym – it means simply North Village in Thai) and consisted of rural migrants and their children. There were 65 children there, around 35 of whom worked regularly or occasionally as prostitutes. Both boys and girls were selling sex and, significantly, they were still living with their parents, who knew what they were doing. The children had a variety of clients but relied in particular on three long-term European clients who had been coming to the slum for several years and bought sex from several of the children. The NGO had set up a small school in the village, provided food, and aimed to ease the children gradually out of prostitution by offering them training for alternative employment and by persuading their parents to reject prostitution as a legitimate occupation.

Finding a fieldwork site was one of the easier parts of the fieldwork, however, and when I started to collect data I uncovered immediate problems, notably the age of some of the children. I had expected to be working with older children or teenagers and I had hypothesised that some of these may not have been considered children within their own communities. However, instead of the 12–16-year-old age range I was expecting, most of the children were much younger, some as young as six. Clearly, this posed huge ethical and practical problems: is it possible to interview a six-year-old in a language with which the researcher is not entirely familiar, and more importantly, it is ethically correct to do so? I certainly tried to include the younger children in my research, spending long periods of time playing with them, discussing their experiences and experimenting with techniques such as body mapping (asking them to draw me pictures of themselves and marking on them any place where they sometimes felt hurt), asking them to show me the places in their community which were important to them, or following their daily routines closely and taking detailed notes on how they spent their days.

However, not all of these techniques were successful – younger children did not always want to draw for me, or even to play with me, and having an intrusive stranger in their midst was clearly an irritant and annoyance to them at times. Often they did not have the vocabulary to talk about what they did or they had started prostitution only recently and had little idea of what it actually involved. Sometimes I was wary of asking too much and imposing my own views or understandings on them and communicating to them the disgust I felt at what they had to do. The children I knew best, therefore, were usually older and more articulate and also had a longer history of prostitution. They were also children with whom I had the closest personal relationships and who were prepared to trust me. In this respect it is instructive to note that although both male and female prostitution occurred in the village, the boys were considerably less willing to talk about it to me than the girls, thereby causing me to place greater emphasis on the girls' experiences. One of the reasons that the boys may have found it harder to talk to me (and vice versa) was that we shared few common interests. I did not want to play computer games and I could not play football and knew little about its stars – particularly those from Manchester United – who were their most intense passion, and they were consequently not interested in hanging out with me. All of the children, however, remained childlike, often getting bored or irritated with me or laughing at my attempts to play their games or speak their language, sometimes being quite spiteful and sometimes very affectionate (for greater detail on the problems of methods during this fieldwork, see Montgomery, 2007).

Child prostitution in Baan Nua: my findings

I found that perhaps the most obvious answer to the question of why the children sold sex and why their parents allowed them to was that it was the quickest and most lucrative way of earning money. There were few jobs available to uneducated children from the slums and work such as scavenging on rubbish tips for scrap metal, begging, or selling food in the street were often tried but rejected as dangerous and frightening. Children spoke of their fears of rats on the rubbish dump where some of them scavenged or of being mugged by older street children who would take any money they earned from begging. In the circumstances, prostitution was the highest-paying job available and was sometimes seen to have other benefits, such as the chance to eat well and stay in good hotels or apartments. Yet the children themselves rarely justified it in these terms and consciously downplayed its monetary aspect. Prostitution carried a stigma and children were often reluctant to admit that they did sell sex, preferring euphemisms such as 'being supported by a foreigner', 'going out for fun with foreigners' or 'having guests'. It was clear, however, that some clients were customers who simply bought sex and these sorts of relationships were disliked and rarely talked about. What the children preferred to discuss were the European men whom they claimed as 'friends', who came back to the slum several times over the season and who had been visiting them for some years. These men were in contact with the children between visits and often sent money when requested to do so. This enabled the children to claim that they had some sort of reciprocal relationship with them and that sex was only a small part of the relationship. They deliberately downplayed the importance of the money to them, preferring to emphasise the friendship and the ongoing relationship rather than the commercial transaction. They never set a price for sexual acts and money that was given to them after sex was always referred to as a present. Sometimes a client would not leave cash but would pay in kind, for example through the rebuilding or refurbishing of a girl's house. Given this, it was easy for the children to deny prostitution; they argued that the men who visited them were not clients but friends who helped out whenever they needed it.

In the modern western ideal, parents are expected to make sacrifices for their children, to protect them and nurture them, and children are viewed as having limited responsibilities to their parents or others. In contrast, I found in Baan Nua that this sense of duty was reversed, and children were thought to owe a debt of gratitude to their parents for giving birth to them. Children were expected to look after parents, to go to work so that their parents did not have to, and to support their parents in whatever way they could and these obligations were lifelong. Drawing on culturally valued traditions of filial piety and family obligations allowed these children to reject the identity of prostitute and emphasise instead their own self-image as dutiful sons and daughters, fulfilling their obligations to their parents. A powerful mitigating circumstance for many of them was the financial support they provided for their families and when they did speak about selling sex (however obliquely), they referred explicitly to ideas of obligation and gratitude to their parents. I was always told that being supported by foreigners was a means to an end, a way of fulfilling the filial obligations of duty and sacrifice for their families and therefore retaining self-respect. These reference points gave the children strategies for rationalising prostitution and for coming to terms with it. They had found an ethical system whereby the public selling of their bodies did not affect their private sense of humanity and identity. When I asked one 13-year-old about selling sex, she replied, "It's only my body, but this is my family." She could make a clear conceptual difference between her body and what happened to it and what she perceived to be her innermost 'self' and her own sense of identity and morality. Betraying family members and failing to provide for parents were roundly condemned but exchanging sex for money, especially when that money was used for moral ends, was not blameworthy and violated no ethical codes.

Challenges and problems

All these findings I have written up at length elsewhere (Montgomery, 2001). I have discussed them extensively at conferences and, on the whole, been given very positive and affirming feedback. However, I was often left uneasy, knowing that behind the confident façade of academic expertise, there were other stories and interpretations and things I felt much less confident in talking about and which, I felt, would show me and my work in a less favourable light. One particular incident has always troubled me.

Sompot was an eight-year-old boy who was sometimes bought for sexual services by foreign men. He was affectionate and cheerful and always seemed to be laughing; he was also a small, skinny boy, often covered in sores and not in good health. Arriving in Bann Nua to be greeted by a bear hug by him was often the high point of the day but always tempered by ambivalence. It was very hard to reconcile the charming, scruffy little boy who asked me continually about Manchester United and whether I could take him to England to see them with the child who was regularly sexually abused by foreign men for money. Not only could I not bear to think too much about what they did to him, but I was also painfully aware that sometimes when he would run to me for a hug, especially after he had sniffed glue and his lips were sore and his nose runny, I would involuntarily flinch and turn my head away in disgust.

One day Sompot came home to his mother after visiting a client. There was fresh blood on his trousers but he seemed in high spirits. The other children crowded around him and teased him, saying "Sompot is having a period – he is bleeding!" Sompot laughed and not one of the other children appeared to be shocked with what had happened to him, despite my horrified reactions. For the first time in the field (I had then been there around nine months) I lost my temper and swore at his mother in a mixture of Thai and English. She looked at me as if I was being particularly stupid and said "It's just for one hour. What harm can happen to him in one hour?"

That night I went back to the tiny room I rented next to a drop-in centre for adult sex workers and cried before deciding I had had enough of fieldwork, of anthropology, of social constructionism, of cultural relativism, of ideas about children's agency, of children's rights that meant nothing in reality, of the ignorance and stupidity of people, and of my own helplessness. Reading through my diary for that night – not my carefully constructed and meticulously neutral fieldwork notes – I can still see the rage and self-pity coming through. The entry is filled with expletives, hatred of everyone around me, and anger at the whole notion of undertaking fieldwork on such a horrible topic, in a place I hated, among people I despised. I decided there and then to give up and come home.

Three months later and my resolve had failed. I did not return home but soldiered on, determined to finish my PhD and not let down my funders, the workers at the small NGO who had helped me and introduced me to these children, my supervisor, or myself. I tried to pride myself on my stoicism and commitment while dismissing my tears as self-indulgence. Seven years later my book on Baan Nua was published. I had thought about including this incident but worried it might be seen as invasive, sensationalistic, or even voyeuristic, so I alluded to it only in passing. It was briefly summarised in the following paragraph with no further mention made of the context.

> For many outsiders, the complicity of mothers in their children's prostitution is regarded as the ultimate betrayal of family relationships and an abdication of the parental role of protection and care. To the people of Baan Nua, however, there is no such feeling. The responsibilities of parents towards children are seen very differently; no-one in Baan Nua believes that they are harming their children by allowing them to work as prostitutes. Life is difficult for all of them and children, just like their parents, have to do the best they can. When I asked Pen, Sompot's mother, why she sold him, she looked at me blankly and replied 'It's just for one hour. What harm can happen to him in one hour?' (Montgomery, 2001, p 85)

In retrospect, keeping the reason for my question out of it seems unnecessarily coy and even obfuscatory. Parents did seem to have very different attitudes towards such incidents, which they viewed entirely in physical, rather than psychological, terms – there was no belief that long-term damage could be inflicted on a child in 'just one hour'. Mothers would do whatever they could to soothe any pain but did not see it as fundamentally harmful in the long term to their children or as damaging to their mental health. Yet what was published was not the full truth and did not convey the visceral horror of what had happened to this boy – was I explaining or condoning?

While representing Sompot's story was perhaps the starkest dilemma I faced in the research and writing processes, it was one of very many, and almost every aspect of my research, and my findings, and the way I wrote them up, is problematic. I remain uneasy and unsure about my choice of language. I use the term child prostitute although the children I worked with did not, and other writers have rejected it as implying an agency that children do not have. Child sex worker is considered even worse. Many in the NGO world use 'commercially sexually exploited child' (CSEC), which conveys the abusive nature of the transaction and the unequal power relationships but remains a mouthful to say or write. I chose at the time to use the phrase child prostitute as it was readily understood but, with hindsight, I would certainly try to find a better term which emphasises the abusive and exploitative nature of the exchange (see Ennew, 2008 for a fuller discussion of this problem).

Another difficult problem was the way my research distorts the importance of prostitution in the children's lives. They in fact spent very little time working as prostitutes or talking about it. They spent the vast majority of their time in Baan Nua, playing with friends, attending classes in the makeshift school that the NGO I was involved with had set up, playing handheld computer games, or talking to me. It remains hard to write about these children because I am the one calling them prostitutes, analysing their lives in terms of prostitution, and giving it a significance that it did not necessarily have for them. Asking children slightly esoteric questions about their identities was always going to be problematic and I rarely attempted it but if they had been able to answer such questions, I suspect they would have replied that they were sons and daughters, sisters and friends, residents of Baan Nua, Buddhists, Thai, supporters of the King and Queen, followers of David Beckham, and so on. If they mentioned being a prostitute as part of their identity, it would, I am sure, have come down very low on the scale of who they were and how they defined themselves. Yet to almost everyone else the only important fact about them was that they sometimes exchanged sex for money. It remains a dilemma I have never satisfactorily answered – how can I say I worked with child prostitutes when the child prostitutes themselves always categorically denied that is what they were?

Equally intractable were the ethical problems of what my research was for. I was very struck, before I did fieldwork, by a quote from Jean La Fontaine in her book, *Child Sexual Abuse* (1990), in which she argues that researchers who write about these issues without thinking through the question of interventions lay themselves open to charges of 'academic voyeurism [which are] no substitute for more action on behalf of the victims' (1990, p 17). This charge of academic voyeurism is one that I have always struggled with, perhaps because it seems very close to the mark. This research, like all research with vulnerable populations, raises questions about whether there is a moral requirement on researchers to do something with their research other than make an academic career out of it and asks us to confront the question, in what ways should research findings be used in order to alleviate the difficult situations that children face?

I could always argue that my work has enabled me to describe the perspective of a particular group of vulnerable children and that any outside intervention in their lives, in order to stand any chance of success, must take account of the complex ways that economic activity and kinship relations interact. I could also point out the practical difficulties of intervening effectively and the further ethical dilemmas that this would raise. In Thailand, when I was doing fieldwork, services for families and children were patchy; there were no specialised child abuse teams and I had little idea who I could have brought in to help. Perhaps I could have involved the police, even though I had specifically promised not to, and which might have resulted in either the children or their parents being arrested, or the family being split up. In 1996 the law was changed to allow for the prosecution of parents and procurers and for jail sentences of between two and six years to be imposed on any parent who allowed a child under 15 to become a prostitute and three years for those whose child was between 15 and 18 years old. Yet the children whom I knew would not have asked for help because they feared separation from, or punishment of, their parents. With this in mind I trod very carefully and promised not to involve anyone from outside the community.

Having made that promise, however, I found I could not keep it. After my rage and impotence when I had seen Sompot injured I promised myself that if anything like that happened again, I would act differently. Later on I had an opportunity to prove myself when Sompot once again came back to the village injured. This time it was a broken or badly sprained arm, which was causing him obvious pain. Without hesitation I borrowed an NGO worker's car, took him to the local hospital, and had them check him over. He protested that he did not want to go and told the nurse there he had been in a fight with another boy. When I brought him back, the community and the NGO were in uproar. Having given my word to them, and the children themselves, that I would not draw attention to the slum in which they lived, that I would not call the police or get other authorities involved, I had reneged on all of these promises. I was accused, very forcibly, of interfering where I had no right. Sompot's mother never trusted me again and Sompot himself rarely talked to me after this and once, when I visited him with a western friend, his mother asked me very pointedly, "Have you betrayed us again?"

Maybe I should not have intervened, or not in this way, or not at this point, or not just in Sompot's case but in all the others. There may well have been alternatives and certainly some people who have read my research or challenged me at conferences have disagreed strongly with my approach and have felt that whatever promises I gave and however limited the alternatives, the opportunity to prevent abuse to children should have overridden all other considerations and I should, therefore, have intervened more effectively, in whatever way possible. Others have argued that academic research should not be placed above the protection of children and that in attempting a long-term research project I prioritised my own interests over those of the children. I share these concerns. It is often acknowledged by researchers in informal conversations, but much less rarely publicly stated, that even with the best of intentions, mistakes are sometimes made, and when these involve vulnerable children there are consequences.

My findings also have huge ethical and methodological implications, and, once again, I can offer no easy answers. The use of children as informants revealed things about child prostitution that I could never have anticipated;

my own understanding of the situation became complicated by the children's and their families' own agendas. I found the children's accounts of their lives deeply problematic because what they told me did not fit with my own worldview and also because they did not say what I expected and indeed wanted them to say. I was expecting rage and anger against the men who abused them and yet the children expressed no such feelings. Indeed they would sometimes ask me to help them write letters saying how much they loved these men. I was expecting parents to do everything in their power to prevent harm coming to their children and yet they claimed to see no harm and supported and encouraged children to sell sex. I was expecting children clamouring to have their rights respected (after I had explained what they were) and found no such demand or desire.

The children resisted my claim that their involvement with foreign clients was a form of abuse which violated their rights. They claimed radically different beliefs about the nature of parent/child relationships and what is right for adults to expect of children. The only way out of this dilemma is to say that children do not know what they are talking about, that they lack the wider economic, social, or political understanding that would allow them to see that they are being exploited by both their parents and their clients. One might claim that the children are victims of a form of false consciousness, unable to see their own oppression, or, knowing it, refusing to acknowledge it. Certainly I could find some evidence to justify this view, not least in their extensive drug and alcohol use. Many of the children sniffed glue and used alcohol regularly but when asked explicitly about their drug use, the children always denied that they took drugs to cope with prostitution, once again making my interpretations problematic. In Baan Nua there was limited entertainment: when they were not working some of the young men would occasionally stage cockfights and bet on the outcome but other than that, they did not do much other than sniff glue and drink alcohol. Several children claimed it was boredom not prostitution that made them use drugs.

The idea of agency is also difficult. Certainly, once the children had entered prostitution, they endeavoured to justify it as a legitimate form of work and, within the constraints of adult expectation, they struggled to retain a degree of strategic control over their lives through the money they earned and the belief that this money was ensuring a greater good. This was far from straightforward for anyone, however, and although both parents and children claimed to see prostitution as a way of fulfilling filial duties and obligations, and that it was the most lucrative way of doing this, I sometimes saw hints that suggested that this view was not entirely unchallenged. When a five-year-old girl once told me, for example, "I don't want to go with foreigners, but my grandmother asks me to, so I feel I must," then no matter what the norms of filial duty and obligation, it is hard to see the child's situation in terms of anything other than manipulation and abuse. Similarly, when I asked Sompot's mother why she allowed him to be a prostitute and she told me, "I am his mother. If I ask my son to make money for me, he will go. I don't send him, he wants to go for me," it is difficult to take this at face value and not to detect some coercion. Although the children told me that the money they earned fulfilled filial obligations, there was an obvious degree of manipulation on both sides and a vested interest by both mothers and children to deny that pressure had been exerted on the children. Furthermore, it was clear to see that only rarely was the money actually used for the good of the family. Occasionally, a new roof would be put on the house, or a television bought, but generally the money seemed to be spent on gambling or drink and although the children said that they gave all their money to their mothers, it was also apparent that they had a degree of purchasing power; they bought glue to sniff or drugs to take and they did keep some money for themselves. Yet, I never heard any children comment on this or criticise their parents. Rather children consistently spoke of their pride in being able to help their parents. They told me repeatedly that they were never sent to be prostitutes. They had seen for themselves that the family was in difficulties and they wanted to help.

Personal impacts

The role of emotions and the personal impacts of doing research on the researcher have started to be examined in recent years and this has opened up debates over professional objectivity and personal and professional boundaries in interesting ways (Phelan and Kinsella, 2013; Graham et al, 2014). This too raises an ethical dilemma and there is a large part of me that feels that speaking and writing of my own, often turbulent, feelings about fieldwork is both unprofessional and self-indulgent when the children I knew suffered so much more. However, acknowledging that research with children can be morally and emotionally fraught also allows researchers to be more honest about their experiences and reveals the sometimes uncomfortable and ambivalent relationship between researcher and informants. It underlines the need for reflection as an importance part of the research process and recognises that, in place of scientific detachment, research can involve a way of acting, talking, and being which is sometimes at odds with personal morality. This can have painful and even traumatic impacts. A friend of mine who worked with vulnerable children elsewhere in the world has recently been diagnosed with PTSD after everything they saw and yet still, when we send researchers out to work with vulnerable children, we rarely warn them of the dangers to their own mental health. Even doing fieldwork closer to home can be traumatic. Ten years after carrying out her research among primary school children in England, during which she found herself both being bullied by some of the children and condoning and giggling along with the bullying of others, Anna Laerke eloquently expressed her feelings of uncertainty and distress over her research role. She claims that it 'broke my heart' (Laerke, 2008, p 144) and that

> [w]hile writing has been an exorcism, of sorts, of a fieldwork identity that literally made me sick, a reconstituted and properly dislodged 'me' has yet to materialize. Ten years on, I am still in the grip of it … writing about [my fieldwork] has produced a gradual sedimentarisation of two feelings: anger and sadness. (Laerke, 2008, p 144)

Such feelings are ones I recognise all too well although I would also add guilt and uncertainty to anger and sadness. Many years after I completed this research, the city I now live in, Oxford, was rocked by a 'grooming' scandal where young girls, mostly under the care of social services, were being sexually abused by gangs of older men. This brought back very painful memories and reflections for me and it became increasingly clear how badly these girls had been let down by those who should have cared for them. Social workers talked about prostitution as a lifestyle choice; the girls talked of the abusers as 'boyfriends' and of having no one else to look after them. This all sounded both horribly familiar and horribly wrong and made me question, once again, the entire basis of my findings. Was what I had claimed as agency and resilience under appalling circumstances simply a cover-up for the abuse and victimisation of other highly vulnerable children?

Conclusions

Working with the children of Baan Nua was an enormous privilege – I am still amazed at their resilience, their vitality, their wit, their loyalty, and their strength. They were often good company and much of my time doing fieldwork with them was funny and enjoyable. In the end, of course, I did not change policy or improve these children's lives and my good intentions came to very little. I got an academic career out of Baan Nua, the children got nothing. In the end I have tried to make sense of what I saw there through the well-worn and even clichéd defence that understanding is not the same as condoning. The children's rejection of the idea of abuse and exploitation can be seen as a denial of their true feelings and as a way of refusing to face the unpalatable facts of their existence, but it can also be understood as a strategic way of exerting some control and agency in their lives. Whatever my personal feelings of anger and pity, I remain unhappy about seeing these children only as victims, exploited by both western men and their own blindness to their true situation. The children themselves specifically rejected this categorisation and although their choices were extremely restricted, they did struggle to take some control over their lives. I felt that it was important to believe the children when they talked about this and to see their attempts to control certain aspects of their lives as active and informed choices among very limited, and very hard, options.

I was, and still am, a firm advocate of child-centred research and of children's rights although I also accept that believing in children's rights is not always enough to protect them or prevent harm. I still consider children's participation in research to be important and their role as informants vital and that research should always aspire to be ethical and rights based. Simply because mine was not does not mean that we should not try to do much better in the future. I still believe that children deserve, and have the right, to be understood and that the success of any proposed intervention depends on a thorough understanding of the interpretations and understandings of children who are to be affected by programmes of assistance. I remain wary of interventions based on claims about children's best interests when children themselves have, more often than not, not been consulted.

While fully supporting the impetus for child-centred research, researchers also have to acknowledge that it does not always give them the answers that they want and that their own ideas about children may be profoundly challenged. In the end it is only comparison across cases and a full and honest account of problems that will enable a comprehensives discussion of the ways in which we can develop discussions of the ethical issues which arise when researching with children in difficult circumstances. It is my hope that this chapter contributes in some way to that discussion.

References

Alderson, P. and Morrow, V. (2020). *The Ethics of Research with Children and Young People: A Practical Handbook*. London: Sage.

Allerton. C. (2016). *Children: Ethnographic Encounters*. London: Bloomsbury Academic.

Ennew, J. (2008). Exploitation of children in prostitution. Paper presented at the World Congress III against the sexual exploitation of children and adolescents, Rio de Janeiro, Brazil, 25–28 November 2008. ECPAT International.

Graham, A., Powell, M.A., and Taylor, N. (2015). Ethical research involving children: Encouraging reflexive engagement in research with children and young people. *Children and Society* 29(5): 331–43.

James, A. and Prout, A. eds (1997). *Constructing and Reconstructing Childhood: Contemporary Issues in the Sociological Study of Childhood* (2nd edn). London: Falmer Press.

Kovats-Bernat, C. (2008). *Sleeping Rough on the Streets of Port au Prince*. Gainesville, FL: University Press of Florida.

La Fontaine, J. (1990). *Child Sexual Abuse*. Cambridge: Polity.

Laerke, A. (2008). Confessions of a downbeat anthropologist. In Armbruster, H. and Laerke, A. (eds) *Taking Sides: Ethics, Politics and Fieldwork in Anthropology*. Oxford: Berghahn.

Mayall, B. (2013). *A History of the Sociology of Childhood*. London: UCL/IOE Press.

Montgomery, H. (2001). *Modern Babylon? Prostituting Children in Thailand*. New York: Berghahn.

Montgomery, H. (2007). Working with child prostitutes in Thailand: Problems of practice and interpretation. *Childhood* 14(4): 415–30.

Phelan, S.K. and Kinsella, E.A. (2013). Picture this … safety, dignity, and voice – ethical research with children: Practical considerations for the reflexive researcher. *Qualitative Inquiry* 19(2): 81–90.

Index

References to figures appear in *italic* type.
References to endnotes show both the
page number and the note number (59n3).

A
academia, emotional support within 17–18, 25
academic voyeurism 106, 165–6
action as a result of research, responsibility for 104–6
activism, young people's involvement in 109–10
see also social action, youth
agency
 adult control and children's 146–7
 of child prostitutes in Thailand 167–8, 169–70
 participation, voice and 97–101
 as relational 108–9
 and 'voice' in practice 102–4
anonymity of participants 36, 85

B
Balagopalan, S. 43, 44, 46, 57, 64
Bergmark, U. 143
Berriman, L. 107
Bhabha, H. 53, 57
Bhadra, B. 65
BikeStormz 109
Boggis, A. 83, 86
boka child 45, 46, 53
Bourdieu, P. 57, 90, 91
boyd, D. 12, 21
brought self 6
Budhwar Peth, children in red-light area of 64, 65–6
 emotional challenges 71–2
 mapping tool 73–4, *74*
 meeting participants 68
 self-portrait tool 76–8, *77*, *78*

C
care, ethic of 142–3, 144, 145
 colliding with safeguarding discourse 148–50, 151, 152–4
Carroll, K. 143, 144

child prostitution in India 73
child prostitution in Thailand 157–71
 absence of guidance and advice on ethics 159
 challenges and problems 163–8
  academic voyeurism 165–6
  agency of children 167–8, 169–70
  dealing with unexpected attitudes of children and parents 163, 164, 166–7, 168
  distorting problem of prostitution to children 165
  drug use 167
  identities 165
  making interventions and reneging on promises 166
  responding to very troubling incidents 163–4, 166
  terminology 164
 data collection 160–1
 denials of prostitution 162, 165, 169–70
 findings 161–2
 impact on researcher 168–9
 inspired by 'New Social Studies of Childhood' 158–9
 practical realities 159–62
  finding a fieldwork site 159–60
  working with boys 161
  working with very young children 160–1
 prosecution of parents 166
 sense of filial duty 162, 167, 168
 terminology 164
child protection, child's voice in context of 117–37
 component structures and relationships 128–30, *129*
 conceptual framework 120–8, 131–2
 child–practitioner relationship 121, 122, 130
 'ecosystem' of relationships 120, 121
 national and global policy trends 121, 127–8

INDEX

organisations and state governing bodies 121, 125–6
practitioner and organisation relationship 121, 122–3
practitioner and other agencies in field 121, 123–4
practitioner and state governing bodies 121, 124–5
statutory state services and state/national government 121, 126–7
differences between child participation and child voice 118, 119
interagency work 124
mismatches between policy and practice 131
models of child participation in child protection 130–2
narrow constructions of child's voice 118–19, 130
political nature of child's voice 119–20, 130
child protection concerns
'defensible position' covering 16–17
as obstacles to research with children 10–11, 13, 15, 25–6
and principles of 'do no harm' 10–11, 25
see also safeguarding
childhood
adult imaginaries of 57
attitudes in Thailand to 163, 164, 167, 168
colonial notions of 64–5
concept of angels and devils 13, 25
construction in post-colonies 44
in context of Global North 44, 63
essentialism and children at peripheries 43–4
gaze on 'other' 56–8
Indian 44–6, 65
  sociology of 64–5
North–South tensions over notions of 42–3
protecting dominant constructs of 29, 35
and sexuality 34–6
situated within a 'walled garden' 139–40, 151
South Asian 63–4
undermining agentic construct of 35
children's rights 37, 97, 100–1, 127
child protection concerns outweighing 10–11, 13, 25–6
to participate in research 158–9, 170
Clark, J. 3, 15, 24, 82, 98, 101, 108, 110
clinical supervision 25
co-production methodologies 106–10, 110–11
comfort through touch, providing 143–4
anxiety over 152–3
colliding with discourse of safeguarding 148–50, 152
mechanisms of control 152
from multiple perspectives 151–2

community, participatory research on *see* participatory research on community in Suffolk
conferences, presenting research at 23, 90, 163
conflict zones, research in *see* Kashmir, children in Indian-administered
consent
concerns over young children's 145–6
obtaining disabled participants' 85
obtaining oral 49
selection of participants and 103–4
withdrawal of 86
Coombs, S. 140, 141, 151
CREATE 123
Crossover Youth Practice Model (CYPM) 124
Cube of Hope activity 50, *51*

D

data collection
with disabled young people 85
ethics of 34, 36, 106–7, 160–1
online and offline 12–13, 14–15
with very young children 160–1
death
children's relationship with 139–41
talking to children about 147–8, 151
'defensible position', forming a 16–17
design, reflexivity in choosing research method and 88–90
dharma 47, 59n3
Dickson-Swift, V. 17, 18, 23, 91, 141, 143, 144, 150
digital methodologies
failing to get approval to go ahead 12–13
lurking online 13–14, 15–16, 18, 19, 24, 25–6
offline research methods to contextualise 14–15
'participant-driven' 24
disabled young people 82–95
anonymity of participants 85
disseminating findings 90, 92, 93
emotional work 90–2
informed consent 85, 86
listening to voices of young disabled people 83, 85, 87, 89, 92, 93
marginalisation in research 82–3
reflexivity
as an embedded research process 86–7
as part of ethical processes 84–6
in research design and method 88–90
storytelling 88–90
taking time out from study 86–7
dissemination of research findings 90, 92, 93
Dogra rule 66
Dolev-Cohen, M. 34, 36
Dominey-Howes, D. 11, 17, 18, 21, 22, 24
drawing exercises 70–1, *70*

E

emotional impact of fieldwork on
    researchers 11, 17, 25, 91, 168–9
  support from academia for 17–18, 25
  taking a break 22, 73
emotional labour 7, 8
  angst around safeguarding practice 152–4
  in carrying out sensitive topic research with children 138, 143–5, 148, 150, 151
  definitions 144
  foregrounding researchers' own identities 143
  research as 90–2
emotions of research participants 91
epistemological reflexivity 54, 58
ethic of care 142–3, 144, 145
  colliding with safeguarding discourse 148–50, 151, 152–4
ethical approval, gaining
  childhood and sexuality research 33, 34–6
  considering harm to researcher in 8, 18, 25
  moral dissonance between young people's agency and 104
  reflexivity as part of process in 84–6
  social media and requirement for 10, 14, 24, 25
ethics
  addressing reflexivity as 67–71
  of data collection 34, 36, 106–7, 160–1
  and impact of research on researchers 168–9
  of perceived inaction, navigating 104–6
  of reciprocity 54–6
ethnomethodology 50, 59n6

F

family opposition to researchers' work 64
feminist research 2, 3, 89, 138, 142
field assistants 54
focus groups 14–15
  online research following information in 15–16
Fook, J. 117, 118, 121, 122, 123, 126, 130, 131

G

Gallagher, M. 98, 105, 108
gangs
  local projects to tackle violence 109
  research online *see* online research with gangs
gatekeepers 103, 104
Gillam, L. 84, 85, 87, 90
Graham, A. 96, 168
graveyard, playground space incorporating a *see* playground incorporating a graveyard,
'grooming' scandal, Oxford 169
Guillemin, M. 84, 85, 87, 90
guilt of researcher 17, 19, 20, 21, 72, 169

H

Hanna, E. 11, 17, 18, 19, 22
Haynes, K. 84, 86, 88
Hill Sabar, children of
  (re-)imagining and 'Indian' childhood 44–6
  boka 45, 46, 53
  Cube of Hope activity 50, *51*
  'double apartheid' 46
  engagement with formal education 45–6
  epistemological reflexivity 54, 58
  ethics of reciprocity 54–6
  field assistants 54
  informal education 50
  Kharia language 49, 54, 59n4
  lack of academic research with 52
  'Life, a Tree' sensory exploration tool 50–1
  reflexive 'turn' on research 48–54
    relationality of difference 52–4
  representation and 'representability' 53–4
  research as a site for reflexivity 46–8
hosts
  fearing for safety of 67–8
  respect and gratitude towards 72
Hyslop, I. 127, 130, 131

I

identities of researcher
  emotional labour and foregrounding 143
  in interactions with respondents 68, 69, 72, 80
  multiple selves in research 5–7
  see also positionality
India
  Adivasis (First Inhabitants) 45, 49
  boka child 45, 46, 53
  emergence of sociology of childhood 64–5
  indigenous communities 45, 49
    categorisation 58n1
    orientalising of 'other' childhood 44–6
  National Education Policy 46
  sex work in 63, 64, 65–6
  see also Budhwar Peth, children in red-light area of; Hill Sabar, children of; Kashmir, children in Indian-administered
Indian Constitution 58n1, 66, 67
Indian flag drawing 70–1, *70*
Indian Forest (Amendment) Bill 2019 58–9n2
indigenous research
  acknowledging 'other-ness' 56–9
  advancing phases of enquiry 49–50, 59n5
  decolonising 53
  ethics of reciprocity 54–6
  links with colonialism 54
  as a site for reflexivity 46–8
  see also Hill Sabar, children of
informed consent
  concerns over young children's 145–6
  obtaining disabled participants' 85
  obtaining oral 49

selection of participants and 103–4
withdrawal of 86
Ipswich 101–2
see also participatory research on community in Suffolk

J
Johnson, V. 101
juvenile justice system
  construction of children in 13
  research on girls in US 24
  youth 'voice' in 124

K
Kashmir, children in Indian-administered 66–7
  concerns for safety of hosts 67–8
  drawing exercise 70–1, *70*
  family opposition to researcher working in 64
  mapping tool and gendered differences 74–6, *75*, *76*
  as an outsider in 67, 69, 72
  self-portrait tool 78–9, *79*
  taking a break from 72–3
Keddell, E. 127, 130, 131
Kharia language 49, 54, 59n4

L
La Fontaine, J. 165
Laerke, A. 169
'Life, a Tree' sensory exploration tool 50–1
Lundy, L. 99, 100, 107, 110
lurking online 13–14, 15–16, 18, 19, 24, 25–6
Lyttle Storrod, M. 12, 24

M
macro systems 128, *129*
mapping tool 73–6, *74*, *75*, *76*, 80
mental health of researchers 168–9
  ethics committees and neglect of 8, 18, 25
  taking a break to protect 22, 73
meso systems 128, *129*
messiness of doing research 92–3, 110
methodology
  co-production 106–10, 110–11
  reflexivity about 56–8, 88–90
  sensitive research 141–5
  see also digital methodologies
micro systems 128, *129*
Montgomery, H. 161, 163, 164

N
nested systems theory 128
Nieuwenhuys, O. 65
Nordic Barnahus Model 124

O
online abuse, reporting concerns of 16, 17, 34

online research with gangs 11–28
  aims of research 11–12
  data collection 12
  'defensible position', forming a 16–17
  focus groups 14–15
  and future research 24–5
  lurking online 13–14, 15–16, 18, 19, 24, 25–6
  Plan A 12–13
  positionality and trauma 21–2
  presenting research at conferences 23
  recovering after research 22–3
  researcher safe spaces 20, 21
  signs of stress 18–20
  stress management 21
  vicarious trauma 11, 16, 17–18, 23
    addressing issues of 24–5
    disclosing experiences of 25
    recovering from 22–3
  witnessing abusive imagery online 11, 16, 17
Orgad, S. 12, 14
'other-ness', acknowledging 56–9
outsider, researcher as 67, 69, 72
Oxford 'grooming' scandal 169

P
parents, dealing with unexpected attitudes of 163, 164, 167, 168
participation in research, children and young people's
  child protection issues limiting 13, 15, 25–6
  children as researchers 100
  children's right to 158–9, 170
  criticisms and concerns 98, 99–100, 105, 110
  defining participation 98–9
  differences between child voice and child participation 118, 119
  influence of human rights movement on 127–8
  models of practice 99–100, 100–1
  popularity of practice tools and guides 119
  and principles of 'do no harm' 10–11, 25
participatory research on community in Suffolk 101–11
  agency and 'voice' in practice 102–4
  agency, voice and participation 97–101
  children as researchers 100
  co-production methodologies 106–10, 110–11
  exploring young people's perceptions 101–2
  issues over consent 103–4
  navigating ethics of perceived inaction 104–6
  participation as relational 106–10
  workshop of participatory activities 107

personal theory of action 47–8
playground incorporating a
    graveyard, 138–56
  children's relationship with death 139–41
  ethic of care colliding with safeguarding
    discourse 148–50, 151, 152–4
  issues around informed consent 145–6
  losing and regaining control over power
    balance 146–7
  methodology 141–5
  talking about death 147–8, 151
police
  children drawing themselves as
    officers 77, 77
  fear of 76
positionality 2
  and adult-child power relationship 68
  co-production methodologies and 109
  and previous experience 142–3, 145, 149
  researching with Sabar 49, 52
  researching with young disabled
    people 86, 87
  trauma and 21–2
'Post-Modern Anthropologist' 157
postcolonial research
  acknowledging 'other-ness' 56–8
  constructions of 'other' childhoods 44–6
  as a site for reflexivity 46–8
power
  co-production and shared 108
  losing and regaining control over balance
    of 146–7
  negotiations of 49
  reciprocity to diminish disparities of 54–6
  relationship between adult and child in
    research 68
  young people navigating dynamics of 105
prison research 20
promises, breaking 166
prostitution
  in India 64, 65–6
    child prostitution 73
  see also child prostitution in Thailand
publishing of research, dilemma over 90,
    92, 93

R
reciprocity, ethics of 54–6
reflexivity 1, 3–4
  about methodology in postcolonial
    research 56–8
  in adopting co-production
    methodologies 109, 110
  as an embedded research process 86–7
  as ethics 67–71
  as part of ethical processes 84–6
  reflexive 'turn' on research 48–54
  research as a site for 46–8
  in research design and method 88–90

Reinharz, S. 5–6
respect for research communities,
    demonstrating 69, 72
Richards, S. 3, 15, 24, 30, 82, 83, 98, 101,
    104, 108

S
safe spaces, researcher 20, 21
safeguarding
  discourse, colliding with ethics of
    care 148–50, 151, 152–4
  see also child protection, child's voice in
    context of; child protection concerns
safety
  participants' feelings of 68, 71, 75
  of researcher 64, 72
  and hosts 67–8
Said, E.W. 46, 54
self-care practices 73, 91–2
self-portrait tool 76–9, 77, 78
self-reflexivity 48–9, 68
selves in research, multiple 5–7
sex workers
  in India 64, 65–6
  child 73
  see also child prostitution in Thailand
sexting, children and adolescents 30–4
  data collection 33, 34
  discussions with parents 33–4, 36
  gaining ethical approval to study sexuality
    and 33, 34–6
  inside and outside romantic relationships 35
  learning about sexuality 29–30
  prevalence 31
  risks 32
Sinha, P. 48
situational self 6
social action, reciprocity and 56
social action, youth 96–116
  agency and 'voice' in practice 102–4
  agency, voice and participation 97–101
  children as researchers 100
  co-production methodologies 106–10,
    110–11
  exploring young people's
    perceptions 101–2
  issues over consent 103–4
  navigating ethics of perceived
    inaction 104–6
  participation as relational 106–10
  responsibility to rally for action on
    research 106
  workshop of participatory activities 107
social media
  abusive images and videos 11, 16, 17
  concerns over following young people
    on 12–13
  lurking on 13–14, 15–16, 18, 19, 24, 25–6
  tours with research participants 24

training for practitioners in issues on 22–3
see also online research with gangs
storytelling 88–90
stress management 21
stress, signs of 18–20
supervision of sensitive research 24–5
'Swerve Sunday' 109

T

Thailand, child research in *see* child prostitution in Thailand
time out from research, taking 86–7
to protect mental health 22, 73
tools of research with children
  Cube of Hope activity 50, *51*
  drawing exercises 70–1, *70*
  'Life, a Tree' sensory exploration tool 50–1
  practice tools for children's participation 119
  in sensitive contexts 73–9, 79–80
  mapping tool 73–6, *74*, *75*, *76*, 80
  self-portrait tool 76–9, *77*, *78*
touch, providing comfort through 143–4
  anxiety over 152–3
  colliding with discourse of safeguarding 148–50, 152
  mechanisms of control 152
  from multiple perspectives 151–2
trauma 168–9
  as 'contagious' 25
  early signs of 18–20
  positionality and 21–2
  recovering from 22–3
  see also vicarious trauma
Tronto, J.C. 142
trust of participants
  gaining 70–1, 91, 122, 153
  losing 166
Tyrrell, K. 101

U

United Nations Convention on the Rights of the Child (UNCRC) 13, 97, 100, 110, 127

V

vicarious trauma 11, 16, 17–18, 23
  addressing issues of 24–5
  disclosing experiences of 25
  recovering from 22–3
voices of children and young people 7–8
  agency and 'voice' in practice 102–4
  agency, participation and 97–101
  child protection issues limiting 10–11, 13, 15, 25–6
  differences between child participation and 118, 119
  ethical frameworks marginalising 33, 35, 37
  inclusion of disabled children's voices 83, 85, 87, 89, 92, 93
  in Indian sociological imagination 64–5
  in South Asia 63
  see also child protection, child's voice in context of
Volunteering Matters 109
vulnerability of children and implications for research 1, 2–3, 36–7, 141

W

Wacquant, L. 90, 91
Widman, L. 33
Winter, K. 122, 123
Women Against Sexual Exploitation and Violence Speak Up (WASSUP) 109
word clouds 18–19, *19*
workshops, collaborative 107
Wright, E.M. 124

Y

YouTube 11, 15–16

www.ingramcontent.com/pod-product-compliance
Lightning Source LLC
Chambersburg PA
CBHW051548020426
42333CB00016B/2147